IMAGES
*of America*

# SS CITY OF MILWAUKEE

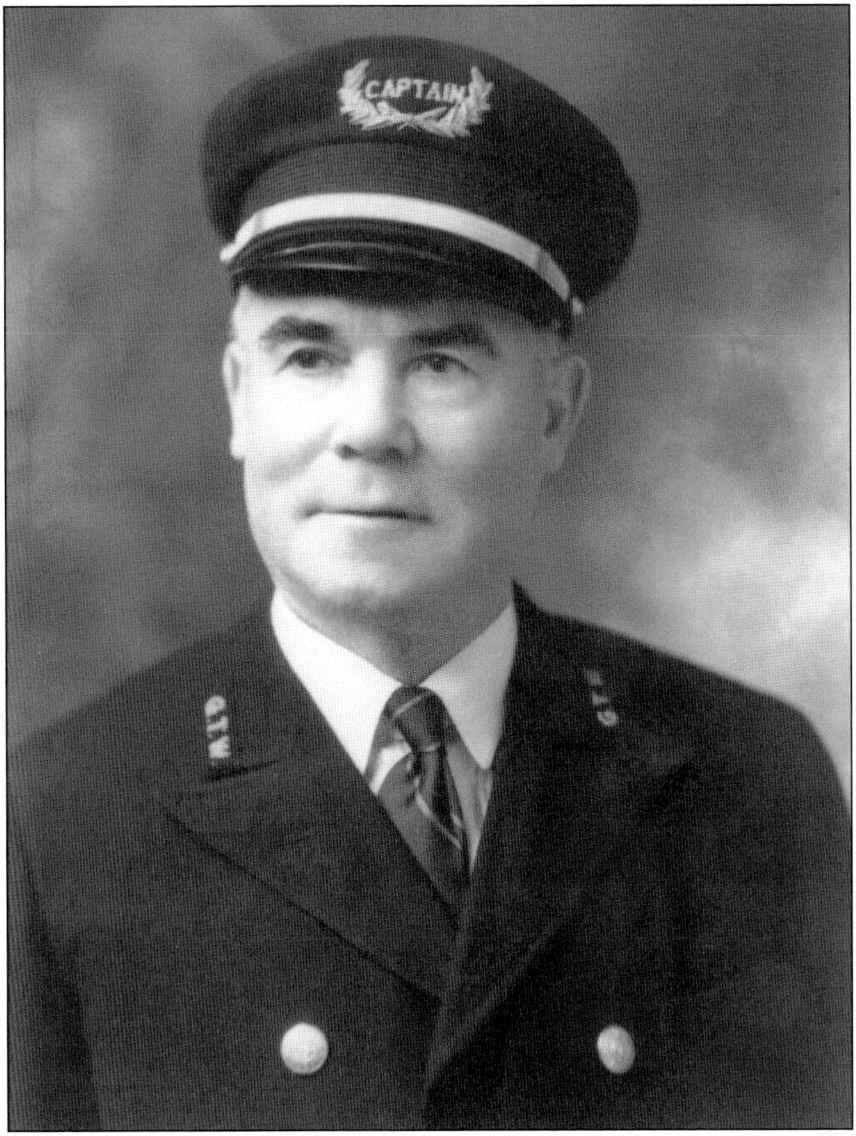

Capt. John F. Cavanaugh, flag captain of the Grand Trunk Milwaukee Car Ferry Company fleet, was appointed as the first master of the SS *City of Milwaukee* when the vessel came out of the Manitowoc Shipbuilding Company yard in January 1931. On April 23, 1936, Captain Cavanaugh suffered a stroke in his quarters while the *City of Milwaukee* was en route to Milwaukee from Muskegon, Michigan. He died the next day in Milwaukee's St. Mary's hospital in the presence of his wife, Ann, and daughter Katherine. (Grand Haven Elks Lodge No. 1200, Dick Fox Collection.)

**On the Cover:** The last surviving example of classic Great Lakes car ferry naval architecture, the *City of Milwaukee* (foreground) lies moored at her lay-up slip in Elberta, Michigan, at the end of the Ann Arbor Railroad's cross–Lake Michigan ferry service in 1982. The ship's twin stacks and traditional profile are a sharp contrast to her heavily modernized, diesel-powered fleet mates, *Arthur K. Atkinson* (center) and *Viking*. The other two ships are actually several years older than the 1931 steam-powered *City of Milwaukee*, which remains largely in her original form. (SS *City of Milwaukee* Archives.)

IMAGES
*of America*

# SS City of Milwaukee

Art Chavez and Bob Strauss

ARCADIA
PUBLISHING

ISBN 978-0-7385-8320-4

Published by Arcadia Publishing
Charleston, South Carolina

Printed in the United States of America

Library of Congress Control Number: 2011928977

For all general information, please contact Arcadia Publishing:
Telephone 843-853-2070
Fax 843-853-0044
E-mail sales@arcadiapublishing.com
For customer service and orders:
Toll-Free 1-888-313-2665

Visit us on the Internet at www.arcadiapublishing.com

*To the memory of Capt. John F. Cavanaugh and Capt. Roland J. Martin, two early skippers of the* City of Milwaukee, *and to all those that sailed aboard and presently work to preserve this excellent ship.*

# Contents

# Foreword

The *City of Milwaukee* has reached her 80-year milestone, but the story that she tells encompasses so many more years than that. Her physical story began in Manitowoc, Wisconsin, after the car ferry *Milwaukee* suffered a terrible tragedy on Lake Michigan. The *City of Milwaukee* was christened and launched November 25, 1930, much as other car ferries before her. I am sure that those who gathered to witness that exciting event never imagined that this ship would live on to become a showpiece of history.

During those 80 years, the *City of Milwaukee* has taken on different roles and has provided many different experiences for so many people. In the years she spent crossing Lake Michigan, she provided employment for many and carried various goods and passengers. As the needs of our nation changed and the era of carrying railcars across Lake Michigan had come to an end, the role of the *City of Milwaukee* was about to change.

It took a special vision to see the importance of saving this ship. This was not only a vision that the *City of Milwaukee* would be rescued, but that she would have the special privilege of preserving and sharing the rich and unique history of the car ferry era. The path to becoming a museum took the patience and hard work of very dedicated individuals. It has been a long journey and has taken many caretakers to reach this juncture in the *City of Milwaukee*'s history.

In the museum, we encounter many people on a daily basis—those who just drive by and are intrigued by the design of the ship and are compelled to take the tour. It was an eye-opening experience for me after my first tour, so it is a pleasure to know that when those people continue down the road they are a little more knowledgeable about our Great Lakes history. Family members of former crew will tour the ship and recall the special times when they were able to cross the lake with a parent who was on duty, proudly working aboard the *City of Milwaukee*. They remember the whistles of the different ships and knew when Dad was coming into port. When they visit, they will often have their children or grandchildren with them. Being able to walk the decks, see the rails, or touch the hull makes the stories the young people hear about Grandpa much more tangible.

One of the most special times is when a former crew member will stop by. Unfortunately, that is becoming an increasingly rare experience. When we are visited by past crew members, our roles as guides are reversed. We are the ones enjoying the stories, and it is rare when we do not learn something new.

I am fortunate to have become one of the people associated with the *City of Milwaukee* who have had the opportunity to play a small part in what we all hope will be her very long history—both as a working steamboat and a living museum.

—Linda Spencer, general manager,
SS *City of Milwaukee* National Historic Landmark

# ACKNOWLEDGMENTS

A large number of dedicated people have given untold time and effort through the years into preserving the *City of Milwaukee* and related activities. They include Ed Andrews, Capt. William Bacon, Jim Baker, Sid and Edna Beechcraft, Bill Beyers, Pat Brandon, John Brandt, Rich Brauer, Daisy Frederickson-Butler, Malcolm Butler, chief engineer Chuck Cart, Dan Cramer, Dick Fox, Doug Goodhue, Roger Griner, Bruce Groeneveld, Vince Hancock, Max Hanley, JoLynn Hanley, John Hausmann, Bill Herd, Dan Hoenecke, Capt. Dean Hobbs, Jed Jaworski, Mark Kalis, Kari Karr, chief engineer Bill Kulka, Kirk Lorenz, Andy LaBorde, Roger LeLievre, Michael Leon, Erich Luedtke, Rollie Martin, Capt. Roland J. Martin, George Micka, Bob Newcomb, Connie Newcomb, Duane Nugent, Stephanie Oden, Ken and Trish Ottmann, Bob and Grace Peppard, Dave Petersen, Glenn Rauth, Paul Rauth, Melissa Read, Tom Read, Ed and Lunora Sadon, Floyd Schmidt, Ed Seng, Jeff Seng, Brad Smith, Linda Spencer, Tom Stoltmann, Bob Strauss, Richard Taber, Debra Townsend, Marc and Jill Vander Muelen, Bob Vande Vusse, Ken Vrana, Wendell Wilke, Craig Wilson, Chris Winters, and Randy and Ron Yeo. There are many others who have given of their labor and financial assistance that we have not mentioned, but word count precludes this. You know who you are, as do we.

Special thanks go out to Tim Foster, for both his commitment to the Society for the Preservation of the *City of Milwaukee* and for use of his excellent postcard collection. The society is grateful for the generosity of the Frank B. Foster Charitable Trust, Gwen Frostic, and West Michigan University. Additional archival illustrations are courtesy of John Snyder and William Vantuono of Simmons-Boardman Publishing, editors of *Marine Log* and *Railway Age*, respectively, and Mark Hallman of the Canadian National Railway. Additional *City of Milwaukee* archival imagery is courtesy of Norma Bishop and Wendy Lutzke of the Wisconsin Maritime Museum at Manitowoc and Grand Haven Elks Lodge No. 1200. Motion picture coverage is courtesy of Brauer Productions, Inc., Lone Wolf Documentary Group, and Debra Townsend.

Images generously contributed by the Wisconsin Maritime Museum at Manitowoc are credited to WMMM. Numerous unmarked photographs from the SS *City of Milwaukee* Archives are from the following photographers: Guy Ellis, Jed Jaworski, George Micka, Roy Nerg, Paul Rauth, Linda Spencer, and Richard Taber. We also appreciated working with editor Anna Wilson and publisher John Pearson at Arcadia Publishing. A large number of the photographs in this book are from the SS *City of Milwaukee* Archives and will be credited as CofM throughout.

# Introduction

The *City of Milwaukee* survives as the last classic, twin-stacked, triple-expansion-engine-powered Great Lakes railcar ferry based on a design profile and deck layout developed by the renowned Manitowoc Shipbuilding Company. This class of ship can be considered a refined version of an earlier generation of lake ferries conceived by naval architect Robert Logan. One of only 38 stern-loading Great Lakes rail ferries constructed between 1892 and 1953, the ship has the lineage to stand as the best possible candidate to represent the historical midway point in the evolution between early and modern Great Lakes car ferry design. The fact that the *City of Milwaukee* symbolizes the first type of vessel to successfully carry loaded railcars across deep, open waters—the technology of which was adopted by ferry operators throughout the world and directly owes its existence to the tragic loss of the *Milwaukee*, a Robert Logan boat of the first order—greatly adds to the relevance of the ship and justifies its status as a national historic landmark.

Virtually unchanged from her original configuration, the *City of Milwaukee* serves to educate students and the general public about the rich legacy of the Great Lakes railroad ferries and their dramatic exploits fighting through storm, ice, and economic decline. That the ship still exists and is not a mere footnote in maritime history is a complex story, best left to be told by the people who were directly involved in saving the vessel from an uncertain fate. Suffice it to say once the Ann Arbor Railroad ceased operating the *City of Milwaukee* and the other ferries in the fleet in 1982, a group led by former car ferry sailor Jed Jaworski worked diligently to acquire it from the State of Michigan and preserve the oldest of the three-ship fleet. In 1978, the state earlier had purchased the *City of Milwaukee* from the Grand Trunk Railroad (GT), who then leased her to the Michigan Interstate Railway, then the operator of the Ann Arbor Railroad.

In 1984, the City of Frankfort, Michigan, purchased the ferry from the state for $2, with the intention of working with the ship's preservation group to turn the *City of Milwaukee* into a museum and tourist attraction. Frankfort in turn sold the ship for $2 to the Society for the Preservation of the *City of Milwaukee* in 1988. In the end, the citizens of the city of Frankfort approved a ballot proposal in 1999 to dock the ship at the foot of Tenth Street, but insufficient water depth, the prohibitive expense of dredging, and the lack of mooring space prompted the move of the *City of Milwaukee* to Manistee, Michigan.

The *City of Milwaukee* last operated under her own steam in August 1981, and since then has hosted thousands of visitors across her decks as a museum ship. In December 1990, the ferry was officially designated a national historic landmark by the secretary of the interior and is one of less than 2,500 historic places that fulfill the requirement that they "possess exceptional value or quality in illustrating or interpreting the heritage of the United States." In that spirit, what follows is a pictorial journey that tells the story of the *City of Milwaukee* and the car ferry fleets that she operated for and of the ongoing efforts to preserve this amazing ship, a virtual time capsule with rich oak-paneled interiors and brass fittings, for future generations.

# *One*

# The Grand Trunk Milwaukee Car Ferry Company

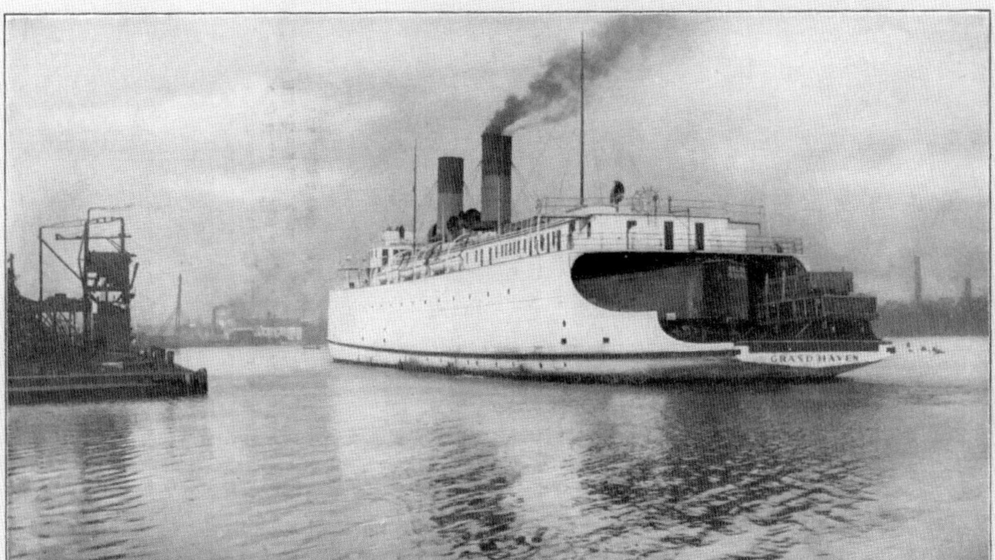


THE GRAND HAVEN—CAR FERRY

The car ferry *Grand Haven* enters Milwaukee harbor. The ship was a greyhound—routinely crossing the lake at 18 miles per hour. In 1903, the Grand Trunk Railroad entered the Lake Michigan rail-ferry trade in partnership with the Crosby Transportation Company—a steamship line running between Milwaukee and Grand Haven, Michigan. Miffed at competitor Pere Marquette Railroad's success at capturing much of the seasonal fruit trade from southwestern Michigan, Crosby saw potential in establishing his own ferry line to Grand Haven in connection with Grand Trunk's trackage. (Bob Strauss.)

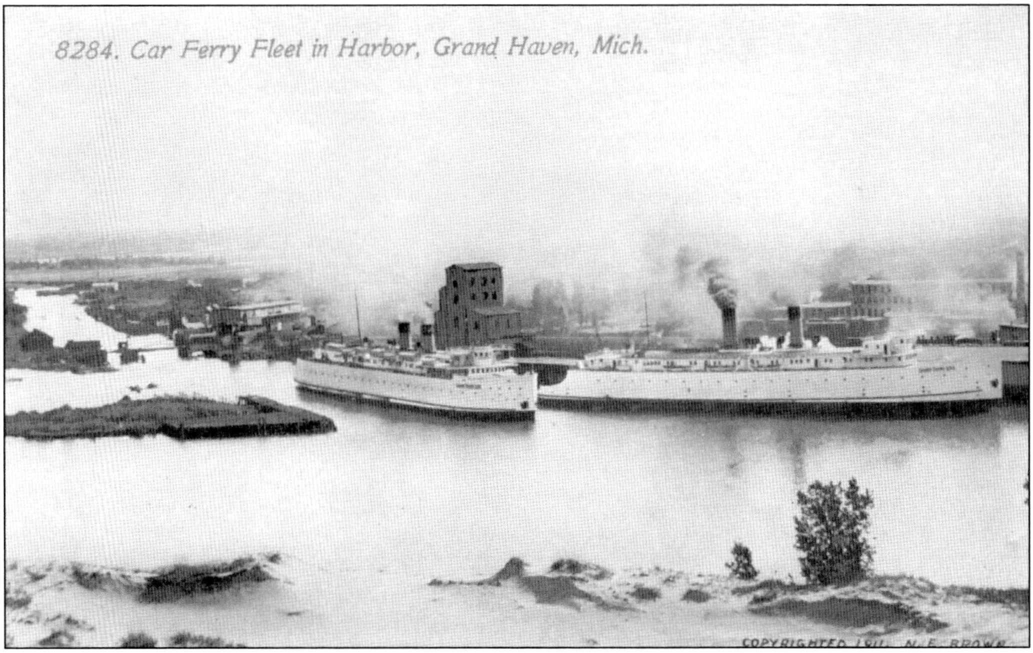


Crosby's Grand Trunk Car Ferry Line was established with a new ferry built in 1903 at Craig Shipbuilding Company in Toledo, Ohio. The 320-foot *Grand Haven* was black, with white cabins and black stacks. After Crosby defaulted in 1905 and with a change in ownership, the ferry appeared with a white hull, buff stacks with black banding, and a red boot-top waterline. The Grand Trunk Railroad bought the ship and maintained the Milwaukee–Grand Haven service. The *Grand Haven* (right) is shown in Grand Haven with the *Milwaukee* (formerly *Manistique Marquette and Northern 1*), which was acquired in 1908. (Bob Strauss.)

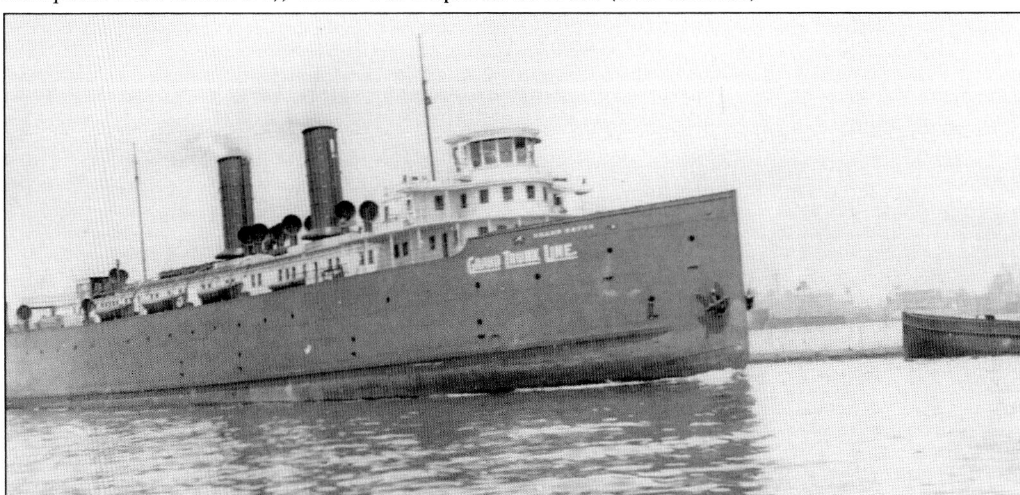


The *Grand Haven* departs Milwaukee harbor in the 1920s. After Crosby failed to build a lucrative traffic level, the Grand Trunk increased freight tonnage capacity with the 350-foot car ferry *Milwaukee*, pursuing customers via its sales staff, an asset that large railroad systems took for granted and a luxury that Crosby could never afford. The Crosby Line continued in the passenger and package freight business after the failed car ferry venture. The firm's owner, Edward G. Crosby, died on April 15, 1912, aboard the White Star liner *Titanic*. (CofM.)

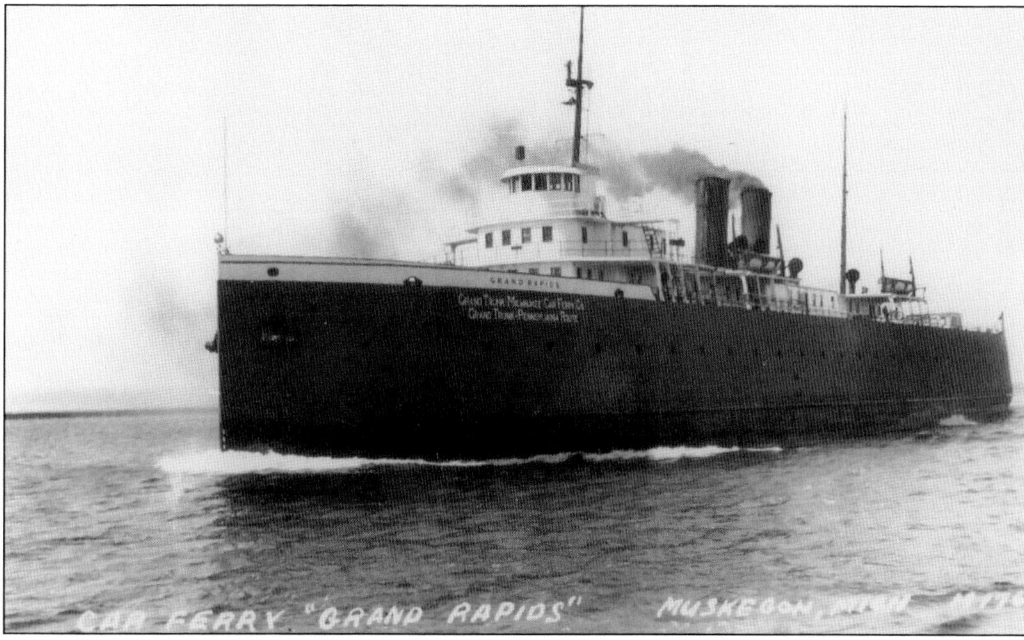


The *Grand Rapids* enters Muskegon in the 1930s. The *Grand Haven* and *Milwaukee* carried for the Grand Trunk into the mid-1920s, but freight capacity was stretched. The railroad leased ferries from the rival Ann Arbor and Pere Marquette operations. With the success of new Pere Marquette car ferries and an Ann Arbor ferry built to the same profile, the Grand Trunk ordered the *Grand Rapids* from Manitowoc Shipbuilding Company in 1926. The ship was christened Saturday, October 23, 1926, at 11:45 a.m. by Merlyn Bowker of Detroit, daughter of Grand Trunk's general manager, C. R. Bowker. (Roger LeLievre.)

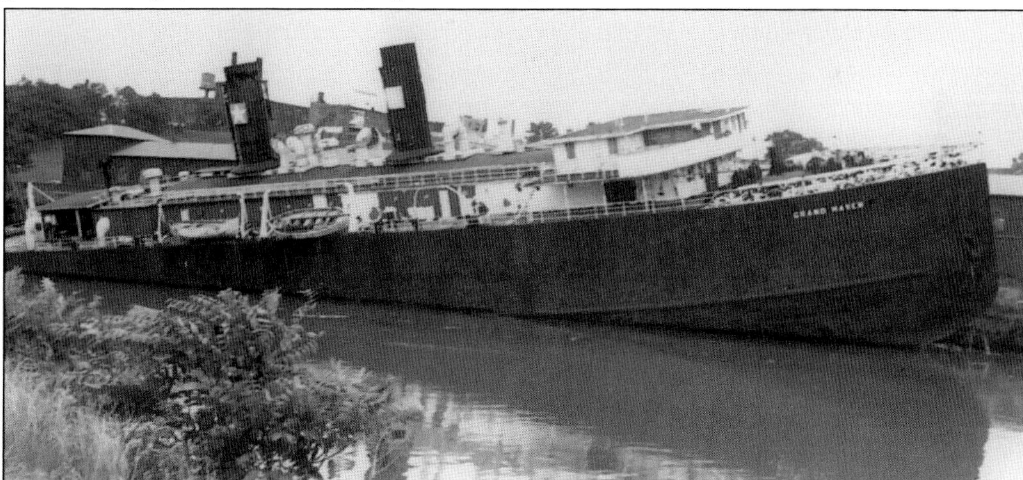

The Grand Trunk Railroad moved toward retiring older vessels with the addition of the *Grand Rapids* and the *Madison*. The *Grand Haven* was used less during the Great Depression and was laid up in Manitowoc harbor during the 1930s. In 1946, the *Grand Haven* sold to the West India Fruit and Steamship Company to ferry railcars between Florida and Cuba. After the Cuban revolution, the *Grand Haven* returned to the Great Lakes and languished at the old Pennsylvania Dock along the Cuyahoga River in Cleveland. Here, she sunk along the bank in September 1969 and scrapped the following year at Hamilton, Ontario. (Bob Strauss; photograph by Andy Sykora.)

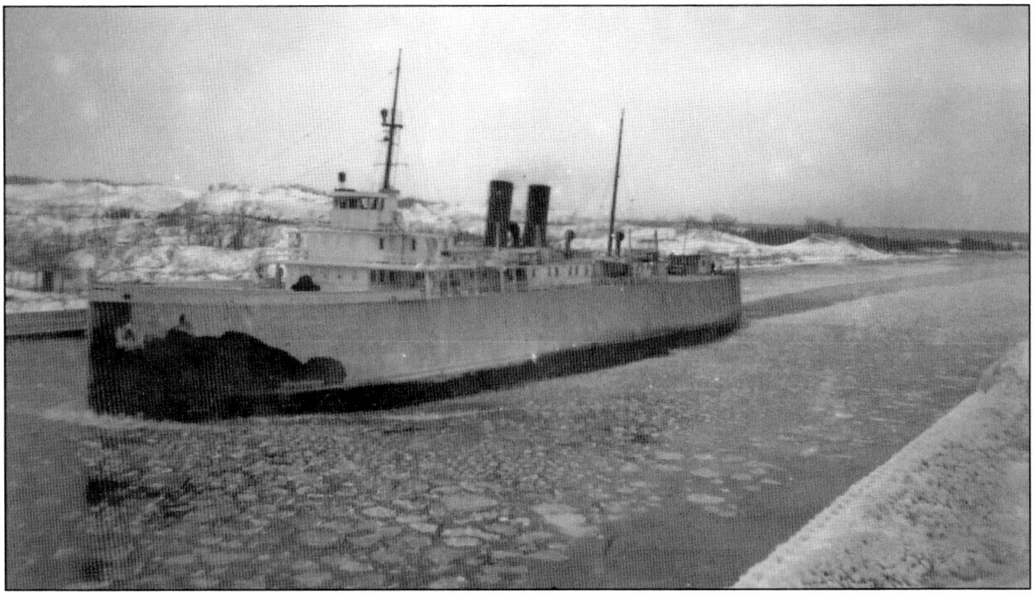

The *Grand Rapids* was 360 feet long with a beam of 56 feet. Powered by a pair of triple-expansion steam engines and a set of Scotch boilers, the ship could attain a speed of 14 miles per hour, besting the first-generation car ferries by a full two miles per hour. (The *Grand Haven* was the exception, capable of 18 miles per hour.) The *Grand Rapids* started a new era of ships built specifically for the Grand Trunk Railroad, just as the road's eastern terminus was switched from Grand Haven to Muskegon, Michigan. The outbound ship pushes through slush ice in the Muskegon channel. (Max Hanley.)

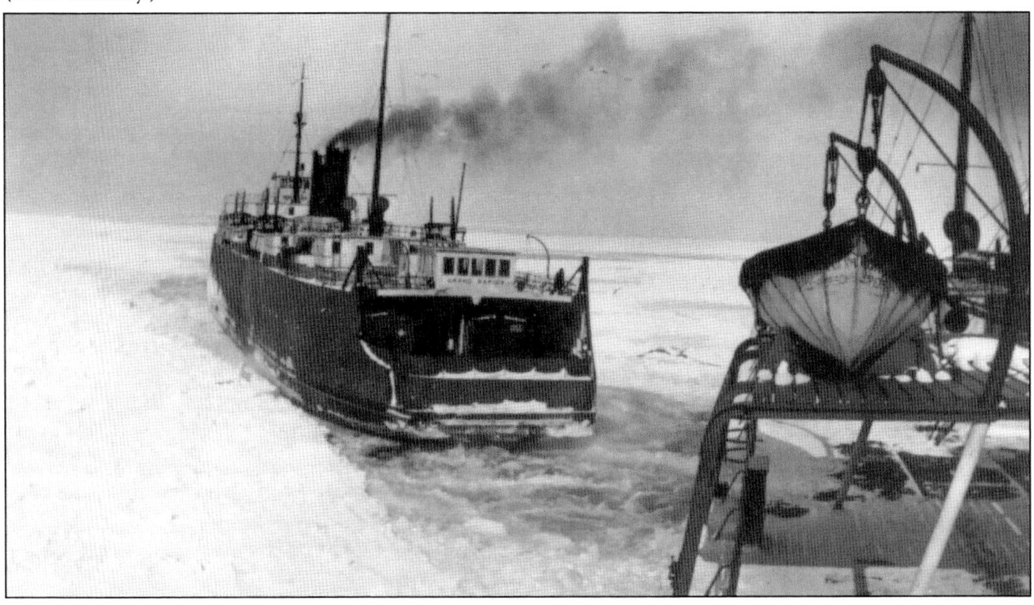

Greater freight movement generated by Muskegon-area customers motivated the Grand Trunk line to move its east-shore Lake Michigan operation from Grand Haven to Muskegon. Grand Haven's river and harbor entrance was troublesome as well: heavy build-up of slush ice and dangerous sandbars caused delays, and ferries suffered damage due to windrowed ice and groundings. The *Grand Rapids* (left) flushes ice from around the *Grand Haven* outside Muskegon harbor. (Bob Strauss.)

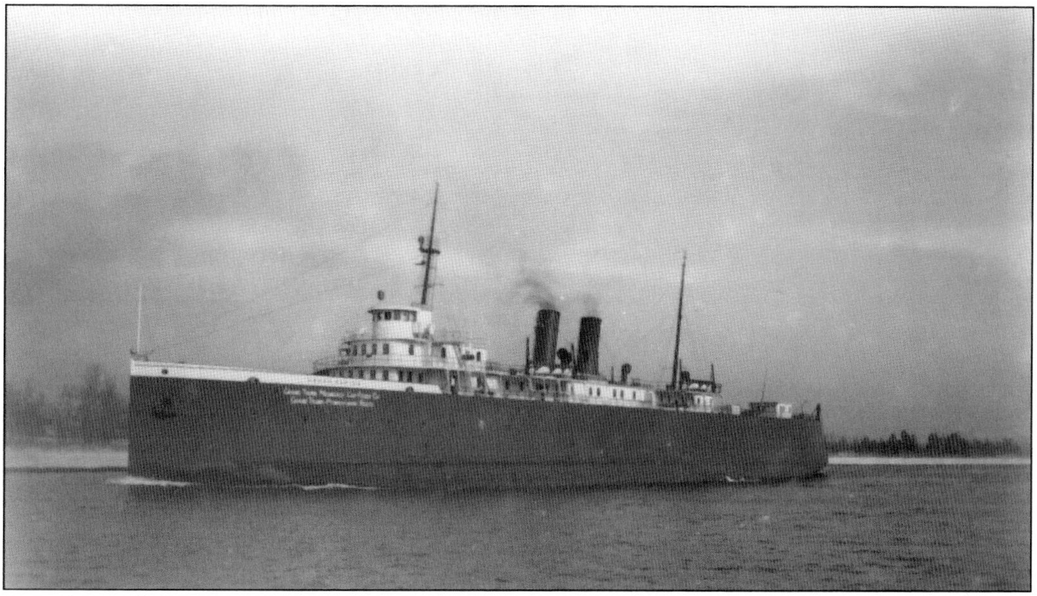

Grand Trunk's move to Muskegon in 1933 coincided with negotiations with the Pennsylvania Railroad (PRR) for joint operation of the ferry service. Beginning in the early 1920s, the PRR sought joint trackage rights or a new fleet of its own to exploit cross-lake traffic. Using GT trackage and car ferries, the PRR operated the fleet jointly from 1936 until 1953. The freight volume that the PRR hoped for never materialized. The *Grand Rapids* wears joint Grand Trunk–Pennsylvania colors at Muskegon during the 1930s. (Max Hanley.)

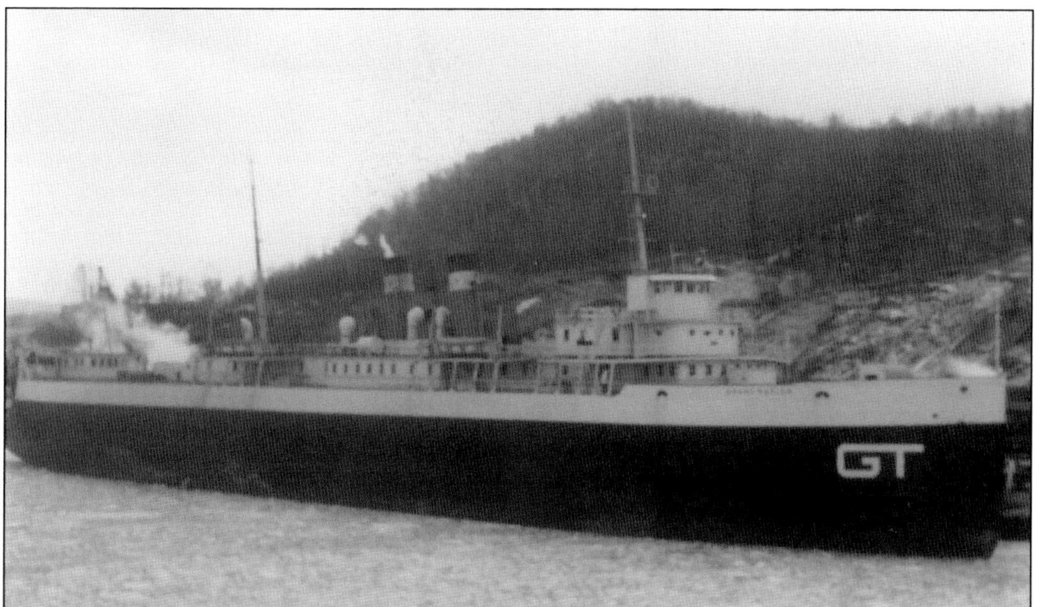


Occasionally the "Big Three" Lake Michigan operators leased ships to one another. Here, in 1966, the *Grand Rapids*, on lease to the Ann Arbor Railroad, sits in the company's west slip, officially in Elberta, across the bay from Frankfort, Michigan. The ship wears Grand Trunk's Canadian National Railways colors—black and white hull and red, white, and blue stacks. The Grand Trunk's "wet-noodle" GT herald is on the bow. (Bob Strauss; photograph by Vaughn E. Braatz.)

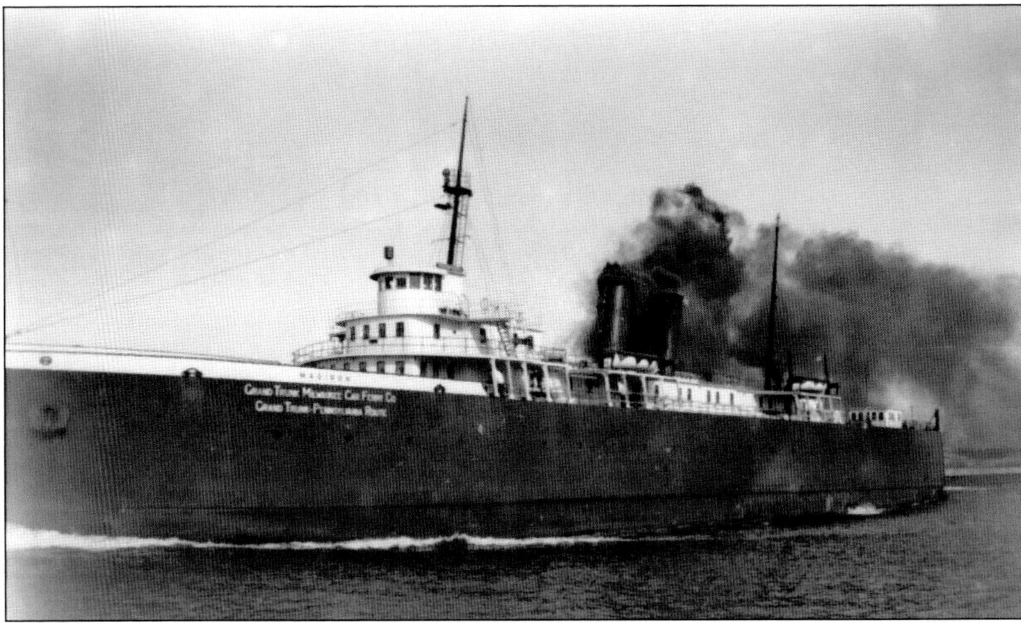

The *Madison* was launched at Manitowoc Shipbuilding on January 19, 1927. Christened just before noon with a bottle of Wisconsin milk by Marion Dixon, daughter of a Grand Trunk Railroad director, the ship was identical to the *Grand Rapids*, launched the previous year. Shown here in Muskegon during the 1930s, the *Madison* took its maiden voyage on March 2, 1927; she carried Nash automobiles loaded inside railroad cars between Milwaukee and Grand Haven. (Max Hanley.)

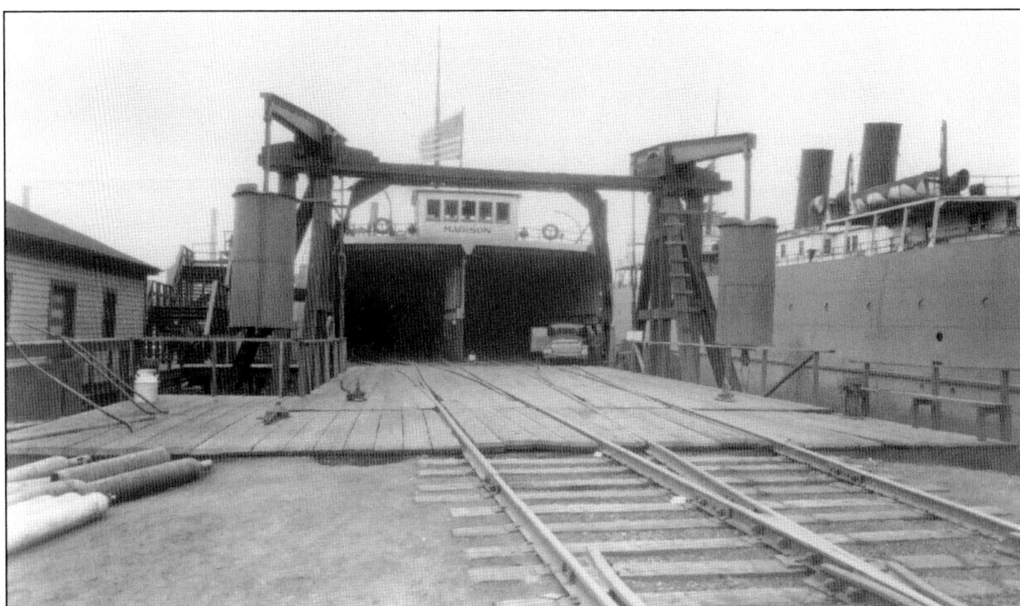

The *Madison* is shown tied up to the west loading apron at Milwaukee. Clearly visible is the rail connection between shore, apron, and ship. Also shown is a passenger automobile on the ship's stern, a rarity for the Grand Trunk. The railroad never actively pursued automobile and passenger traffic like the rival Pere Marquette and Ann Arbor fleets did and stopped carrying them altogether in 1970. (Bob Strauss.)

Our ships do not run on a schedule. Their departures are governed by freight requirements.

GRAND TRUNK WESTERN RAILROAD COMPANY
MILWAUKEE-MUSKEGON CAR FERRY SERVICE

- - - - - - - - - - - - - - - - - - - -

Six and one-half hours across Lake Michigan

| Leave Milwaukee, Wis.<br>1825 South Allis St. | Leave Muskegon, Mich.<br>2100 Lake Shore Drive |
|---|---|
| Central Std. Time | Eastern Std. Time |
| 8:00 A.M. | 5:00 A.M. |
| 2:00 P.M. | 11:00 A.M. |
| 7:00 P.M. | 4:00 P.M. |
| 11:00 P.M. | 11:00 P.M. |

The above schedules are subject to cancellation without notice. They show the time steamers should depart from Milwaukee and Muskegon, but their departure or arrival at the times stated is not guaranteed.

FARES BETWEEN MILWAUKEE & MUSKEGON
(one-way - either direction)

| | |
|---|---|
| Passage Fare | $ 4.50 |
| Stateroom (lower & upper) | 5.75 |
| Lower Berth | 3.00 |
| Upper Berth | 2.75 |
| Private Room | 6.75 |
| Pullman Room | 6.75 |

| Meals: | | |
|---|---|---|
| | Breakfast | $ 1.50 |
| | Noon-dinner | $ 2.00 |
| | Supper | $ 2.00 |

WE DO NOT HANDLE OR CHECK BAGGAGE

For further information -

In Milwaukee: Call SHeridan 4-1901

In Muskegon: Call PErshing 3-2290

WE HAVE NO FACILITIES ON CAR FERRIES TO HANDLE PRIVATE AUTOMOBILES

That passenger traffic was of minor importance to the Grand Trunk operations is evidenced by this 1967 schedule. Bare-bones and typed on a single sheet of paper, it stands in stark contrast to the more elaborate printed color brochures then current with the Ann Arbor and Chesapeake & Ohio (Pere Marquette's successor as of 1947) fleets. It was strictly no-frills, passenger-only service, with no provision for automobiles. (Bob Strauss.)

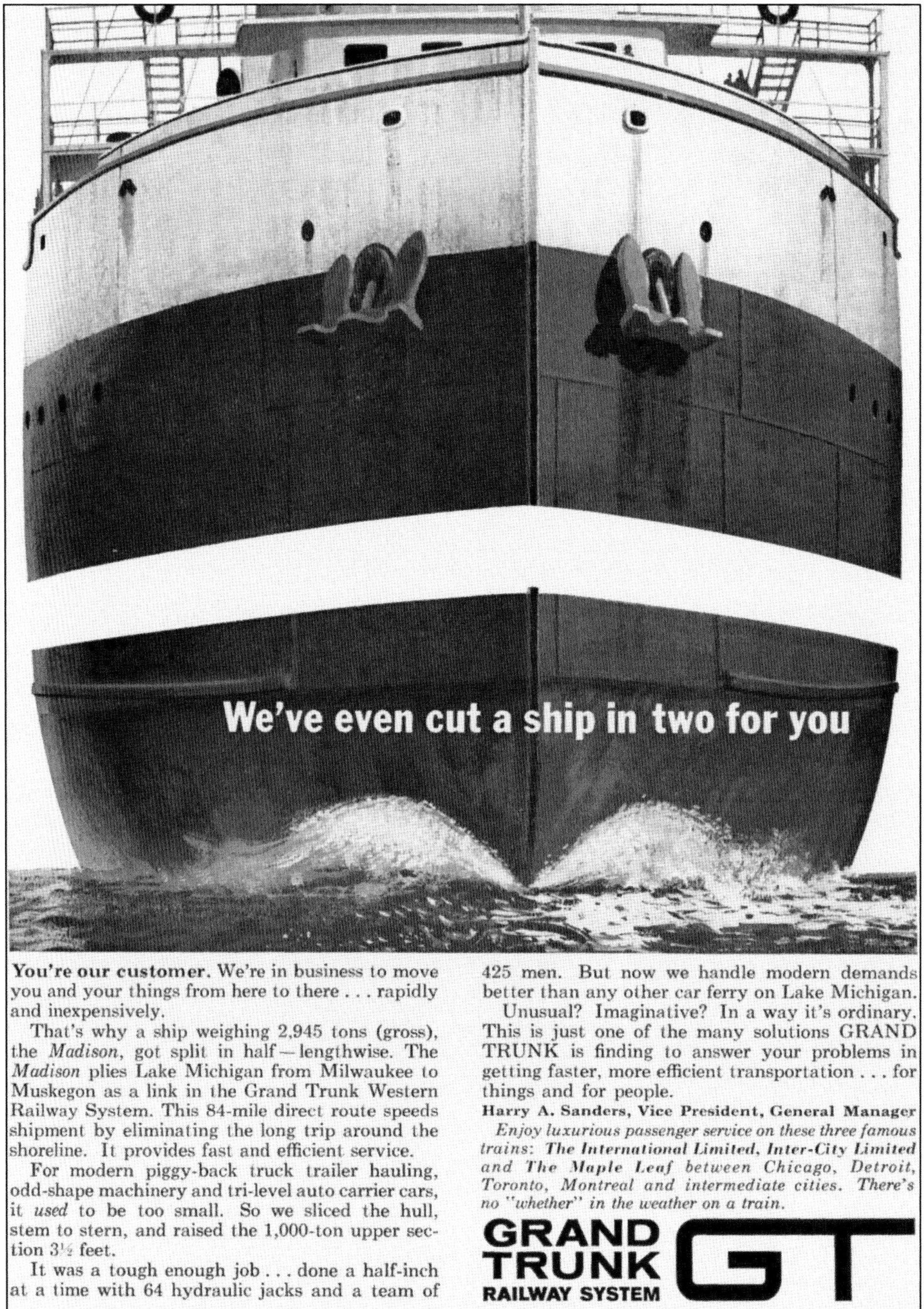


In September 1961, the Grand Trunk sent the *Madison* to Manitowoc Shipbuilding to have her overhead car deck clearance raised 42 inches for an overall space of 19 feet. This allowed the ship to carry new, specialized railcars such as piggyback trailers on flatcars and tri-level automobile carriers. The big job required the shipyard to cut the perimeter of the car deck horizontally and employ 64 manually operated jacks. Two men were assigned to each jack and raised the car deck gradually, a half-inch at a time. The modification cost $600,000. (Bob Strauss.)

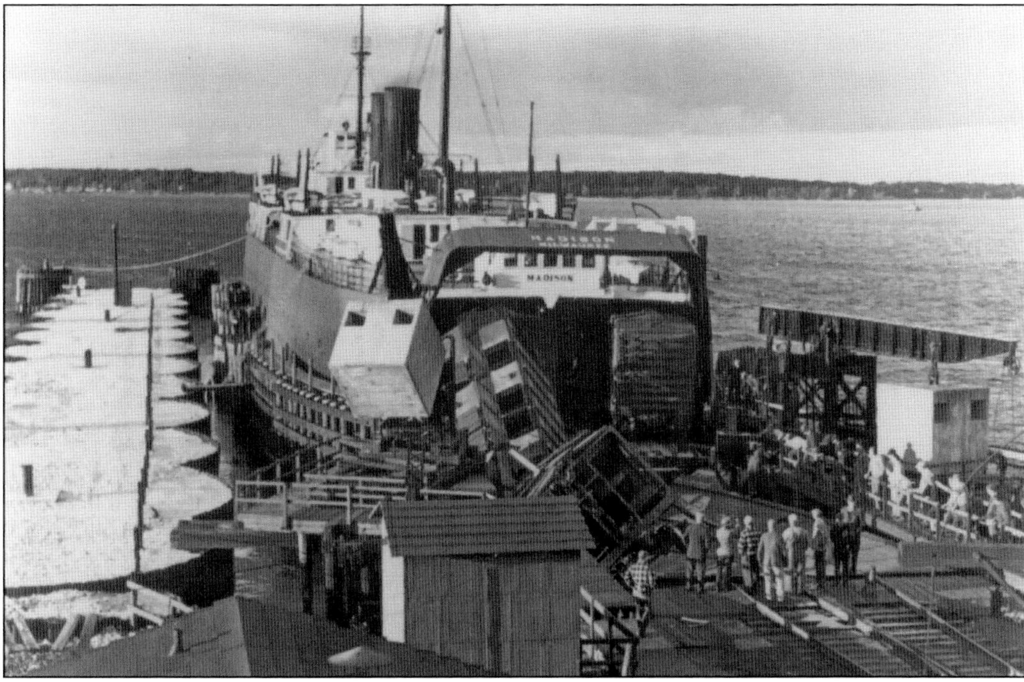

Loading aprons and surrounding structures were susceptible to deterioration, collision, and collapse. Most commonly, a ship was pushed away from the apron by a locomotive during loading, causing the apron to drop to the retaining beam below. More often than not, a railcar would either end up hanging halfway over the ferry's stern or completely in the water. Heavy damage always resulted due to the weight involved, and repair delays lasted from weeks to months. This incident involved the *Madison* at Muskegon in 1949. (Bob Strauss.)

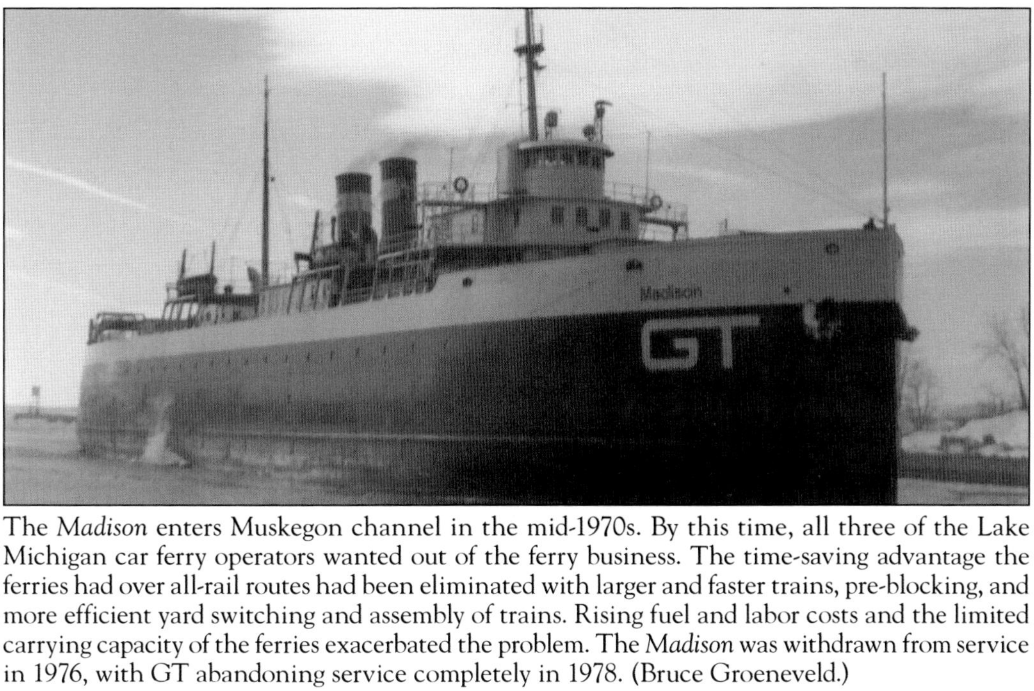


The *Madison* enters Muskegon channel in the mid-1970s. By this time, all three of the Lake Michigan car ferry operators wanted out of the ferry business. The time-saving advantage the ferries had over all-rail routes had been eliminated with larger and faster trains, pre-blocking, and more efficient yard switching and assembly of trains. Rising fuel and labor costs and the limited carrying capacity of the ferries exacerbated the problem. The *Madison* was withdrawn from service in 1976, with GT abandoning service completely in 1978. (Bruce Groeneveld.)

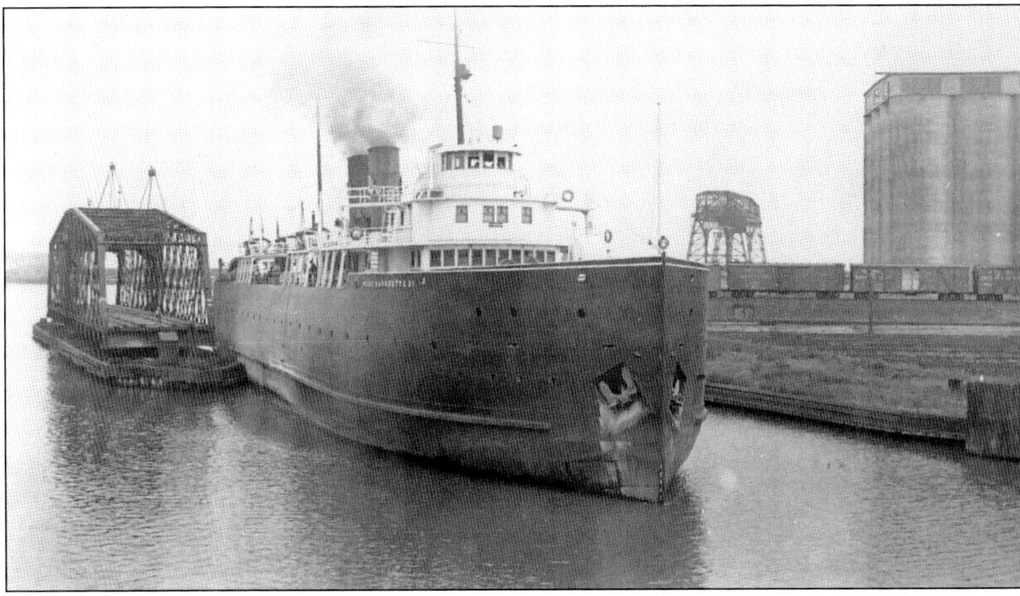

The *Pere Marquette 21*, shown entering Milwaukee's Kinnickinnic River, was the lead ship in the class of six that became the most prolific and successful ferry design used by all three of the modern Lake Michigan car ferry operators. Pere Marquette Railway's design featured a 'tween-deck anchor windlass room enclosed within the forecastle and recessed pockets for storage of the anchors. (Bob Strauss; photograph by M.J. Brown.)

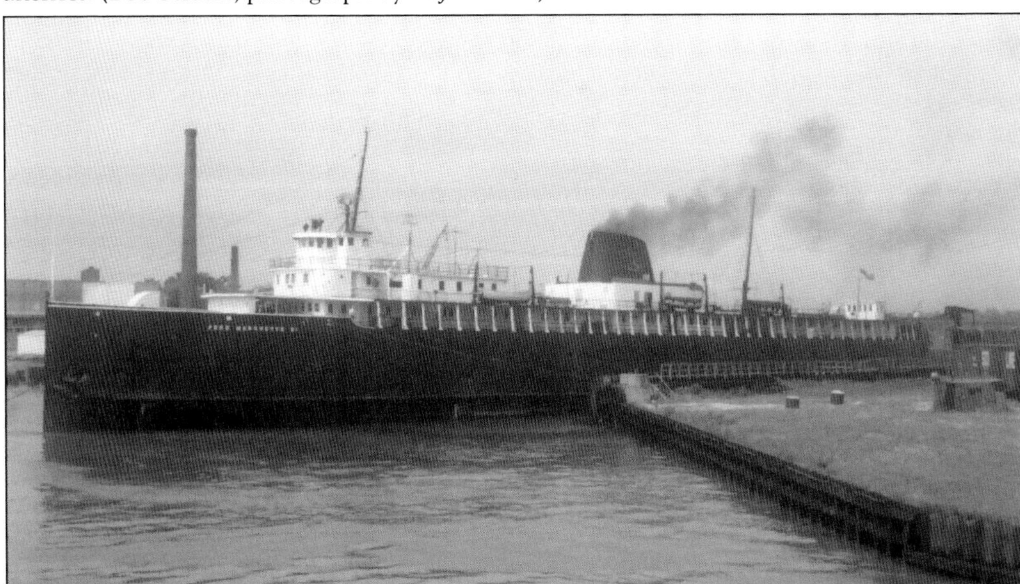

The heavily and frequently modified design of the *Pere Marquette 21* and *22* indicated Manitowoc Shipbuilding's robust design characteristics. The pair gained full-length cabins in 1936; they were lengthened 40 feet and repowered with Skinner Unaflow engines and water tube boilers in 1953–1954. The *Ann Arbor No. 7* was also heavily modified, with diesel-electric propulsion and an exterior makeover, making her virtually unrecognizable. Grand Trunk boats remained unaltered their entire lives, save for conversion from coal- to oil-burning equipment. (Bob Strauss; photograph by Vaughn E. Braatz.)

# *Two*

# Ann Arbor Railroad Car Ferries

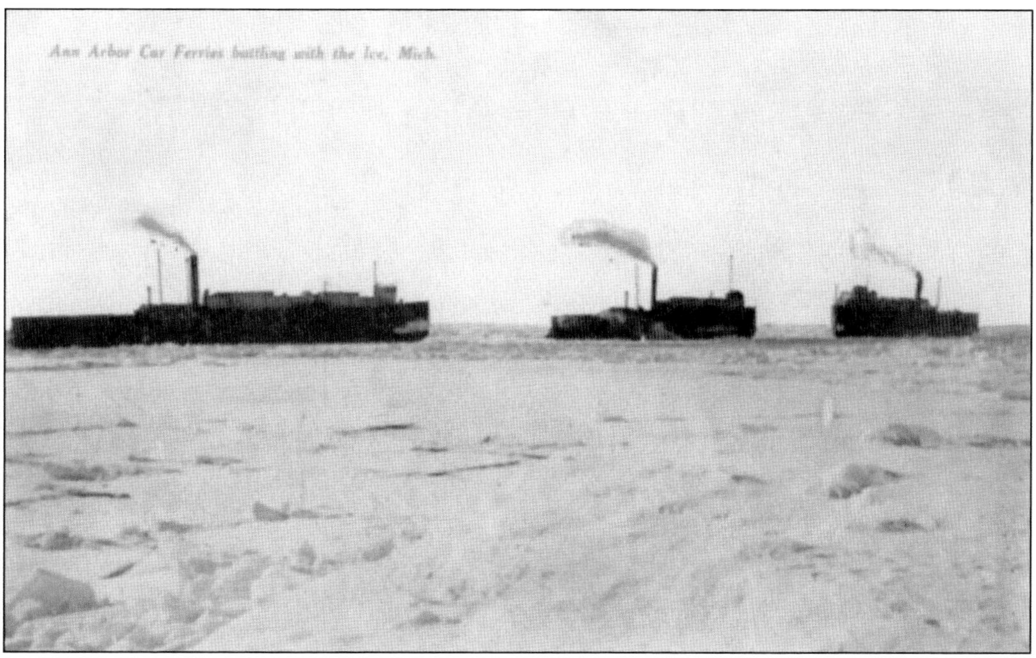


The Ann Arbor Railroad established the viability of cross-lake railroad ferry service with the wooden car ferries *Ann Arbor No. 1* and *No. 2*. Designed and built by Craig Shipbuilding, the pair went through engineers, deck officers, and crew at unusually high turnover rates, due to the hazardous weather and heavy ice the ferries sailed through and the primitive living conditions aboard ship. (Tim Foster.)

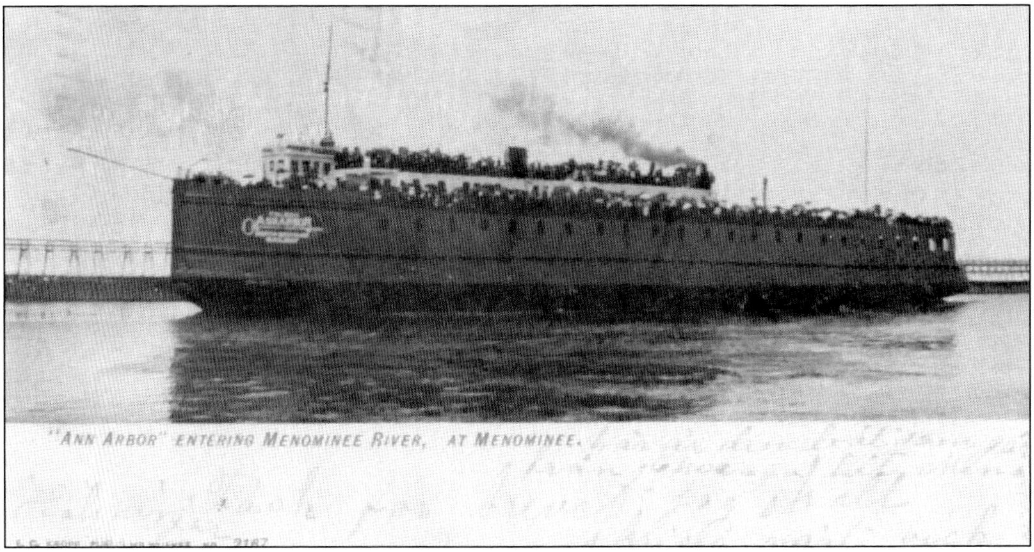


This broadside view shows the boxy layout of the *Ann Arbor No. 2*, on an excursion to Menominee, Michigan. The oak hull had a length of 274 feet, a beam of 52 feet, and a capacity of 24 thirty-two-foot railcars. When the twin *Ann Arbor No. 1* and *Ann Arbor No. 2* entered service, they were equipped with a forward engine powering an icebreaking bow propeller. The large stack aft was for the main boilers, and the stubby stack passing through the cabin was for the forward boilers. (Tim Foster.)

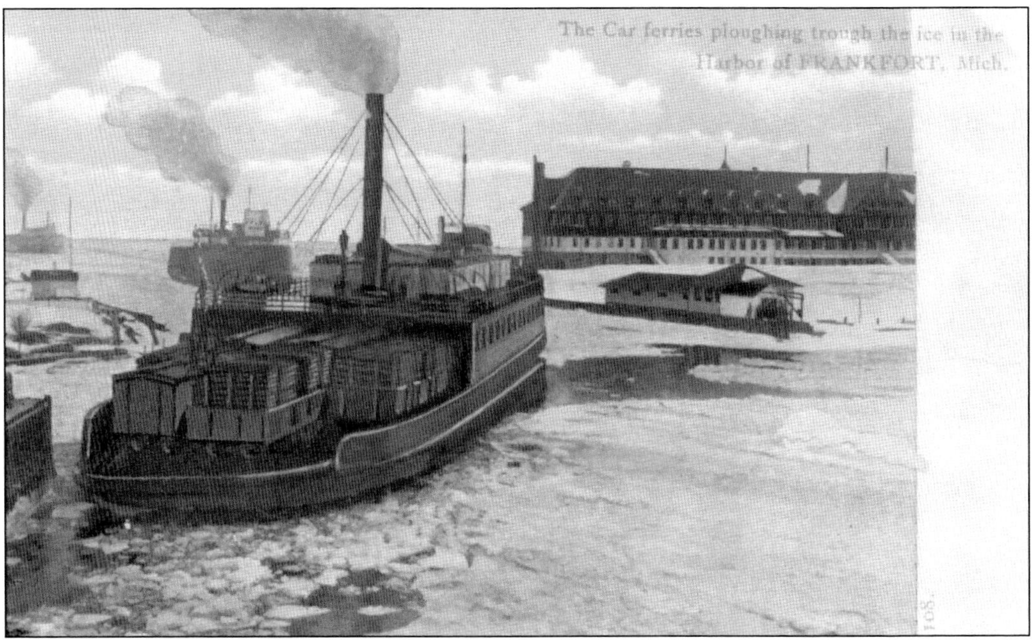


In the planning stages, the wooden Ann Arbor ferries were to be built with an open car deck, with the first 50 feet from the bow enclosed, upon which the cabins would be placed. The car deck would be protected by a gunwale rising 25 feet from the waterline, with an open stern. It was decided to cover the car deck completely; but in actual service, the turnout of the wing tracks on the ships' port and starboard aft quarter required the car decks to be cut back somewhat. This view shows the last 100 feet of the *Ann Arbor No. 2*'s deck cut away. (Tim Foster.)

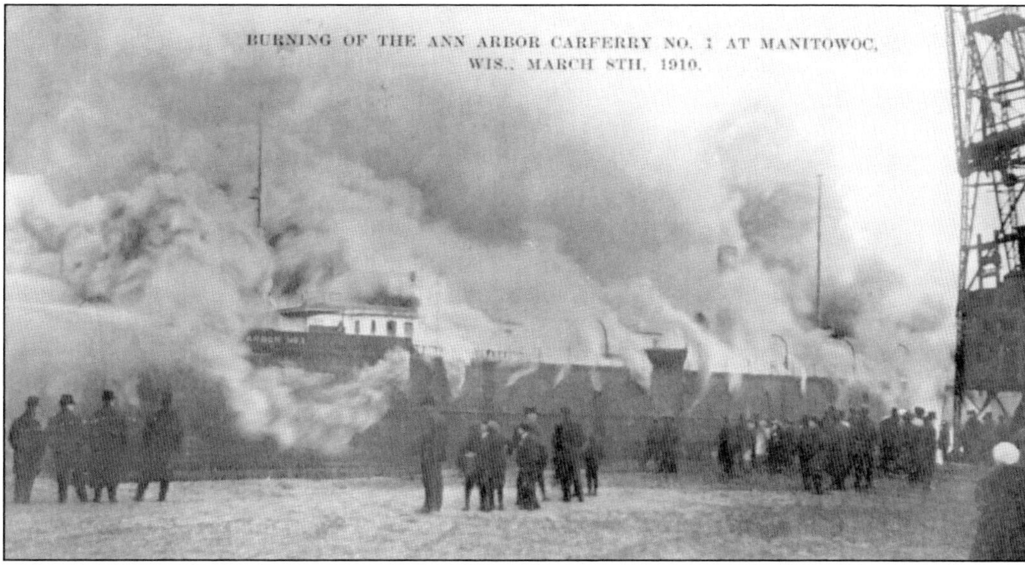


After a dicey 18-year career as an underpowered and ungainly craft, the *Ann Arbor No. 1* ended her days by burning to a total loss at the Chicago & North Western ferry slip in Manitowoc on March 8, 1910. Differing accounts say the blaze was started by a coal dust explosion or an oilcan bursting in the engine room. The humble little ship proved the viability of ferrying loaded freight cars throughout the year in the harshest of climates. The *No. 1* is shown at the height of the blaze. (Tim Foster.)

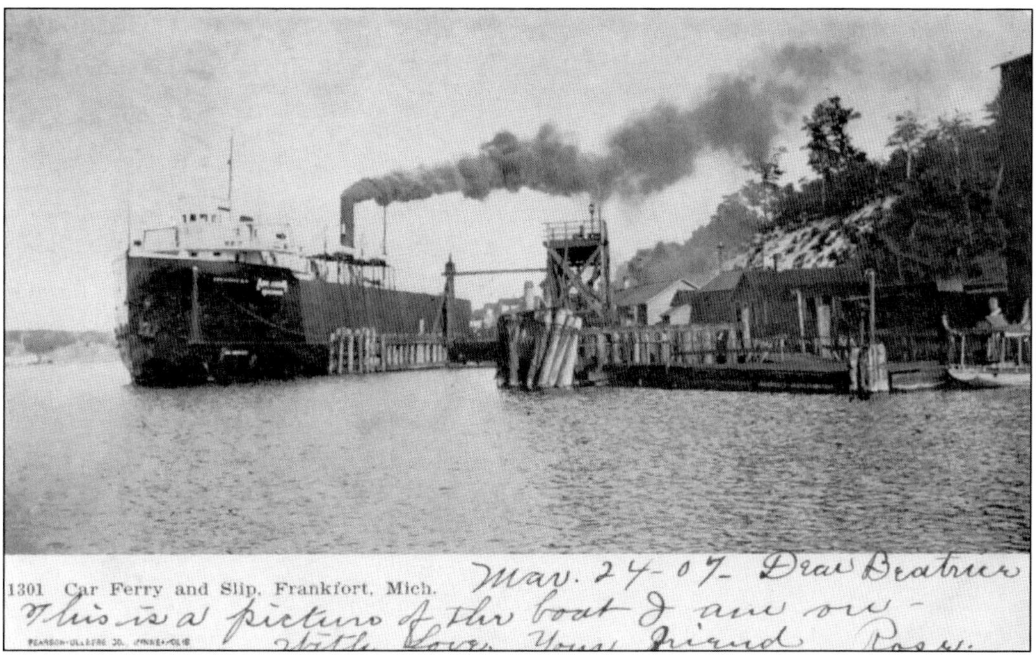


The Ann Arbor Railroad's first steel car ferry, *Ann Arbor No. 3,* was built in 1898 at Globe Iron Works of Cleveland and was designed by Robert Logan, whose highly acclaimed *Pere Marquette* was the first steel cross-lake ferry on the Great Lakes. *Ann Arbor No. 3* was unusual in that it was designed with a forward hold for carrying loose grain and side gangways on the car deck for carrying package freight. The ship is shown at Frankfort harbor in the early 1900s. (Tim Foster.)

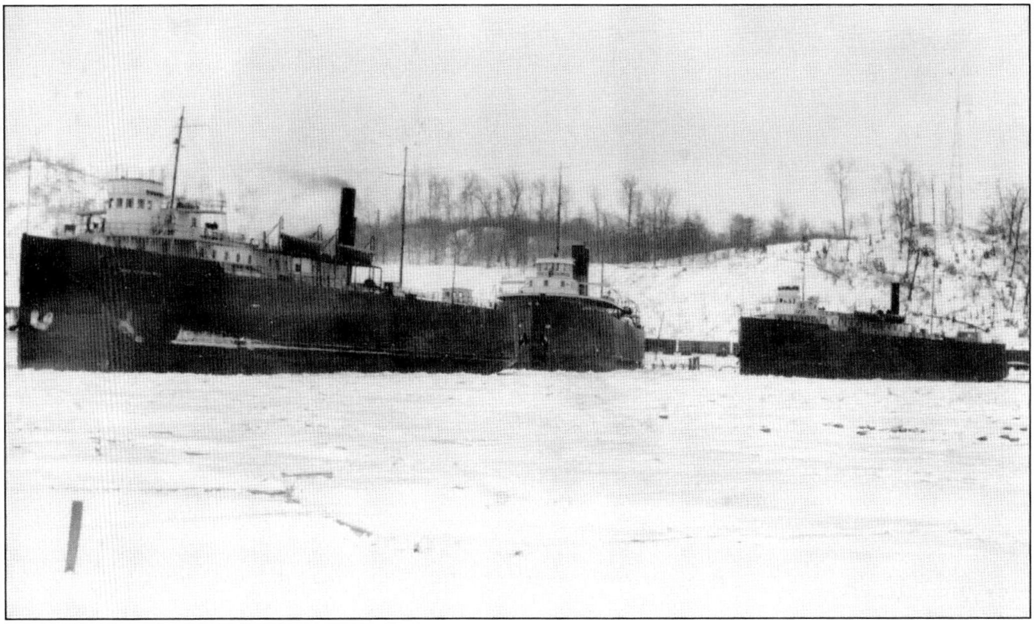

The Ann Arbor car ferry fleet was plagued by heavy ice due to its northern Lake Michigan routes on Green Bay and transiting the Sturgeon Bay Ship Canal. Frankfort harbor was not immune to ice troubles, as this scene from around 1920 attests. Frozen in on Lake Betsie are, from left to right, *Ann Arbor No. 3*, *Ann Arbor No. 5*, and *Ann Arbor No. 4*. (Tim Foster.)

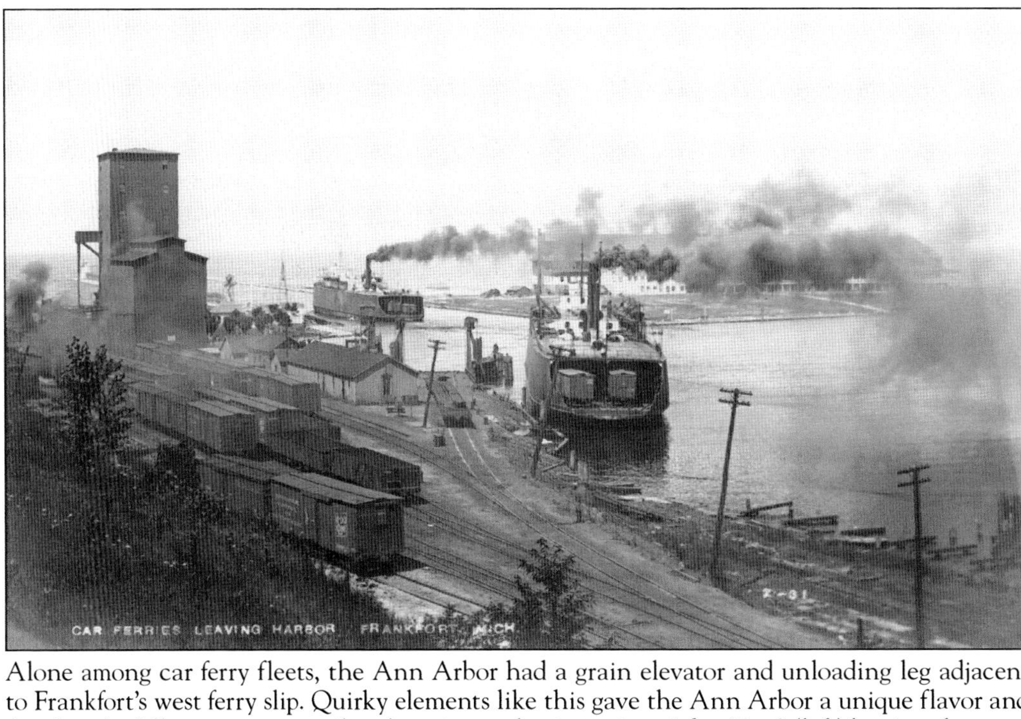


Alone among car ferry fleets, the Ann Arbor had a grain elevator and unloading leg adjacent to Frankfort's west ferry slip. Quirky elements like this gave the Ann Arbor a unique flavor and developed a following among rail and marine enthusiasts. *Ann Arbor No. 3* (left) has just departed the slip, and the *No. 4* is preparing to take its place. (Tim Foster.)

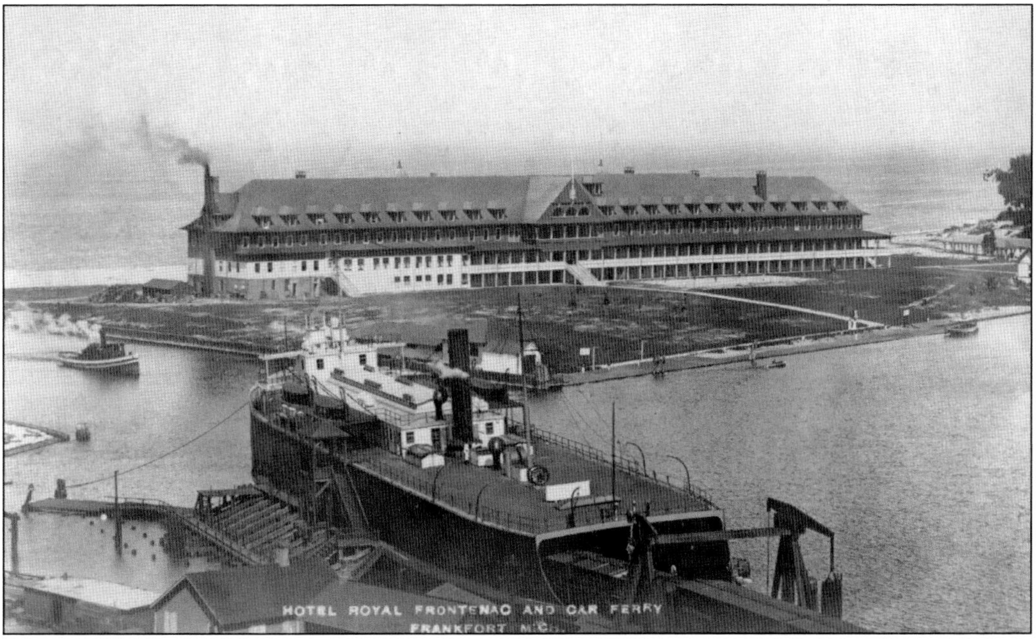


At the turn of the 20th century, the Ann Arbor Railroad built the Royal Frontenac Hotel, which rivaled the magnificent summer resort Grand Hotel on Mackinac Island. As at the Grand, large passenger steamers brought affluent vacationers to the Royal Frontenac from large cities. Opened in 1902, the huge wooden structure burned to a total loss in January 1912 and was not rebuilt. The *Ann Arbor No. 4* is shown taking on a load of cars at Elberta's west slip. (Tim Foster.)

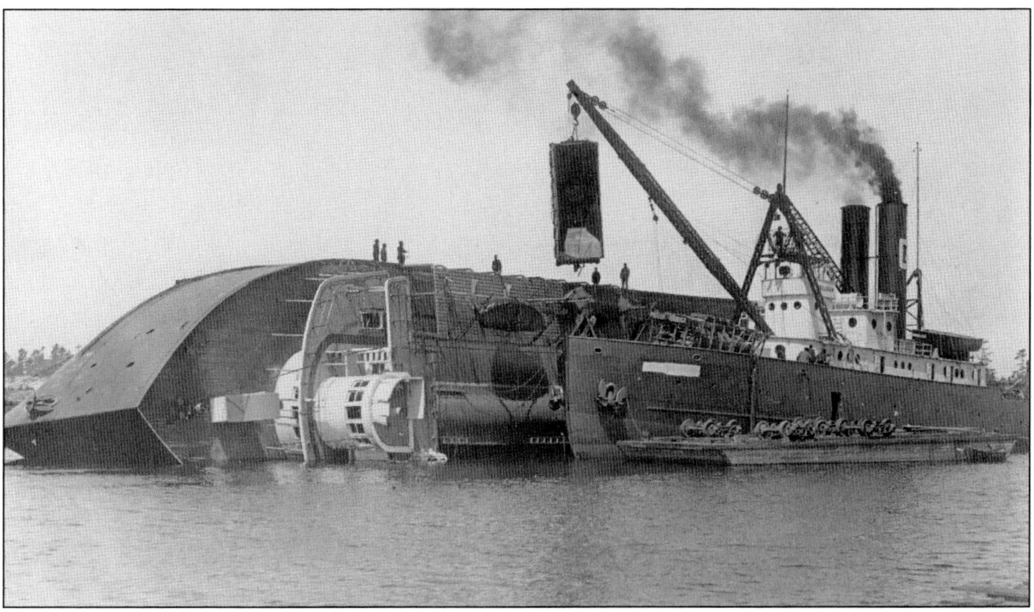

The capsizing of *Ann Arbor No. 4* at Manistique, Michigan, in 1909 was one of two major blows to the Ann Arbor fleet. A miscalculation by the switch crew and the ship's mate while loading heavy iron-ore cars caused the mishap. Too many cars were placed in the ship's port wing track all at once; the listing ship broke the cars couplings, preventing them from being pulled back off. In the second big incident, in 1923, the *No. 4* sank at the Frankfort pier head. (Tim Foster.)

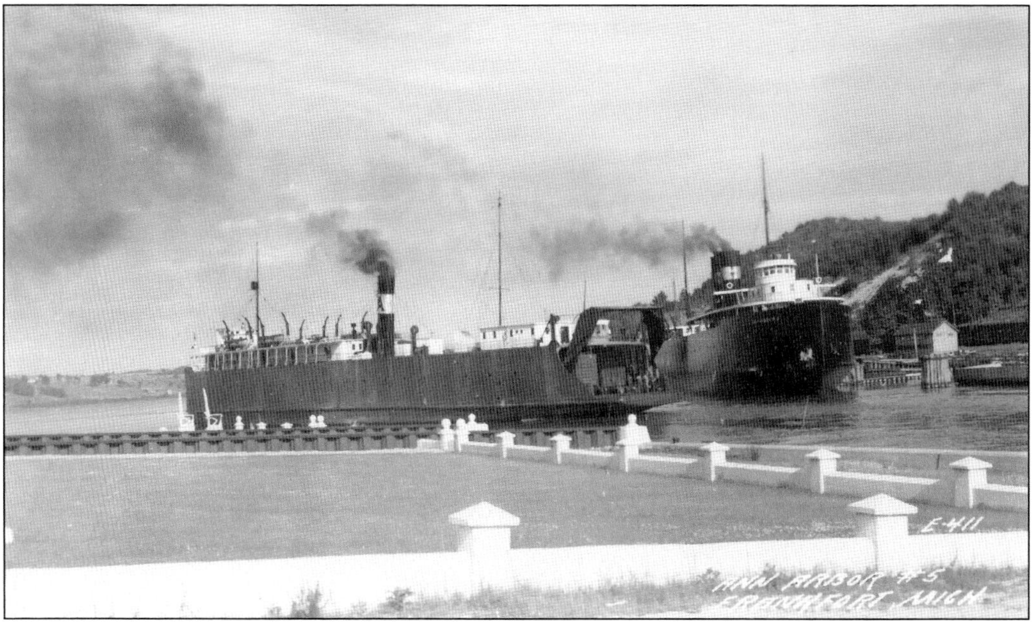


The harbor at Lake Betsie divided two municipalities. Frankfort, the larger of the two, was located on the north shore, and Elberta, the home port and operational base for the fleet, was on the south side. Official documents always stated that the Ann Arbor car ferries sailed out of Frankfort. The picturesque harbor was a tourist destination and offered visitors a clear view of the ferry activity. *Ann Arbor No. 3* is on the left, and the *No. 5* is in the slip. (Tim Foster.)

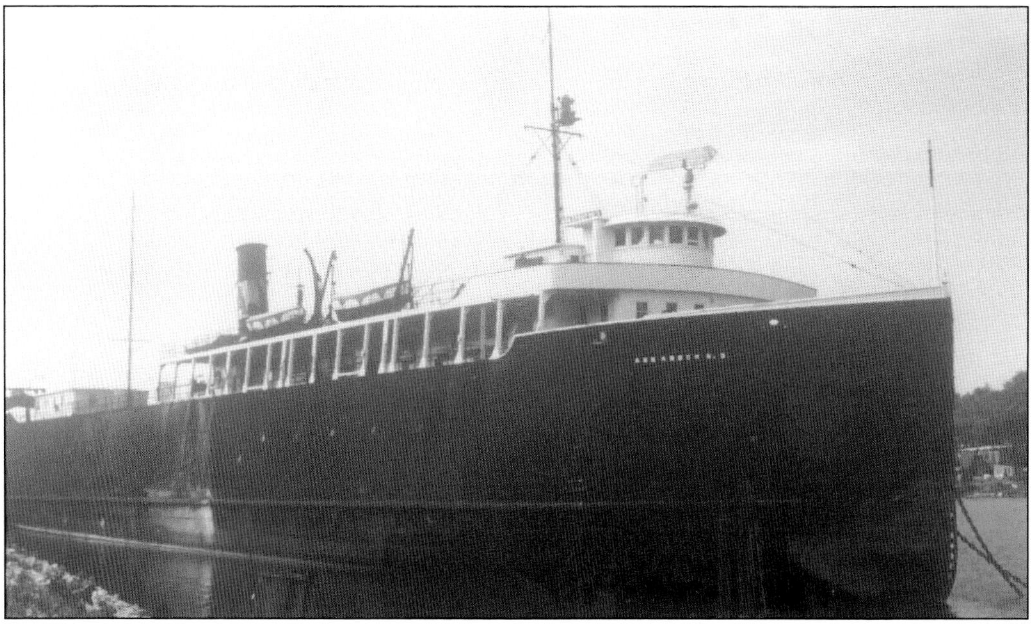

The *Ann Arbor No. 3* led a charmed life compared to her jinxed sister ship, *Ann Arbor No. 4*. Affectionately called the "three-spot" by her crew, the *No. 3* was altered several times, including lengthening, new cabins, and receiving new triple expansion engines. Her original power plant in 1898 consisted of the forward engines from the *Ann Arbor No. 1* and *No. 2*. (Bob Strauss; photograph by Vaughn E. Braatz.)

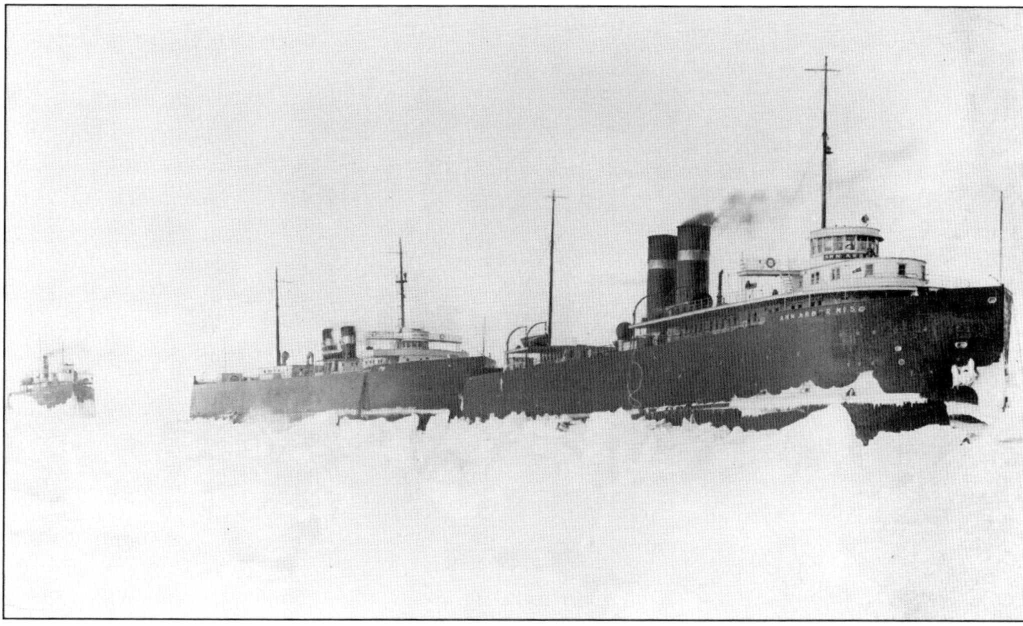

Heavy ice was typically problematic for the Ann Arbor fleet on the sheltered waters of Green Bay, but only on occasion at Frankfort during especially severe cold snaps. From left to right, the *Ann Arbor No. 4*, *No. 6*, and *No. 5* lie in an ice pack off Frankfort in early 1917. Crews were ordered onto the ice to pry it away from the ships hull with spud bars. (Tim Foster.)

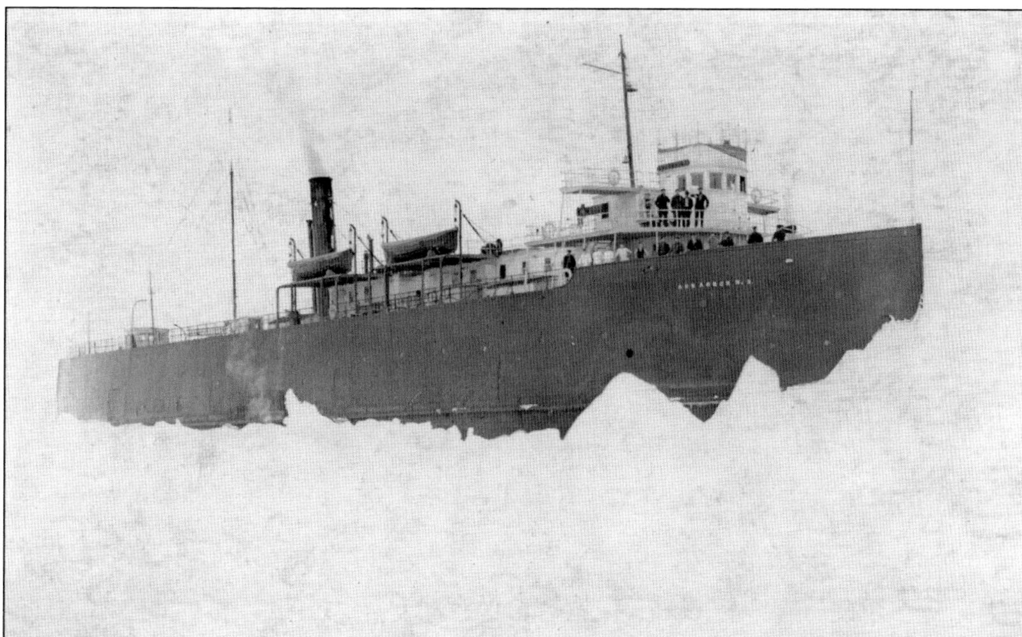

Shown in her glory days breaking heavy ice in the early 1900s, the *Ann Arbor No. 3* was used as an example in the British government's study of the severe weather a car ferry could handle as England attempted to establish rail ferry service across the English Channel. The *No. 3* ended her years as a barge. Renamed *Manistee*, the barge operated on the Great Lakes, and then it found a role in the New Orleans area as a tank-cleaning vessel. (Tim Foster.)

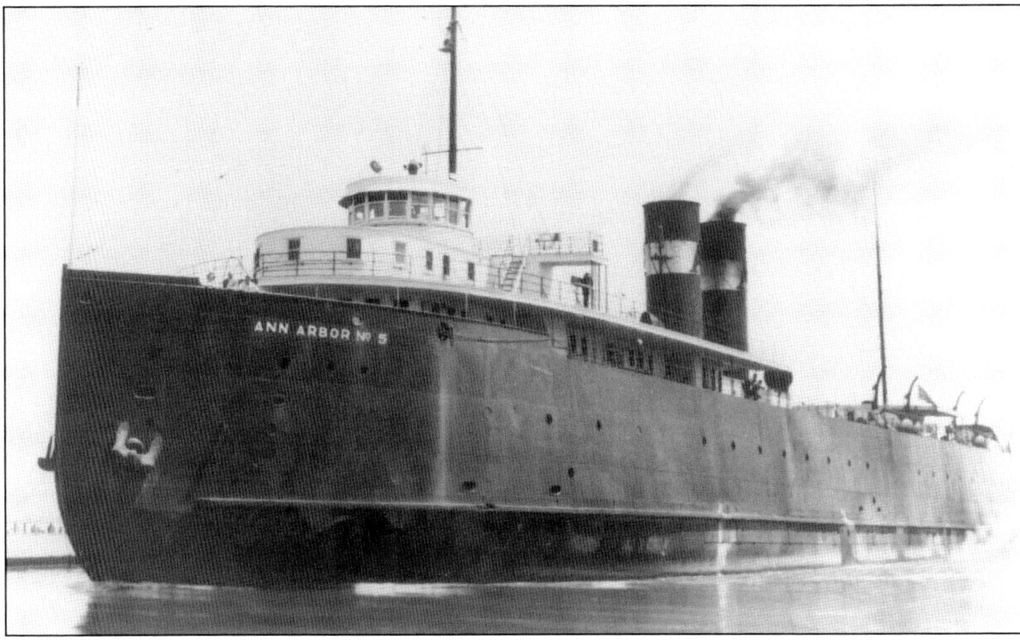


Likely the most famous of the early Ann Arbor car ferries was the *Ann Arbor No. 5*, one of the most successful icebreaking designs of naval architect Frank E. Kirby. Much has been written about this excellent ship, which survived half a century with few mishaps or disasters. In 1918, escaping steam killed four crew members in the *No. 5*'s boiler room during inspection. (Bob Strauss.)

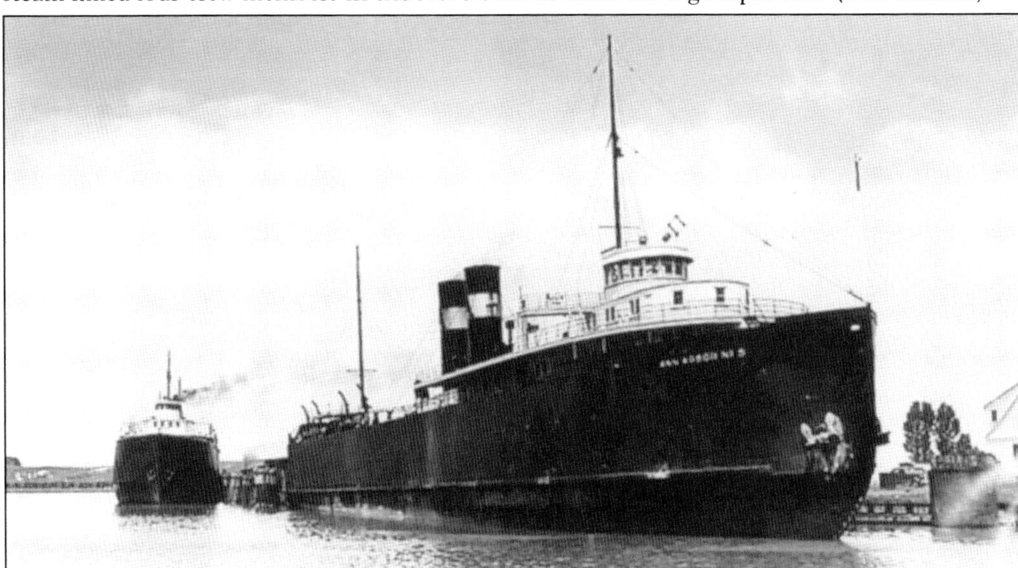

The *Ann Arbor No. 5*, foreground, and the *Pere Marquette 22* take on freight at Kewaunee in the 1940s. The *No. 5* was retired in 1965 and in 1966 sold to Bulk Food Carriers of San Francisco, but she never left the Great Lakes. In 1967, the ferry was acquired by Bultema Dock and Dredge Co., partially stripped for use as a barge, and in 1969 used as a scow and breakwater for the Palisades nuclear power plant near South Haven, Michigan. The hull sank in a storm but was recovered. What was left of her hull broke apart during a tow; the stern section embedded in the bottom of Lake Michigan. A dive team rediscovered the wreck in 2005. (Tim Foster.)

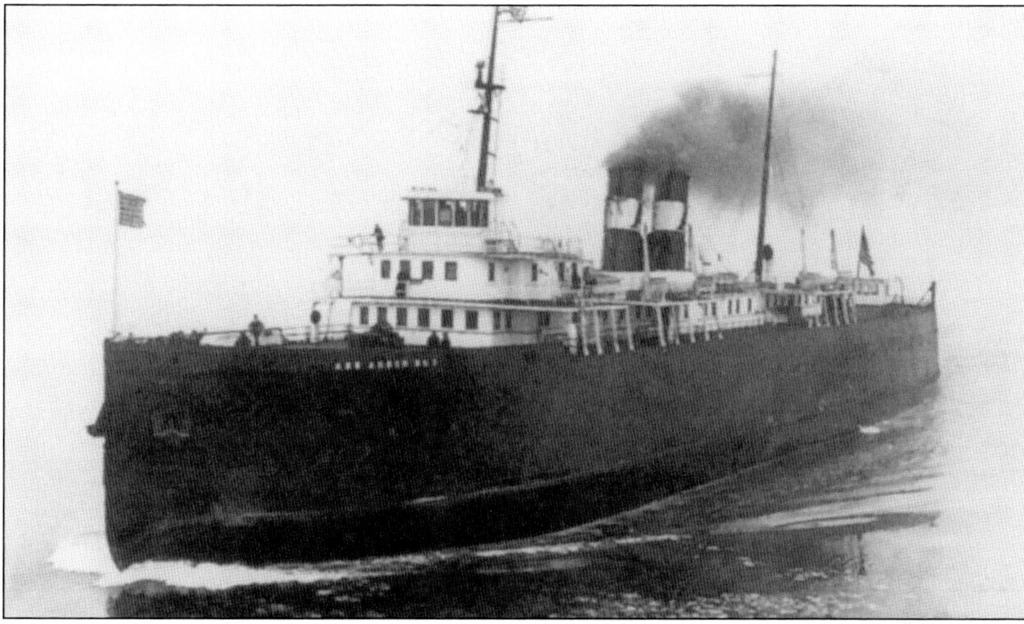

In 1925, the Ann Arbor Railroad ordered one of the new and improved mid-1920s car ferry designs from Manitowoc Shipbuilding Company. *Ann Arbor No. 7* differed from *Pere Marquette 21* and *22* by the installation of tall, panoramic pilothouse windows, shown here, and more importantly, a spoon-shaped, icebreaking prow. Such a hull feature was designed to allow the ship to rise above and cut through heavy ice fields. (Marc Vander Meulen.)

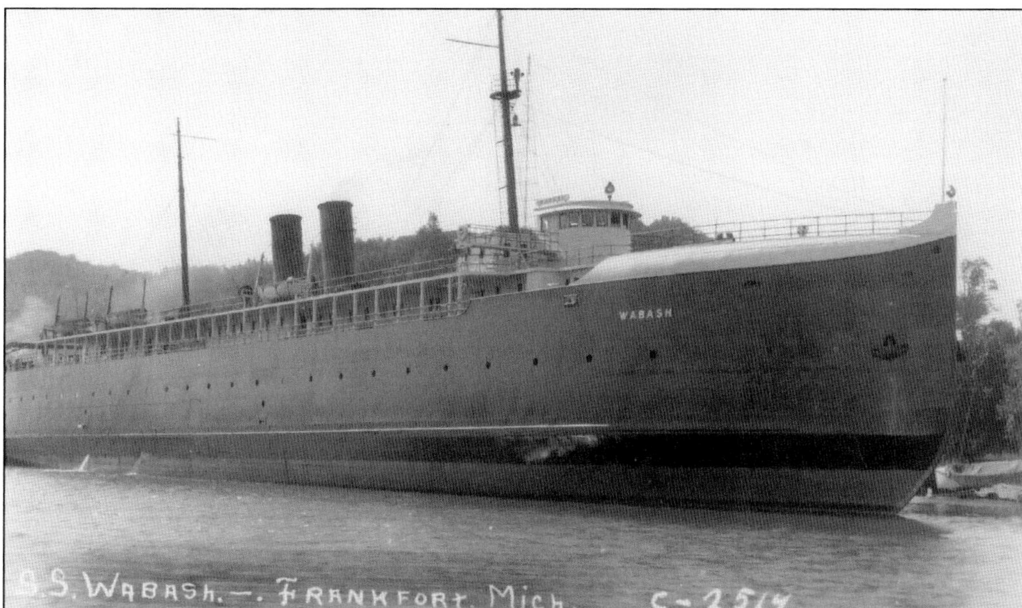


Experiencing significant growth and a need to upgrade its fleet, the Ann Arbor Railroad ordered another ferry in 1927 from the Toledo Shipbuilding Company. The *Wabash* was 380 feet long overall, with passenger cabins that ran the full length of the ship, a first for the fleet. The ship's most significant incident was a minor collision in fog with a Pere Marquette car ferry off Kewaunee in the 1930s. (Bob Strauss.)

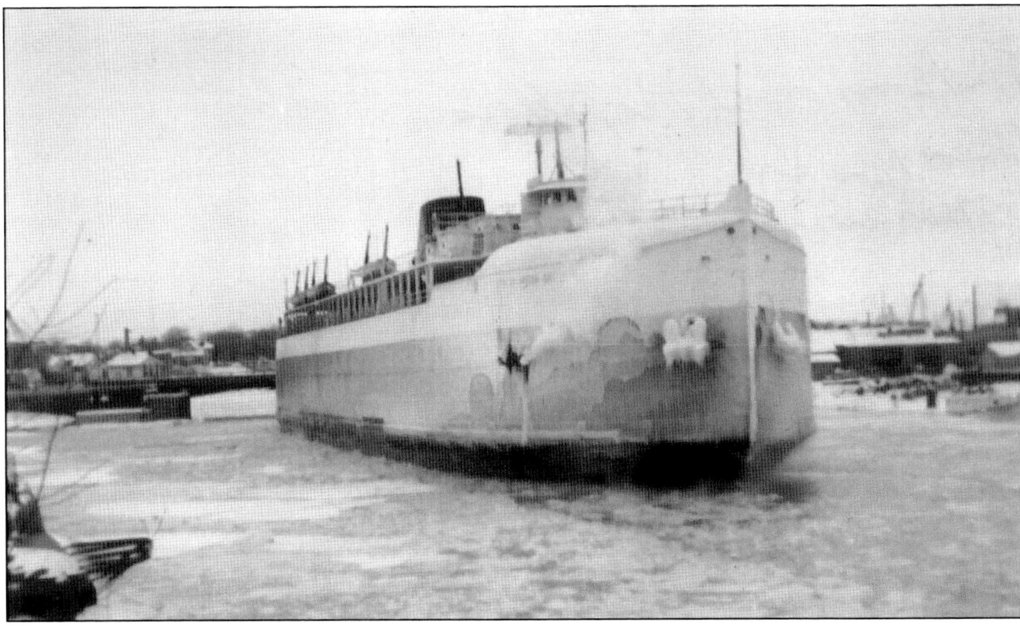

In 1962, the *Wabash* was converted from coal- to oil-burning and received a modern stack and an upgrade to her cabins as part of a fleet modernization program. Renamed *City of Green Bay*, she was retired from service and scrapped in Spain in 1974. The ship was retired, as it needed expensive structural repairs just as the Ann Arbor was abandoning some of its ferry routes. The *City of Green Bay* is shown outbound on the Manitowoc River. (Bob Peppard.)

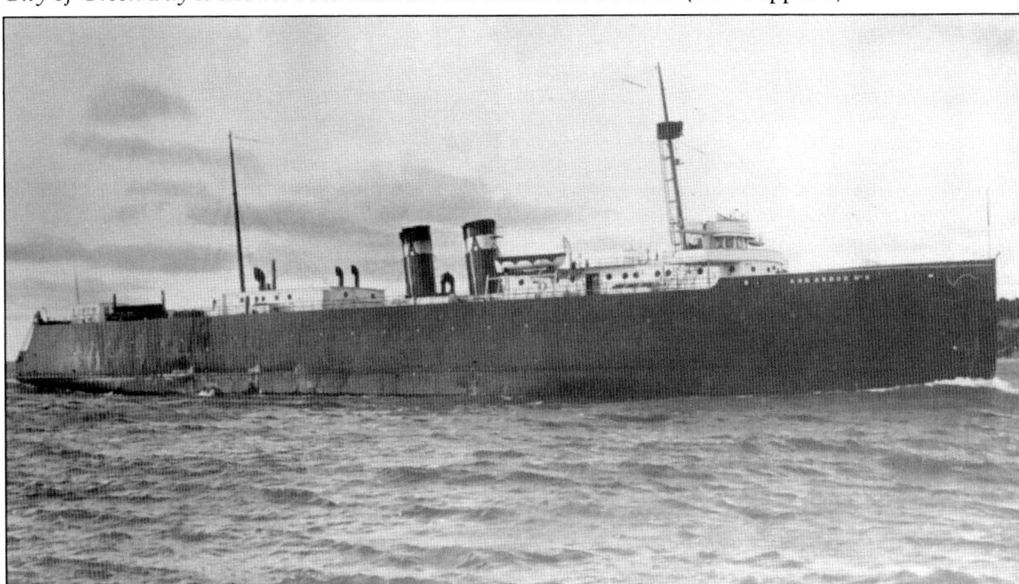

The *Ann Arbor No. 6* was the only ship not built specifically for the Ann Arbor fleet. It was one of two ferries to be built at Great Lakes Engineering Works for the Grand Rapids & Northwestern Railroad. A third was to be constructed, but investors pulled out of the venture during a shaky economic climate. The first ferry, *Maitland No. 1*, went to the Toronto & Hamilton Navigation Company, and the second ship went to the Ann Arbor Railroad as the *No. 6*, shown here at Frankfort. (Tim Foster.)

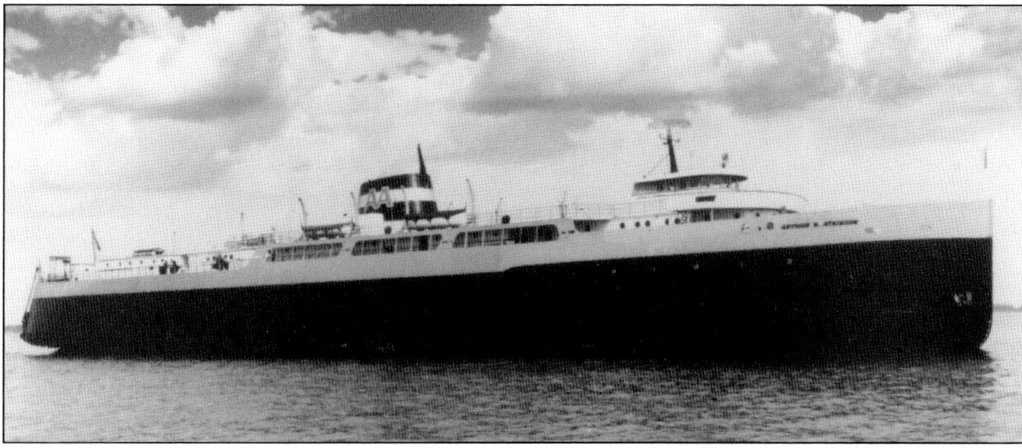

In 1958, failing to finance a new ship, the Ann Arbor Railroad settled on a fleet rebuilding program. *Ann Arbor No. 6* was withdrawn and sent to Manitowoc; her hull was lengthened and car deck clearance raised, and she was converted from steam to diesel propulsion—generally modernized inside and out. The renamed *Arthur K. Atkinson* was nearly four miles per hour faster, with deck space for four additional railcars. Two boilers were retained for steam heat and deck machinery. The ship is shown on her sea trials. (Bob Strauss.)

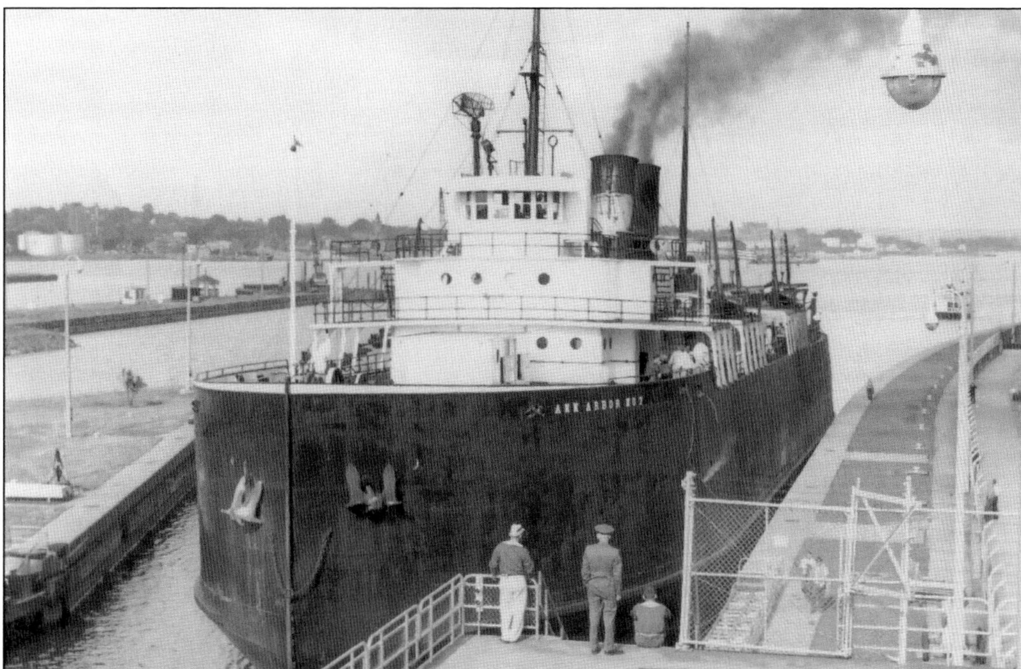

After the 1958 rebuild of the *No. 6* and the refurbishment of the *Wabash* in 1962, the *Ann Arbor No. 7* underwent a complete makeover in 1965 at Fraser Shipyard at Superior, Wisconsin. The ship was raised three feet, six inches, and twin triple-expansion steam engines were removed and replaced by four General Motors EMD locomotive-type 16-567D1 diesels. The boilers were not retained, but new cabins, stack, and pilothouse were added features. The *No. 7* transits the Soo Locks (her only such trip) en route to the Fraser yard. (Roger LeLievre; photograph by Thomas Manse.)

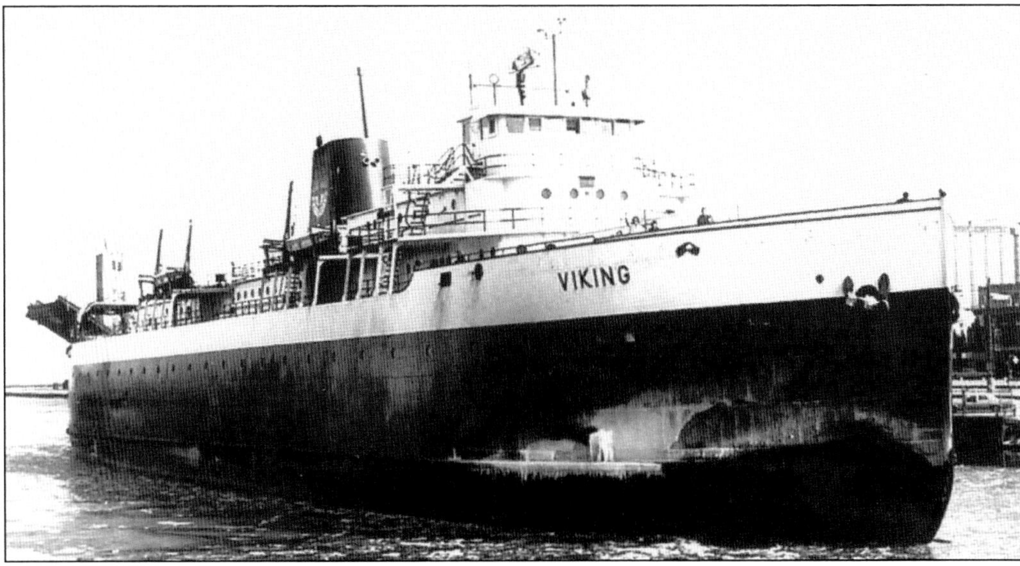

Upon the completion of her 1965 rebuild, *Ann Arbor No. 7* was renamed *Viking*, a fitting tribute to the Scandinavian (particularly Norwegian) heritage of many of the men and women who sailed with the Ann Arbor car ferry fleet. The *Viking* was the fastest and among the most powerful of the cross-lake car ferries, capable of 20 miles per hour at just over 7,000 horsepower. She is shown heading up the Manitowoc River during the 1970s. (Photograph by Roger LeLievre.)

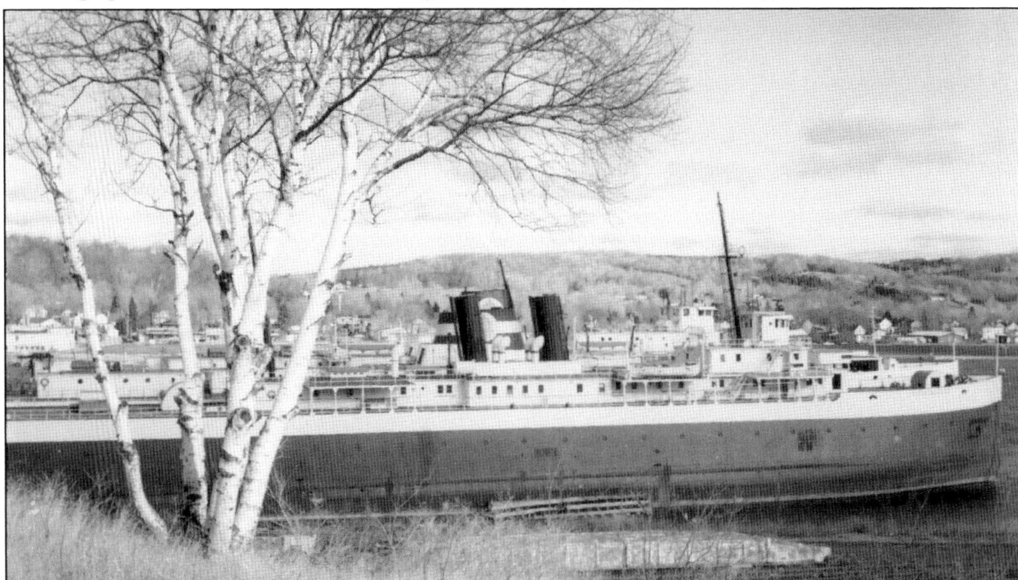

The *Viking* ran from 1965 until the Ann Arbor abandoned the car ferry business in 1982. The *Atkinson* ran from 1958 until 1973, when a broken crankshaft sidelined her until a 1980 repair and reconditioning brought her back to service for two years. The *City of Milwaukee* joined the Ann Arbor fleet in November 1978 after the Grand Trunk Railroad ceased its cross-lake service. A lack of funding subsidies from the states of Michigan and Wisconsin ended Ann Arbor's cross-lake ferry operation permanently in April 1982, just as the fleet was nearly returning to profitability without government aid. From front to back are the laid-up *City of Milwaukee*, *Atkinson*, and *Viking* at Elberta. (CofM.)

# *Three*

# THE LOSS OF THE SS *MILWAUKEE*

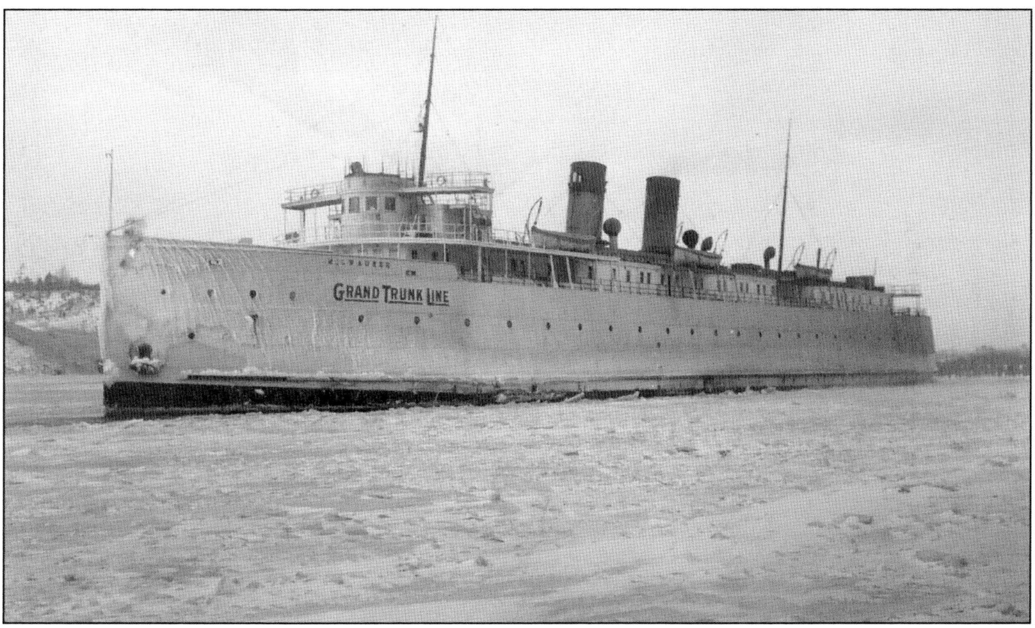


The Grand Trunk Railroad in 1908 bought the *Manistique Marquette and Northern 1* from the railroad of the same name (except the numeric designation of the ship) and renamed it *Milwaukee*. The ship was one of a successful series of ferries designed by Cleveland-based naval architect Robert Logan. For the next two decades, the *Milwaukee* ran dependably on daily schedules ferrying railcars between Grand Haven and Milwaukee before the ship and crew fell victim to the worst tragedy to involve a Great Lakes car ferry. The *Milwaukee* is shown at Grand Haven in 1912 wearing white hull livery. (Bob Strauss.)

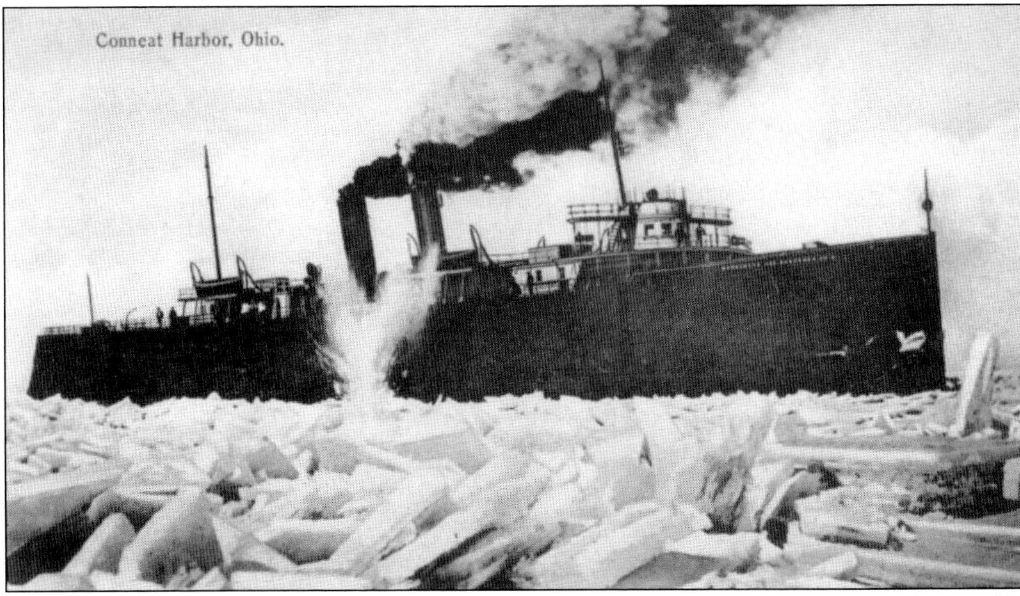


Before disaster struck the *Milwaukee*, two other car ferries with the same hull form, designed by Robert Logan, were lost on the Great Lakes. The first, the *Marquette & Bessemer No. 2*, sank with all 33 hands in a Lake Erie gale on December 9, 1909. Early car ferries were built with open sterns, allowing high waves to wash onto the car deck, flooding the holds below through open ventilation and coal-bunker hatches. Capt. Robert McLeod had complained about this problem not long before he and his men were lost. Here, the ship is dynamited out of an ice pack. (Bob Strauss.)

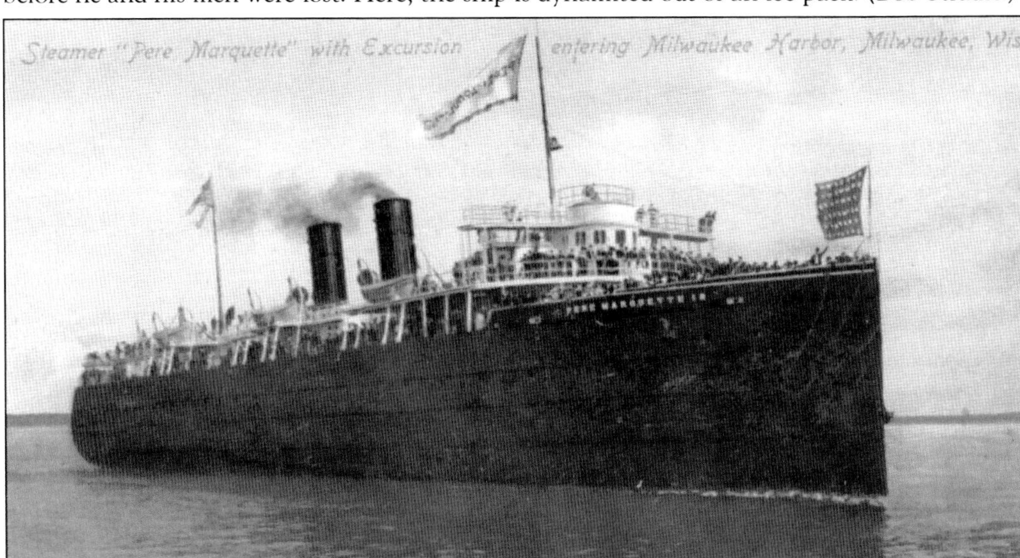


In the second car ferry tragedy on the Great Lakes, the *Pere Marquette 18* (shown at Milwaukee) was lost on September 9, 1910, when she sank in a moderate gale 20 miles off Sheboygan, Wisconsin. A sister ship was standing by. Thirty-three lives were lost, including all of the ship's officers. The *18* took on water from an unknown source; this was first discovered at 3:00 a.m. By 7:30 a.m., the source of the leak was still a mystery, and the ship sank stern-first in over 400 feet of water. The *Pere Marquette 18* had an open stern, which played a role in the sinking. Wreck hunters are currently looking for the ship. (Bob Strauss.)

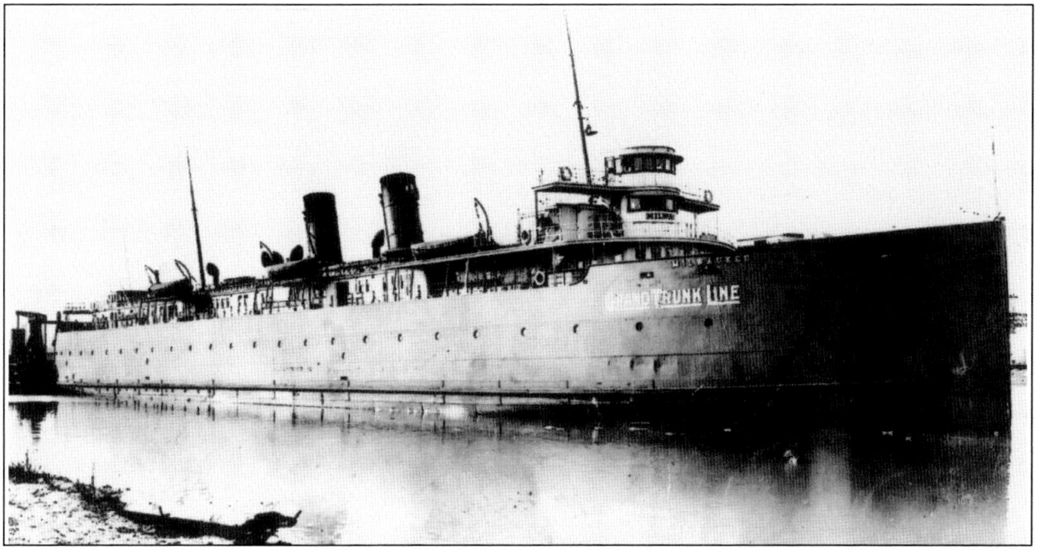

The *Milwaukee* was retrofitted in 1913 with a new steel sea gate. The hinged device lowered to form a solid barrier to deflect waves and lifted vertically over the car deck when in port. In spite of the perceived protection that the sea gates provided, they were not infallible. Early gates were just under five feet tall, allowing some of the heaviest seas to pour in over the top and sides. The *Milwaukee* is shown at her namesake port in the mid-1920s. (Bob Strauss.)

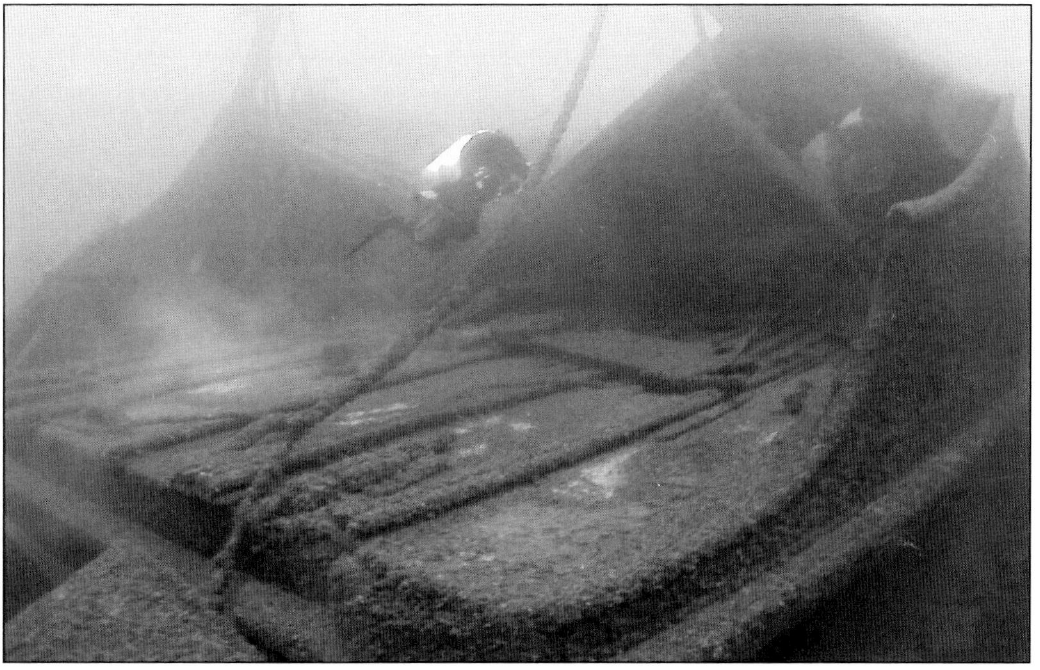

On October 22, 1929, the *Milwaukee* set out from Milwaukee to Grand Haven in the teeth of a massive northeasterly storm, with a cargo of 25 loaded railcars and a crew of 52 men. The ship was not equipped with radio communication (although it had radio during World War I when all Great Lakes car ferries came under government control). The ferry was last seen at 3:45 p.m. rolling and pitching deeply in a trough of massive swells. Within six hours, the ship would go down. The wreck is shown here, seen from the stern. (Photograph by Bob Broton.)

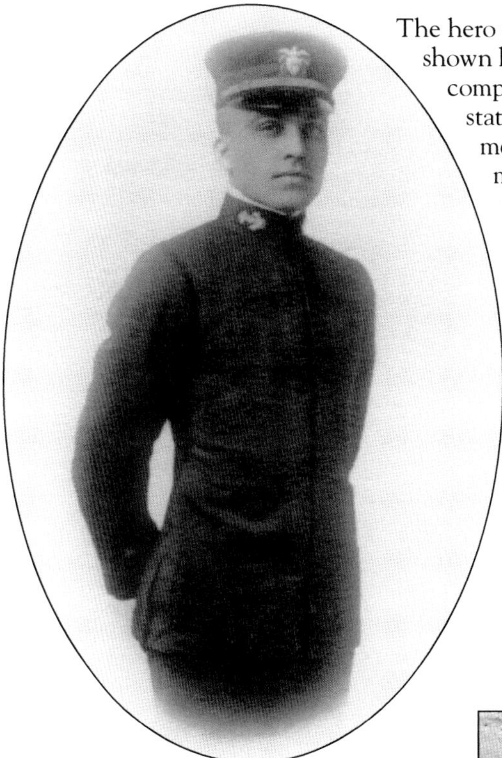

The hero of the *Milwaukee* disaster was A. Richard Sadon, shown here in his early 20s. The 32-year-old ship's purser composed a brief note on official Grand Trunk Railroad stationery. Sadon placed the note in a brass, watertight message carrier and tossed the tube overboard. The message read: "SS Milwaukee, October 22/29 8:30 p.m. The ship is making water fast. We have turned around and headed for Milwaukee. Pumps are working but sea gate is bent in and can't keep the water out. Flicker is flooded. Seas are tremendous. Things look bad. Crew roll is about the same as on last pay day." (Ed and Lunora Sadon.)

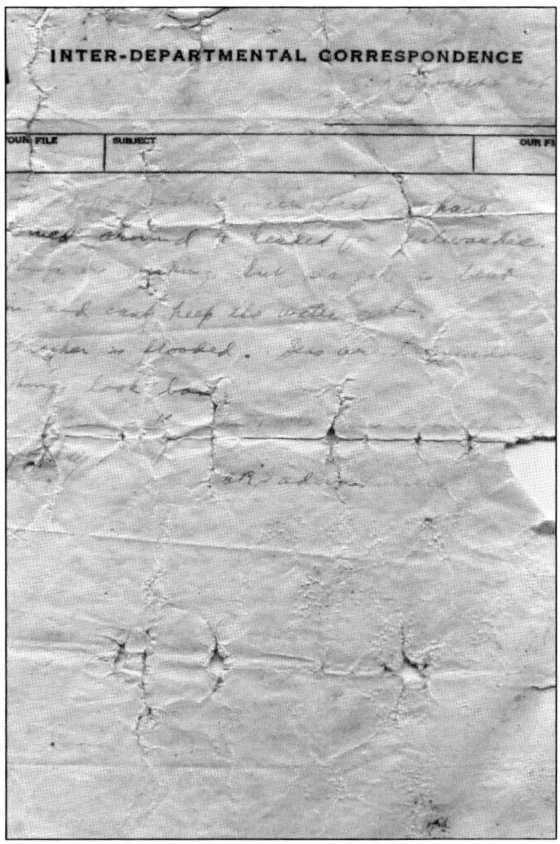

INTER-DEPARTMENTAL CORRESPONDENCE

YOUR FILE | SUBJECT | OUR FI

The term *flicker* in Sadon's message refers to the crew quarters below deck at aft. The message case was found by a Coast Guard beach patrol near South Haven, Michigan, on Sunday, October 27, 1929. In the chaotic horror of the *Milwaukee*'s sinking, a lifeboat was launched; unfortunately, the four men inside died from exposure before they reached shore. A.R. Sadon's note, shown, was rediscovered in 2006 in the files of the Chicago branch of the National Archives. It had not seen the light of day since it was filed and boxed in the 1930s. (National Archives and Records Administration.)

# *Four*

# SS CITY OF MILWAUKEE OPERATIONAL HISTORY

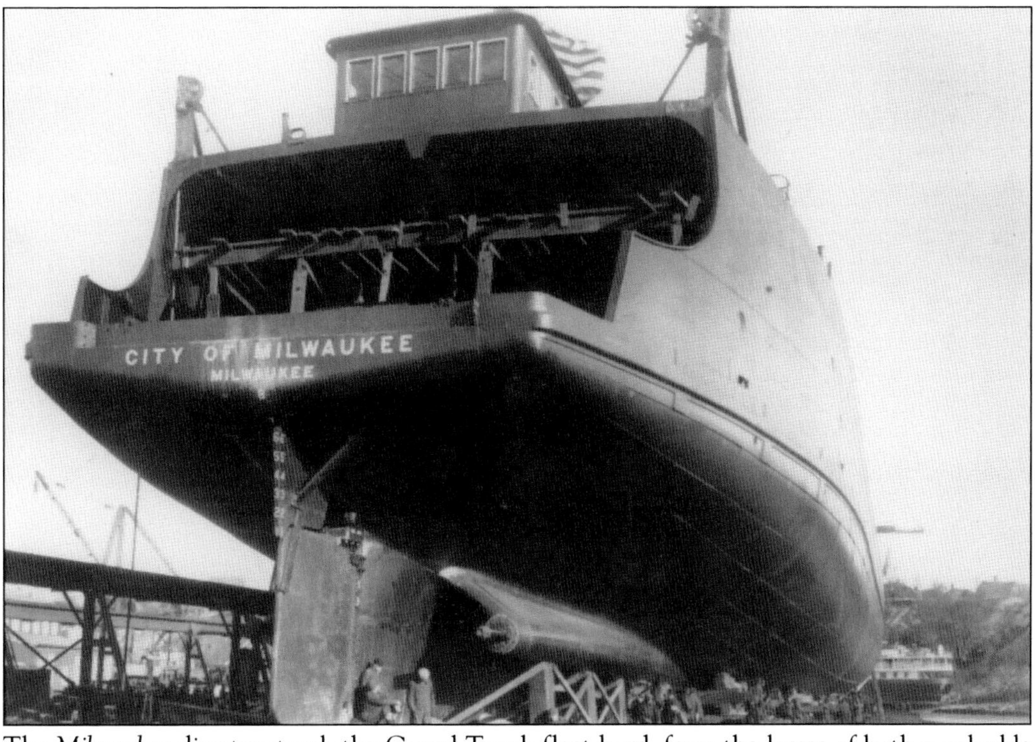


The *Milwaukee* disaster struck the Grand Trunk fleet hard, from the losses of both a valuable asset and the men who sailed aboard her. Especially hard-hit was the fleet's home port of Grand Haven, where nearly everyone knew someone who was on board the ship. Many lost a father, son, or husband. But the reality of running a railroad required a new ship to replace the *Milwaukee*. Manitowoc Shipbuilding again was tasked to build yet another ferry to the design of the fleet's *Grand Rapids* and *Madison*. Shown here on the launch ways, she sports the name *City of Milwaukee*, in honor of both her lost predecessor and the city that she would service. (WMMM.)

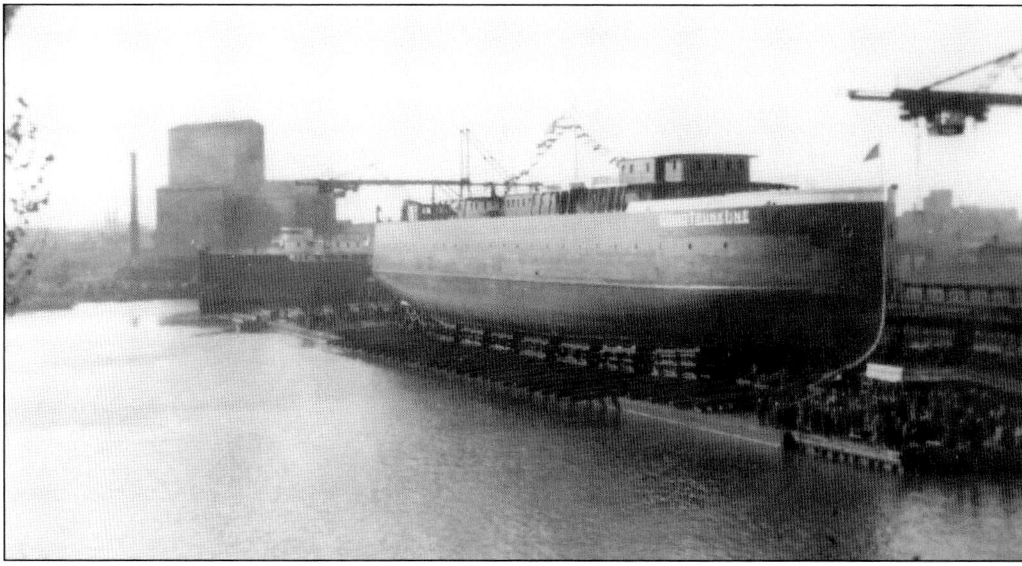

According to the November 25, 1930, issue of the *Muskegon Chronicle*, "A special train brought several hundred business executives, public officials and railroad men [from] Wisconsin, Illinois and Michigan to [the Manitowoc Shipbuilding yards] to witness the launching. . . Following the launching, the Manitowoc Shipbuilding corporation was host to 300 guests at luncheon in the Hotel Manitowoc. The "City of Milwaukee" will make daily round trips between Milwaukee and Grand Haven until spring when its Michigan port will be Muskegon where a new carferry terminal and harbor developments are being completed." (WMMM.)

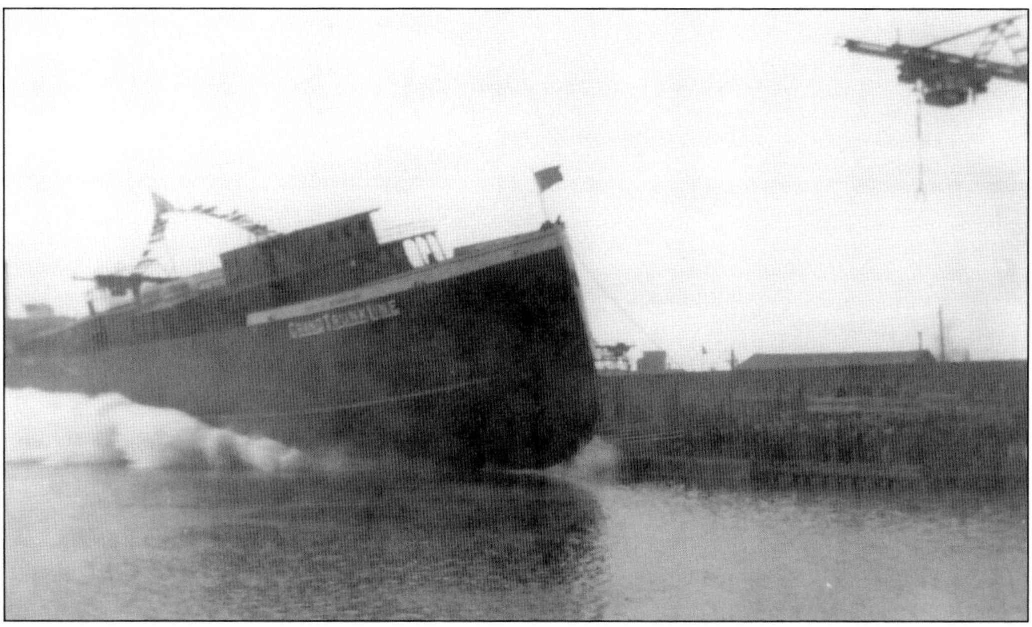

The *Muskegon Chronicle* continues: "While several thousand watched, the new million dollar carferry "City of Milwaukee" rolled broadside down its skids this morning and sent the waters of the Manitowoc River showering high into the air. . . . [T]he giant steel craft was christened in time-honored fashion by Mrs. Walter Wilde, wife of the collector of customs for the district of Wisconsin." (WMMM.)

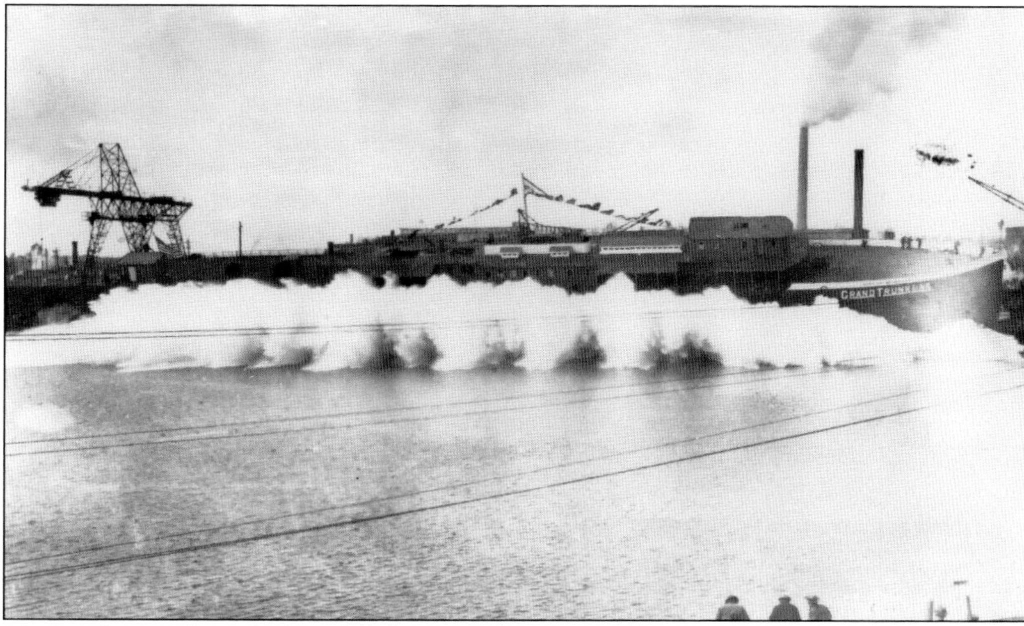

The *Muskegon Chronicle* describes the boat's launch in the November 29, 1930, issue: "With a mighty splash, the new million-dollar carferry, City of Milwaukee, slides sideways down the ways at Manitowoc, Wis., to go into service this winter to replace a ship which foundered with its crew in Lake Michigan last fall . . . The ship will ply between Milwaukee, Grand Haven, and later Muskegon." (WMMM.)

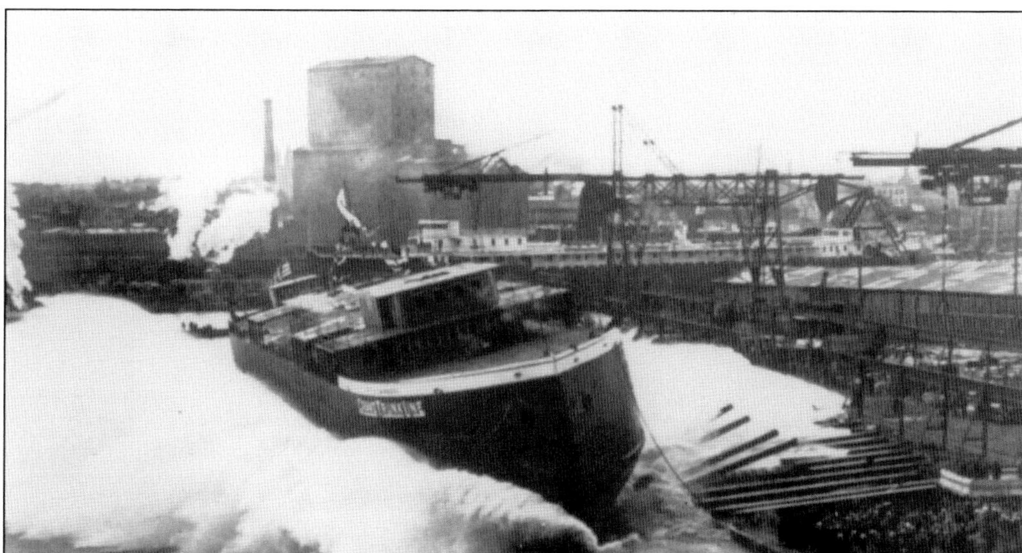

The *Muskegon Chronicle* article on November 25, 1930, states: "With an overall length of 360 feet and gross tonnage in excess of 3000 tons, the new carferry will be able to carry 28 loaded freight cars of the largest type. Its carrying capacity will be 2400 tons of freight and 200 passengers. . . . The new carferry is the last word in ships of its class, has the latest in mechanical equipment and the furnishing of the quarters of both passengers and crew is carried out in the most up-to-date manner. The ship was built largely of the products of Milwaukee and Wisconsin industries and 1200 men were employed in its construction." (WMMM.)

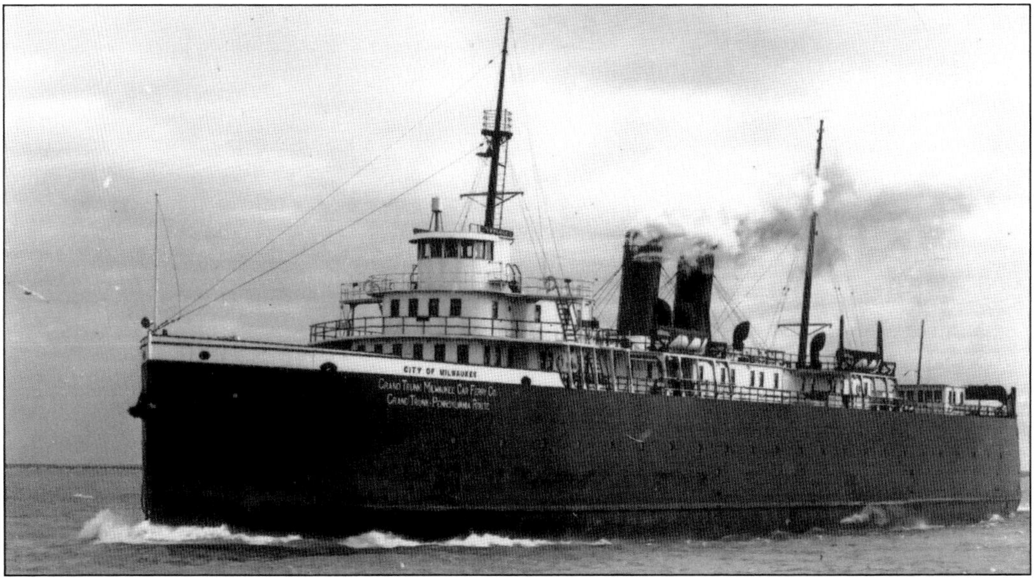

"Her entrance acclaimed by blasts of sirens, whistles, and an accompaniment of hundreds of automobile horns, the new Grand Trunk carferry City of Milwaukee made her first entrance into Grand Haven harbor at 11 p.m. Saturday [January 17]. . . . The run of 84 miles pier to pier was made in five hours and 29 minutes according to the ship's log, departure from Milwaukee being at 5:29 p.m.," reads the *Muskegon Chronicle* article on January 19, 1931. Here, the ship blows her whistle a few years after she entered service. (John W. Hausmann.)

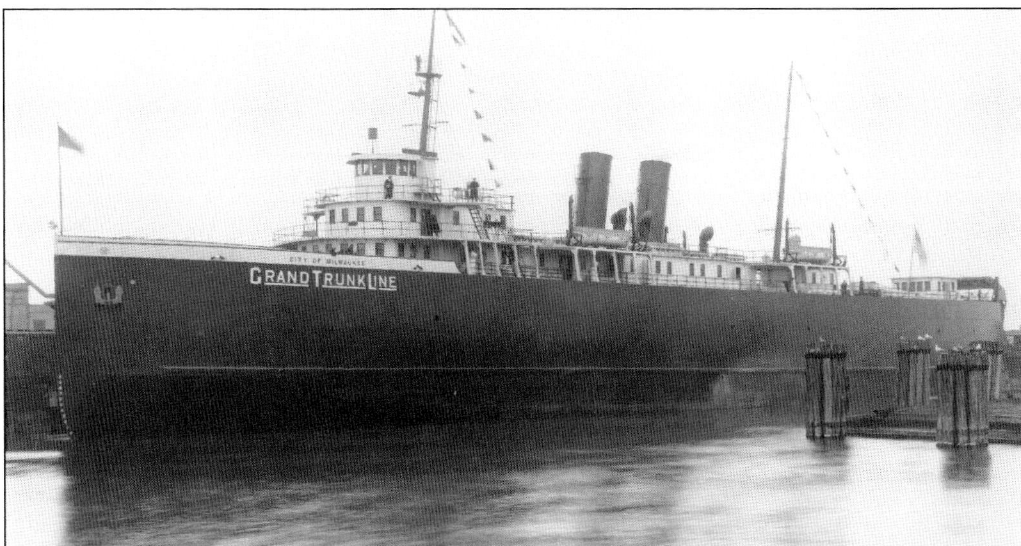


The article goes on to say that "Sunday morning the City of Milwaukee was docked at the warehouse wharf and shortly after 8 o'clock the Chamber of Commerce committee headed by President A.E. Jacobson and Secretary William L. Stribley who was a guest on the first trip across, made inspection. Hundreds visited the steamer during the morning. As flagship of the Grand Trunk fleet, she was decked out with flags and banners including the flag captain's banner of Capt. John F. Cavanaugh her master. The paint work is the same as other Grand Trunk vessels, dark green hull, white upper works and black funnels and masts." (Dick Fox.)

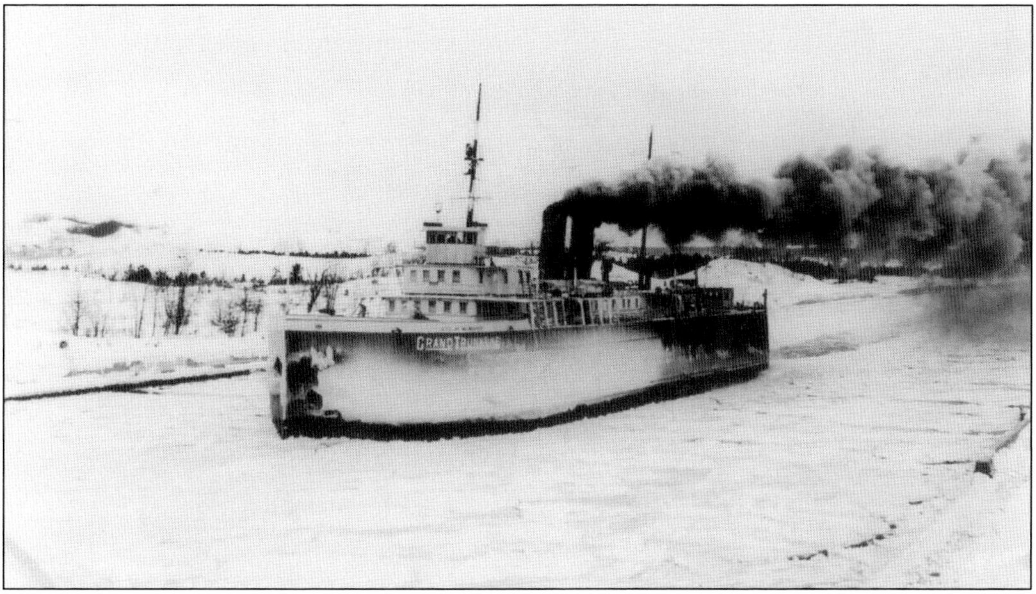

In July 1933, the Grand Trunk Railroad switched its east-bank ferry terminus from Grand Haven to Muskegon. Marine superintendent Charles E. McLaren cited the need for safer and more efficient service due to the narrow, congested harbor at Grand Haven; accidents and delays resulted in $94,000 in losses in 1928. During 1927–1928, the fleet lost 1,184 operating hours in ice delays. Muskegon harbor had a large arrowhead-shaped breakwater and a naturally wide turning basin for the ferries. Here, the *City of Milwaukee* leaves Muskegon in moderate ice. (Art Chavez.)

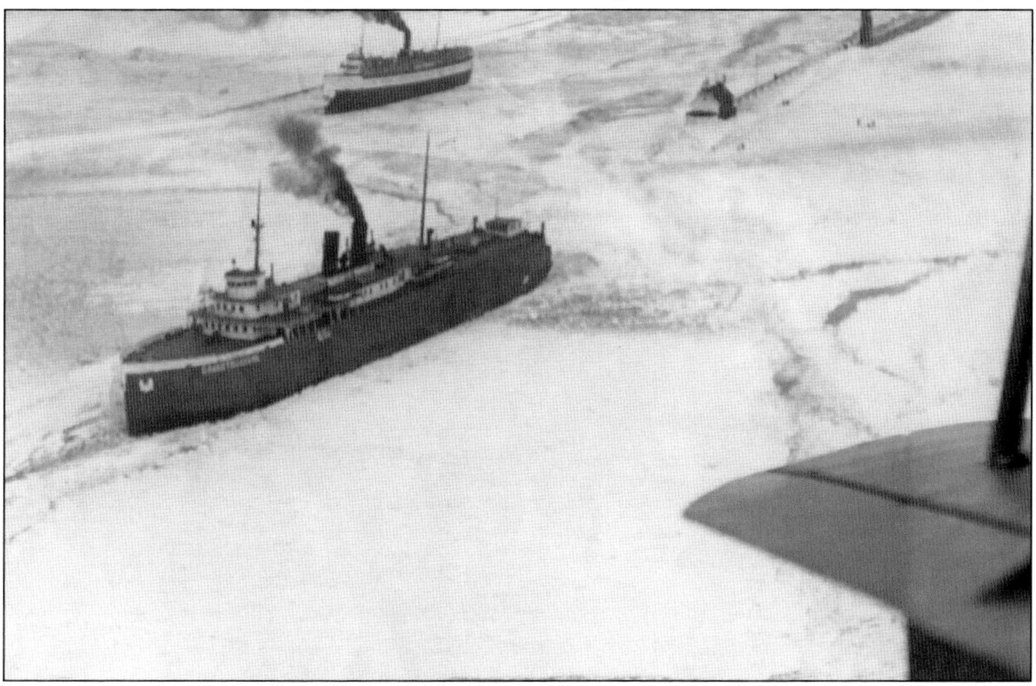

This rare aerial view shows the *City of Milwaukee* working through a heavy ice field off the Grand Haven pier heads. The unprotected outer harbor at Grand Haven was susceptible to sandbar buildup and heavy ice. (Bob Strauss.)

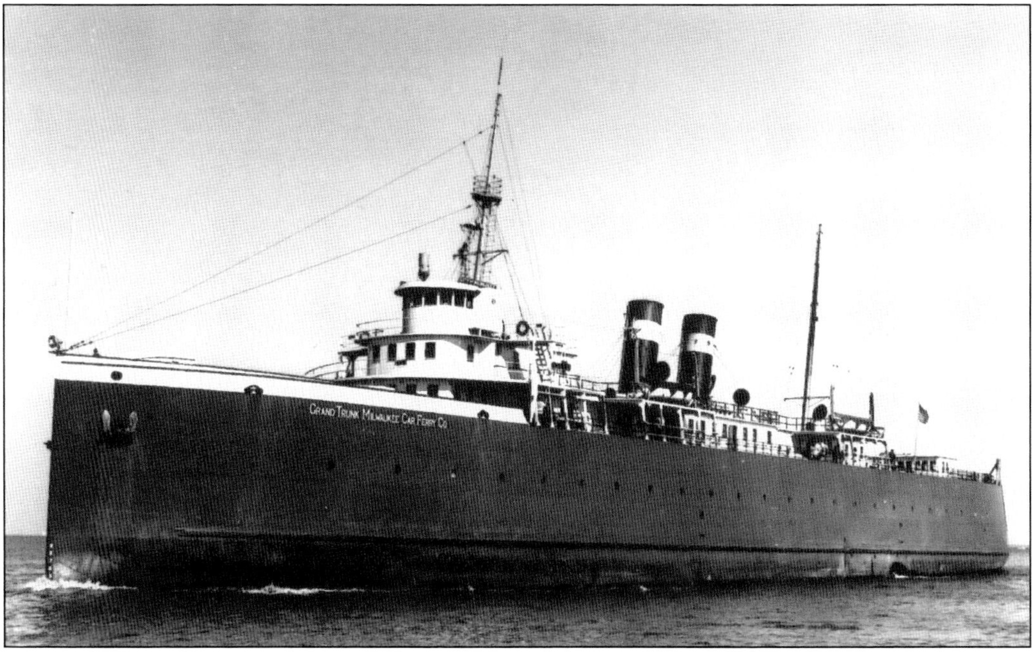


The *City of Milwaukee* is shown in the 1950s wearing the stack colors of the Canadian National Railway: red stack, white band, and blue top ring. For a short time, the hull remained a kelly green, but it was later painted with black with a white upper band. Over the years, several different shades of green were used. (Roger LeLievre.)

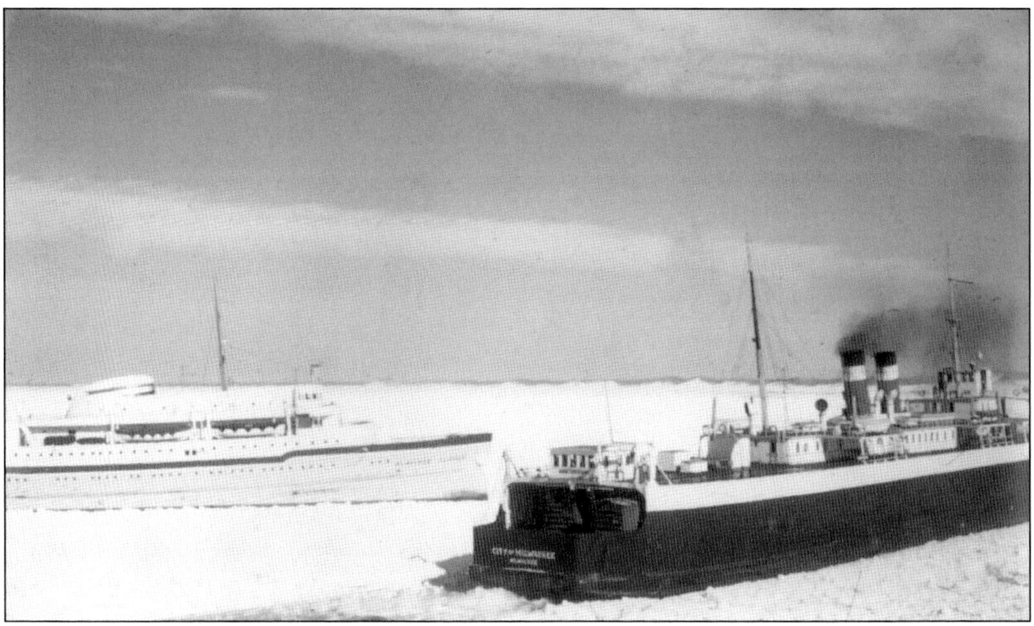

On occasion, heavy ice fields piled up for miles outside of a harbor, sometimes running up and down along the coast as far as the eye could see. These unusual conditions were caused by a prolonged cold snap and a predominant, sustained wind from a given direction. Historically, the east shore of Lake Michigan bore the brunt of these conditions. Here, the *City of Milwaukee* assists the *Milwaukee Clipper* outside of Muskegon. (CofM; photograph by Clarence Klein.)

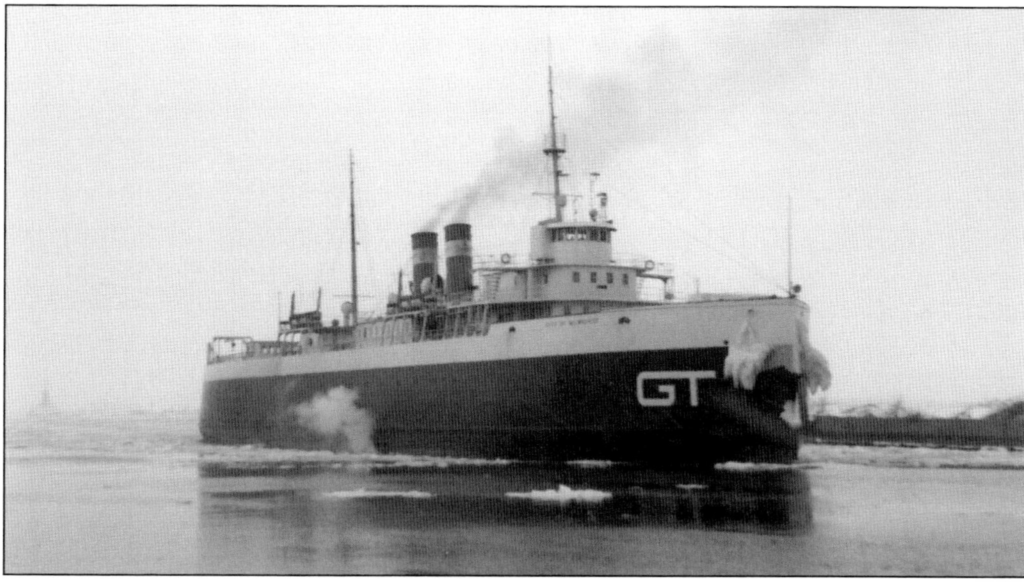


Wearing brows of heavy ice on her anchors, the *City of Milwaukee* enters Muskegon harbor after a wintry crossing from Milwaukee. Typical eastbound loads consisted of automobile frames, malt, beer, tractors, machinery, paper, dairy products, and fertilizer. Westbound cargo included coal, oil, foundry sand, newsprint, glass bottles, salt, and sheet and structural steel. (Photograph by Bruce Groeneveld.)

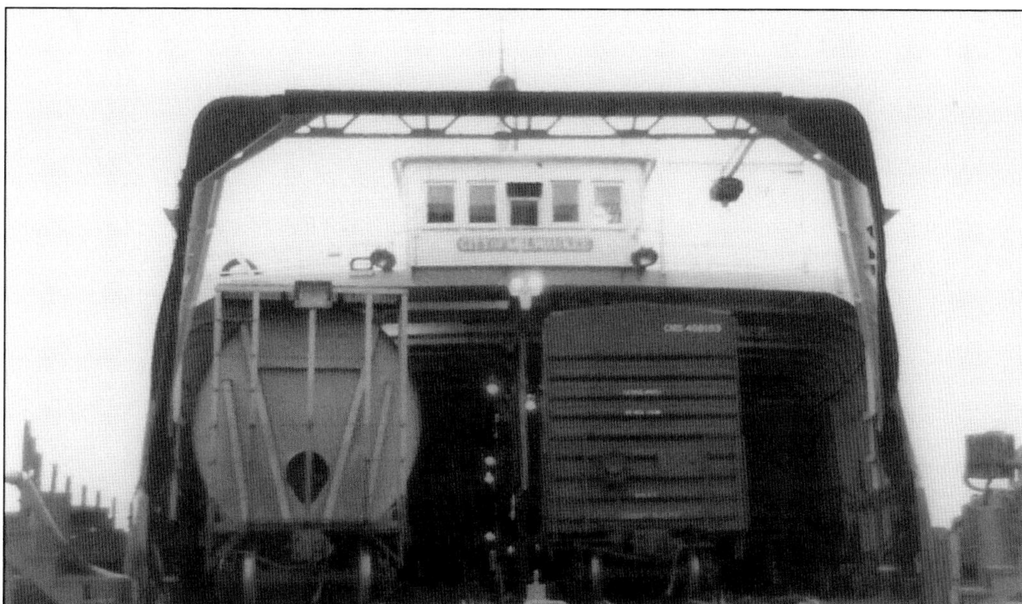

The *City of Milwaukee* awaits a switch crew to unload a cargo of railcars. When built in 1931, the ship was able to carry 28 standard-size railcars. By the mid-1970s, larger cars reduced the ship's capacity to 24. Note the tight overhead and side clearance, especially in the wing track on the ship's port side. Some of the oversized cars had to be carried in the center tracks or, if too high, would have to cross the lake on the *Madison* or Chesapeake & Ohio Railway's *Badger* or be routed through Chicago. (Photograph by Bruce Groeneveld.)

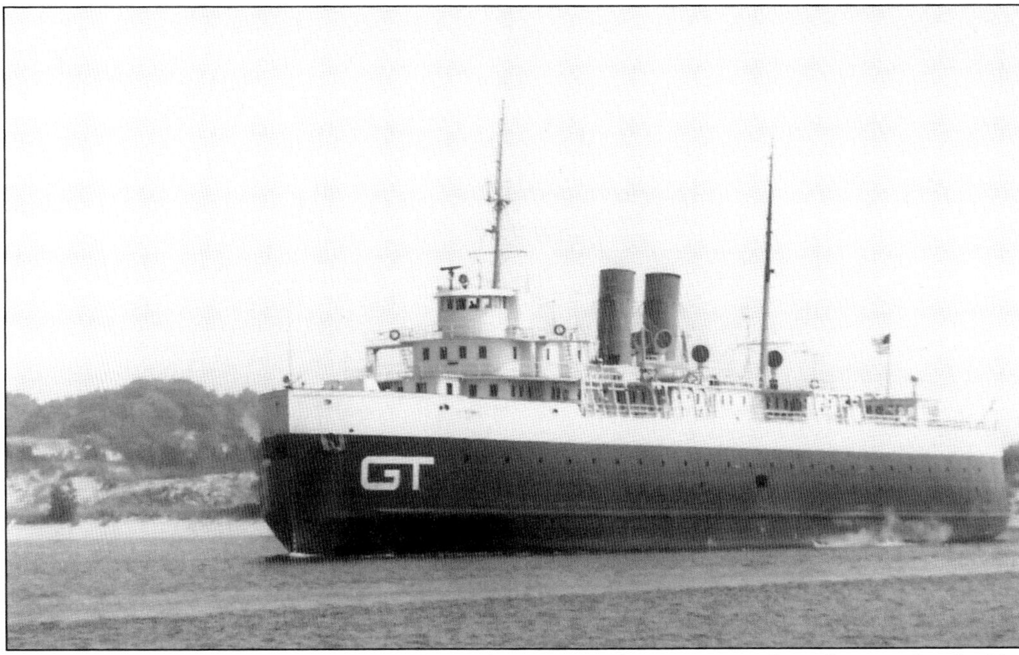


Sporting new stack colors of the Grand Trunk Western's locomotive color scheme—bright blue stacks with a red/orange top band, the *City of Milwaukee* departs Muskegon harbor bound for Milwaukee. The wet-noodle GT herald on the bow first appeared on the ships in 1962. (Photograph by Bruce Groeneveld.)

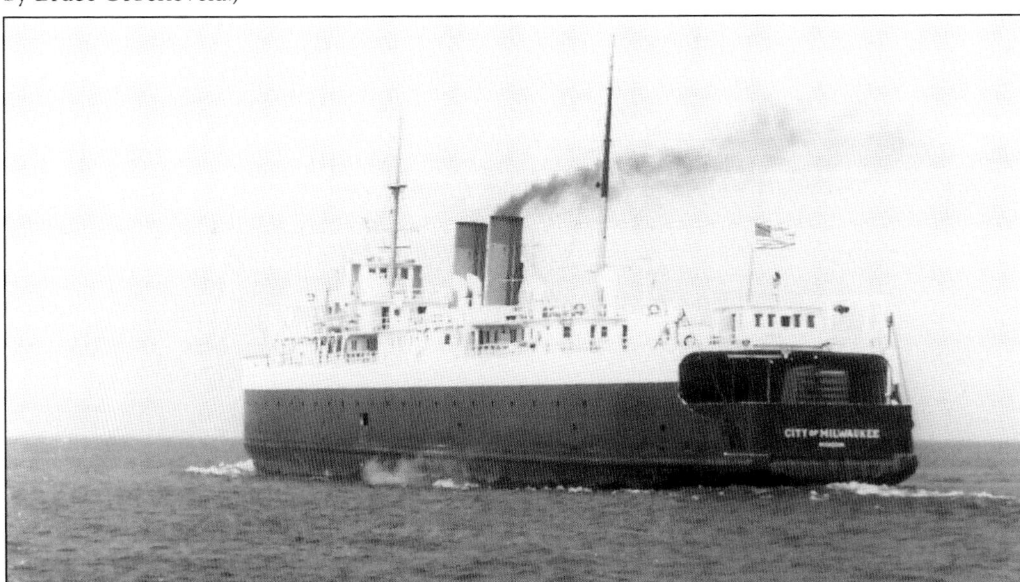

As the ship passes the camera, the stern end is visible, showing off the *City of Milwaukee*'s 10-foot-high sea gate. At the time the ship was designed, the plan was for a five-foot high sea gate. But a year after the Milwaukee disaster, a committee of Coast Guard and car ferry officials convened and decided on a minimum eight-foot, six-inch sea gate height. The Manitowoc Shipbuilding Company subsequently altered the ship's plans and built up the gates with five feet additional framing and shell plating. (Photograph by Bruce Groeneveld.)

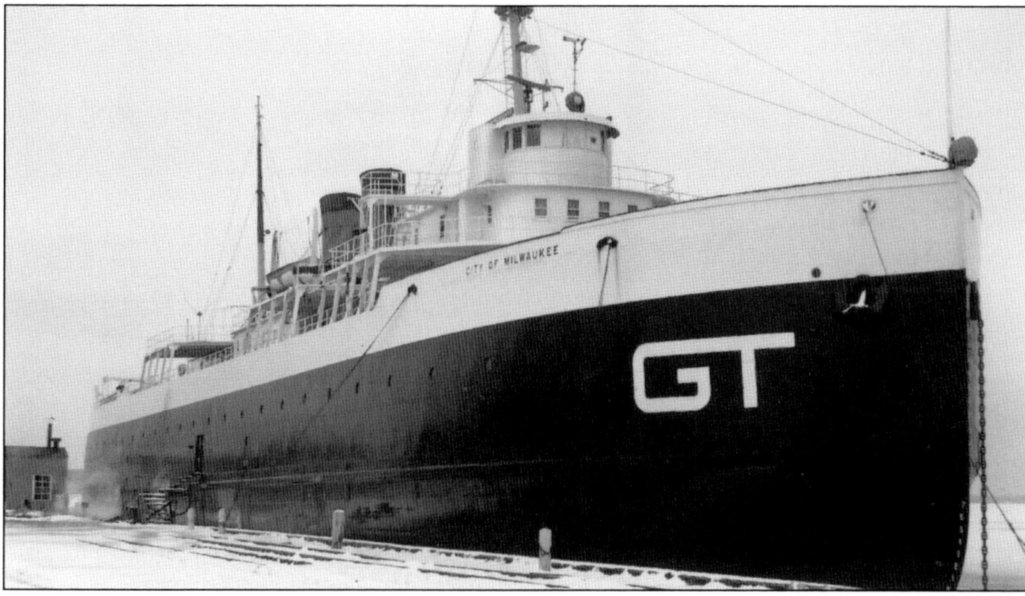


With canvas over her stacks and covers on her pilothouse windows, the *City of Milwaukee* still looks sharp laid-up at Muskegon. To the end, the Grand Trunk Railroad maintained its operational ships with care. Regular painting and cleaning details were a routine practice. Note the crow's-nest platform on the ship's forward mast. This was an unusual feature among car ferries and was shared by the three newest ships in the Grand Trunk fleet. (Photograph by Bruce Groeneveld.)

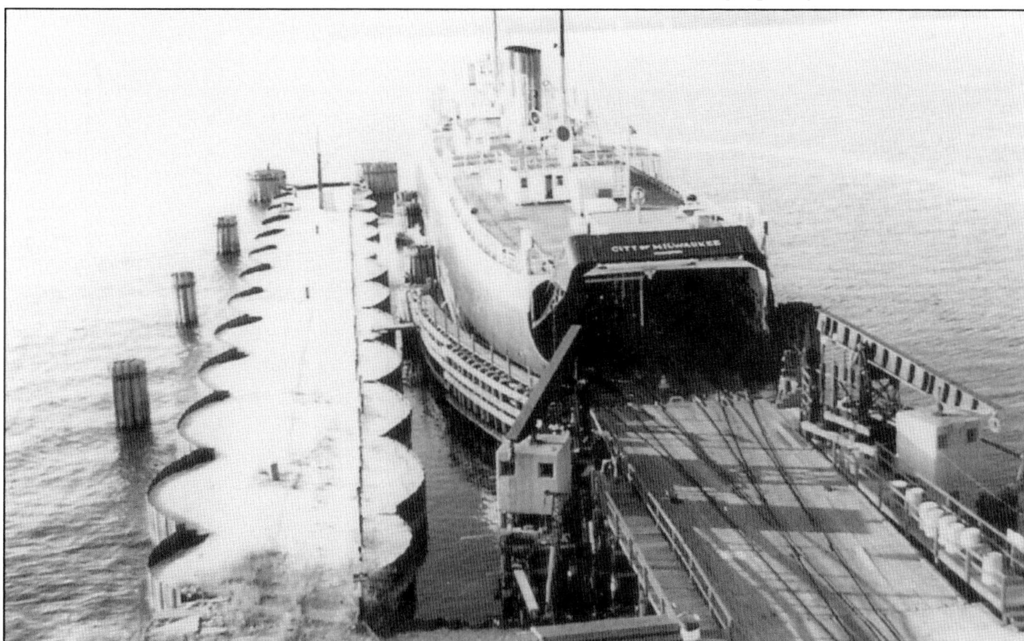

This aerial view shows the *City of Milwaukee* tied up at the slip in Muskegon at the foot of McCracken Avenue. In spite of the four-ship operation in the 1920s and a three-ship operation until the 1970s, the Grand Trunk had only one slip at each port served on the east side of Lake Michigan. On the west side of the lake, the port of Milwaukee had a second slip built in 1927 to accommodate the new *Grand Rapids* and *Madison*. (Photograph by Bruce Groeneveld.)

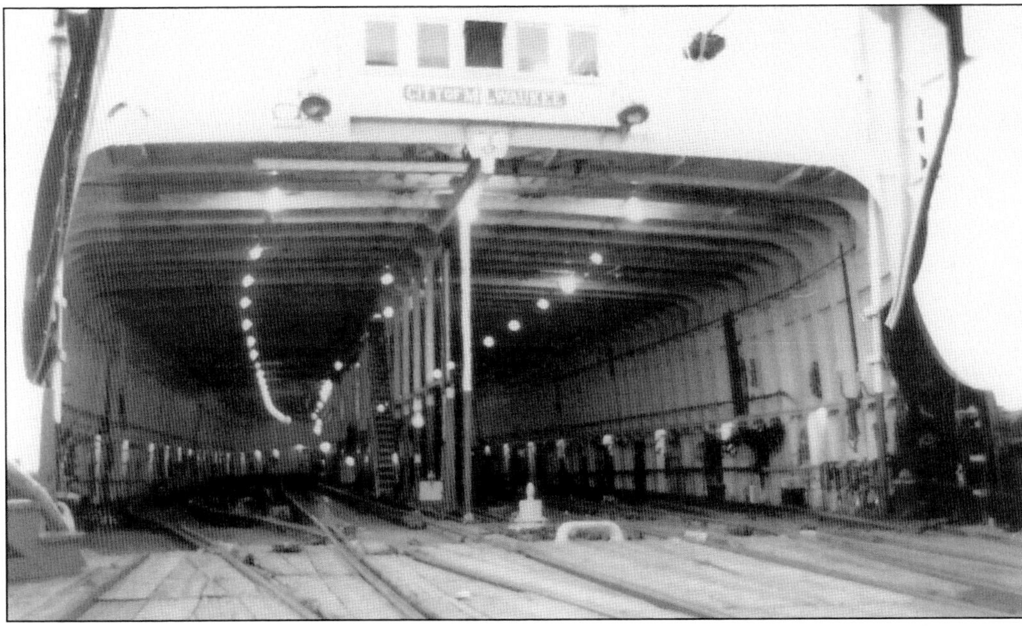

The stern end of the *City of Milwaukee* shows the cavernous, empty car deck as the ship awaits a load of freight at Muskegon during the 1970s. She was always looked upon as the fleet's best boat, in spite of her car deck not being raised to accommodate higher railcars, as those on her sister ships, *Grand Rapids* and *Madison*. (Photograph by Bruce Groeneveld.)

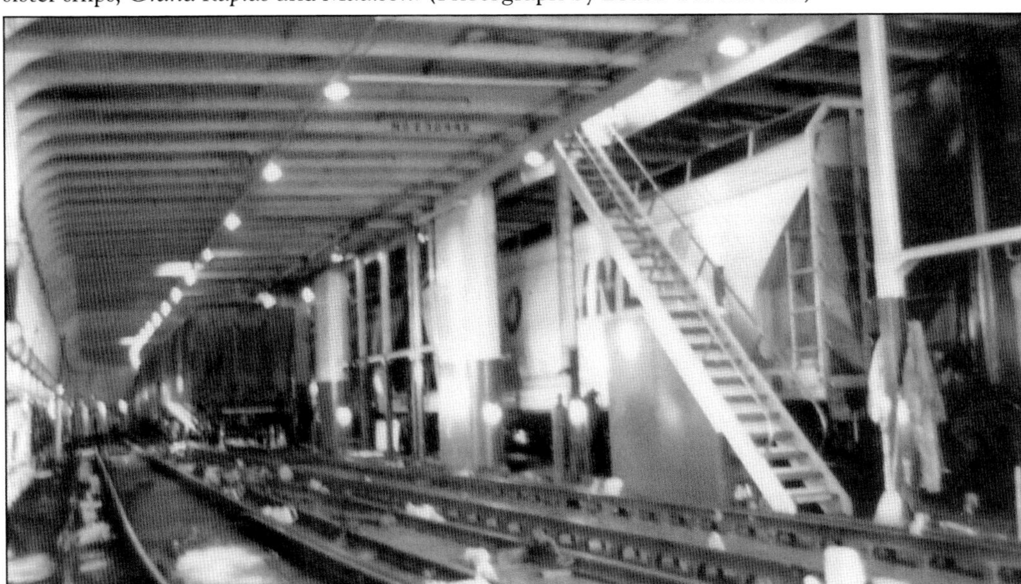

This view shows the ship's car deck with a partial load of freight, an increasing occurrence during the 1970s, as shippers began routing their cargo around the lake rather than across it. No doubt, the railroad was discouraging use of the ferries near the end of the service, and greater efficiencies in rail technology eliminated many of the time-saving benefits once offered by the cross-lake route. With partial loads like this, railcars were often placed alone, making them susceptible to rocking, damaging the ship's stanchions or falling completely over. Full loads allowed adjacent cars to buffer the movement of a car that broke its restraints in a storm. (Photograph by Bruce Groeneveld.)

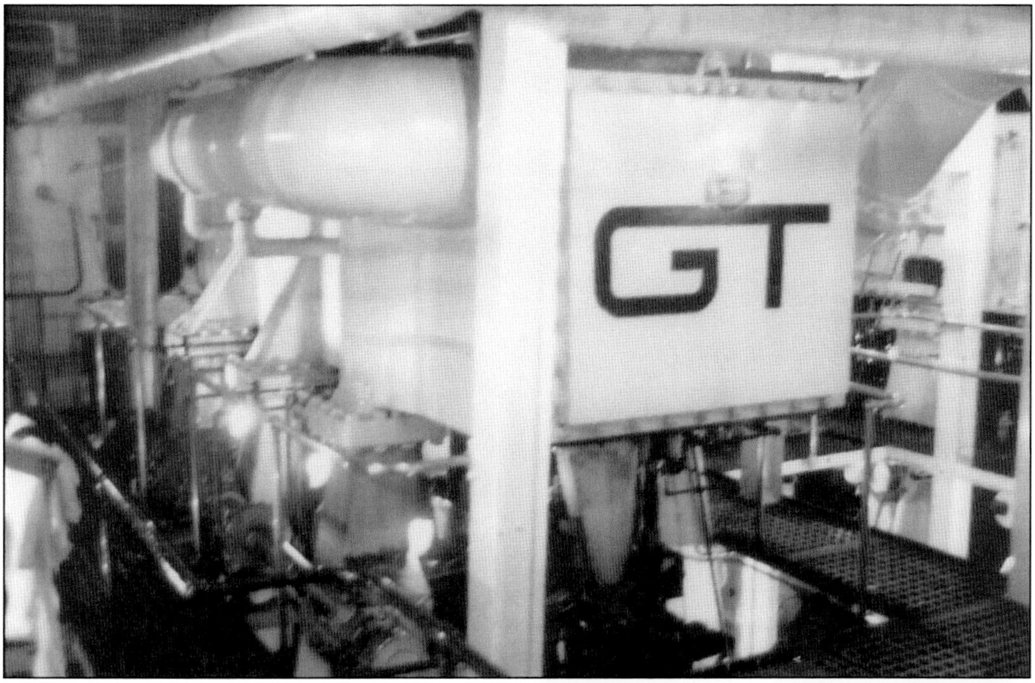


This view shows the engine room near the end of active service for *City of Milwaukee* in the Grand Trunk line. The crew painted the company's wet-noodle GT herald at the top of an engine's cylinder housing. Such company pride was common, as the railroads that owned all three Lake Michigan car ferry lines treated their employees well. It was only during the economic decline of the services that the operators cut back on the amenities offered to their crews. (Photograph by Bruce Groeneveld.)

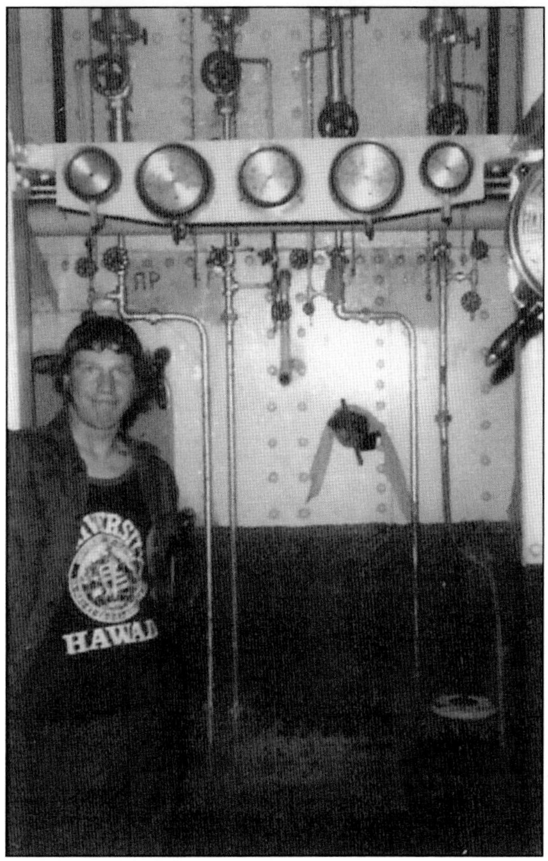

Bruce Groeneveld stands between the engine-control chadburns and beneath gauges indicating that live steam is coursing through the *City of Milwaukee*'s network of piping. In 1947, the ship, along with her two sisters, were converted from coal- to oil-burning steam boilers, which eliminated several coal passers from the crew roster of each ferry. The *City of Milwaukee* routinely topped off her bunkers with 12,000 gallons of No. 5 fuel oil. (Bruce Groeneveld.)

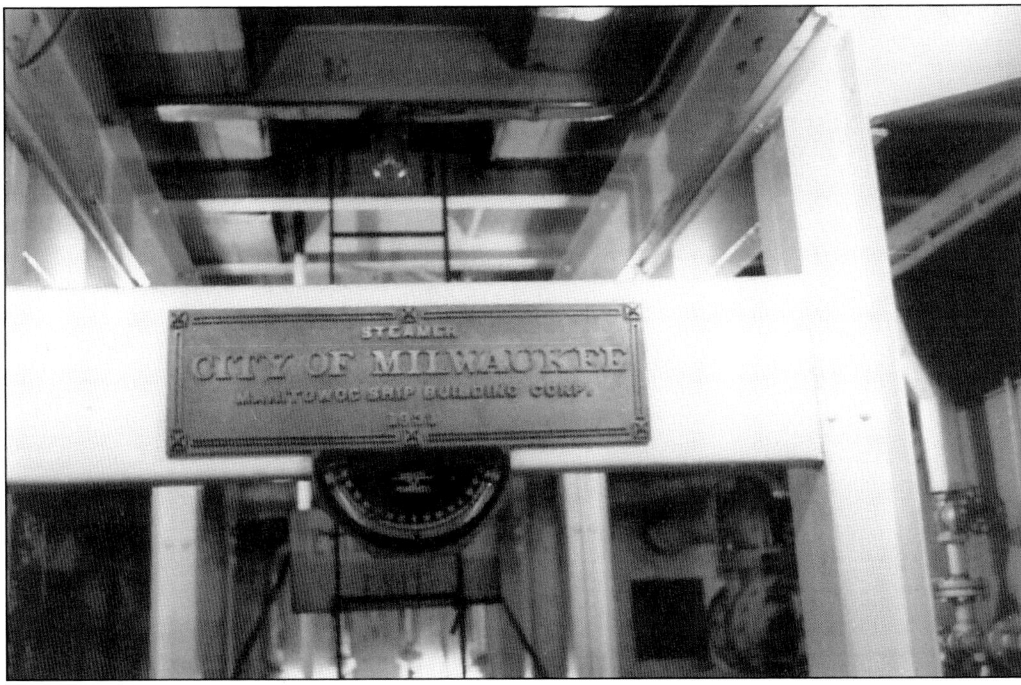


One of two of the *City of Milwaukee*'s bronze builders plates is shown in pristine condition in the center of the engine room. Since the ship was laid up after 1982, parties unknown removed this and an other plate, mounted outside below the pilothouse. Only the forward builder's plate has been recovered. Manitowoc Shipbuilding Company's plates had a characteristic elegant yet simple design. (Photograph by Bruce Groeneveld.)

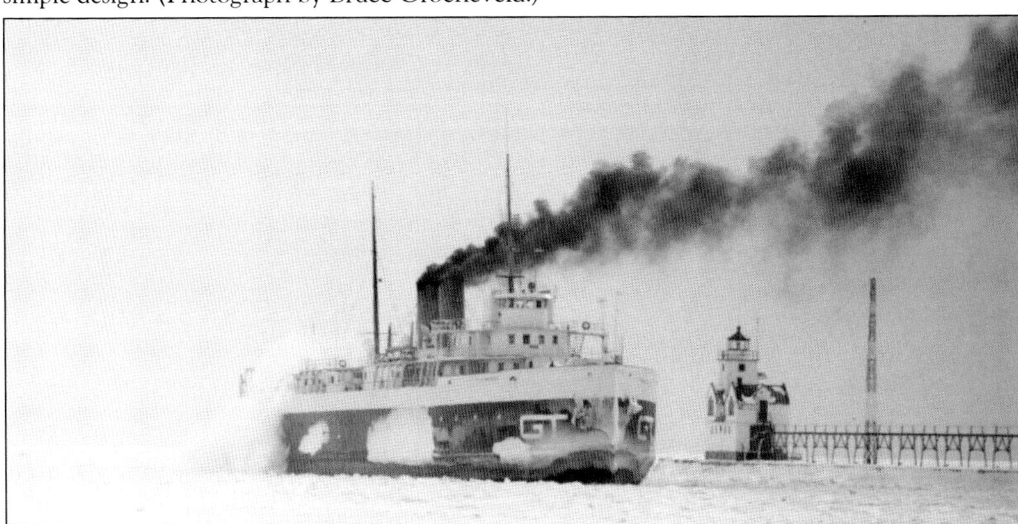

Entering the harbor at Kewaunee, Wisconsin, in February 1979, the former Grand Trunk Railroad car ferry *City of Milwaukee* battles heavy ice and a minus-17 degree Fahrenheit temperature. This classic photograph was taken from a snowbank by Wendell Wilke while the ship was under lease to the Ann Arbor Railroad, by then operated by the Michigan Interstate Railway. The ship was purchased by the State of Michigan for the purpose of being leased to the railway at a favorable rate with an option to buy. (Photograph by Wendell Wilke.)

# *Five*

# MOVING FROM ELBERTA TO MANISTEE

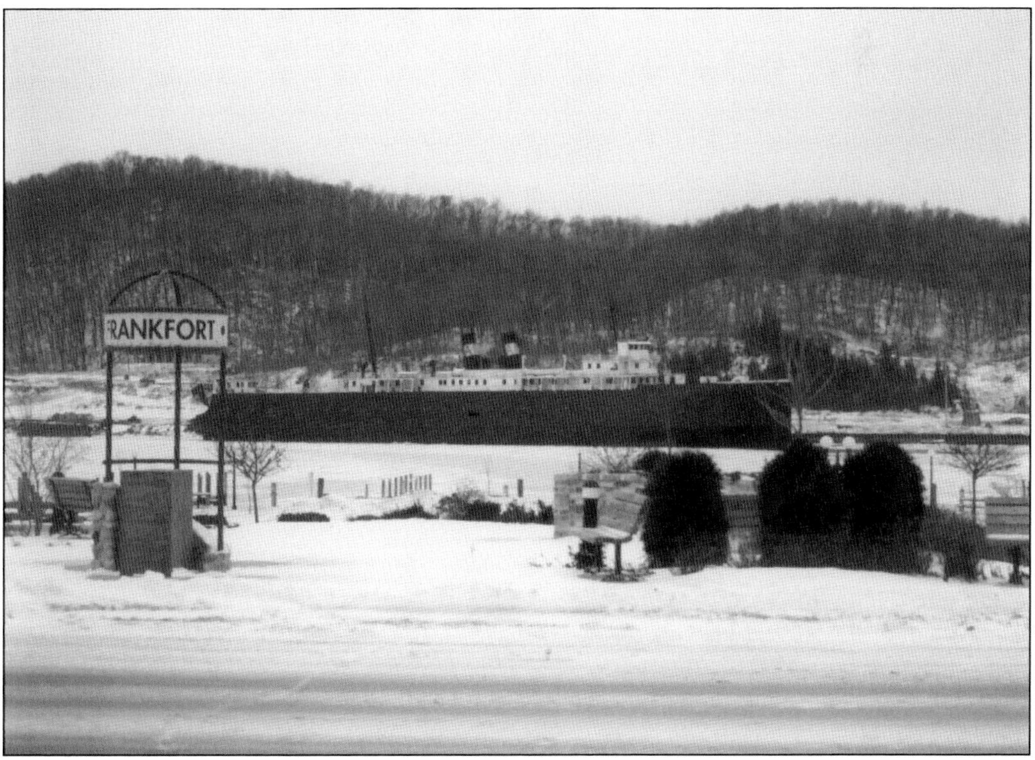


After the Grand Trunk was permitted to abandon its ferry route in November 1978, the Ann Arbor Railroad leased the *City of Milwaukee* from the State of Michigan, which had obtained her from the Grand Trunk. The ferry's new career was short-lived; the Ann Arbor ceased ferry operations in April 1982. At that stage, the ship was laid up with fleet mates *Viking* and *Arthur K. Atkinson*. Jed Jaworski, a former *City of Milwaukee* crew member who had established a maritime museum, looked at his former ship as a potential historic attraction. The ship, painted in Ann Arbor fleet colors, is shown at Elberta, across Lake Betsie from Frankfort. (CofM.)

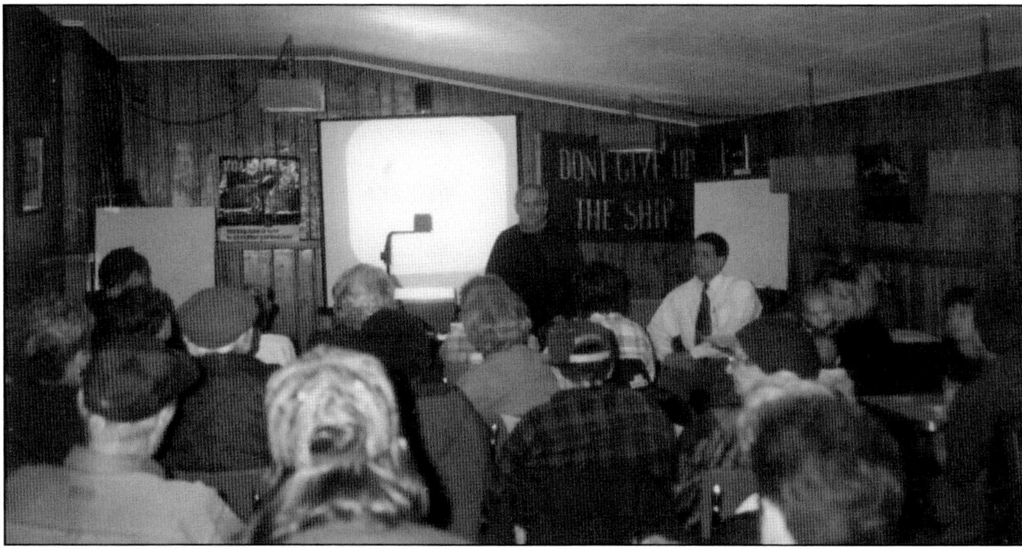

Despite the efforts of Jaworski, marine contractor Erich Luedtke, businessman Kirk Lorenz, and other founding members of the Society for the Preservation of the *City of Milwaukee,* a plan to create a historic interpretive site, with the car ferry as a focal point, failed to come to fruition. In 1999, the citizens of Frankfort approved a ballot proposal to dock the ship at Tenth Street in Frankfort, but insufficient water depth required a move to Manistee. Here, a meeting to discuss the move convenes at Elberta's Mayfair Tavern, known as Pea Soups to the old Ann Arbor crews. (CofM.)

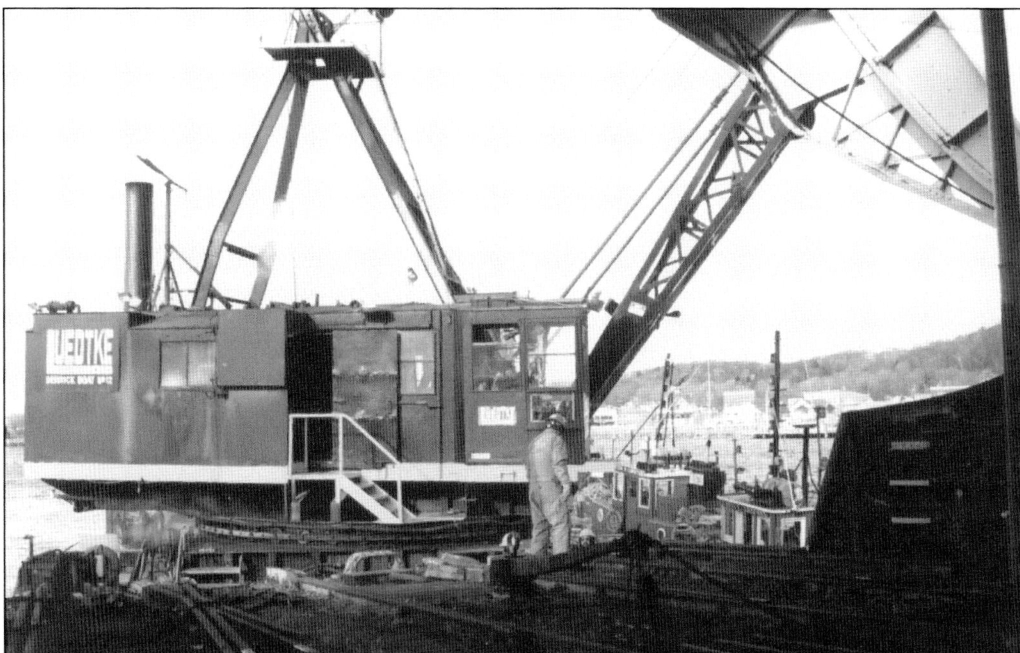


Moored at various locations on Lake Betsie since 1982 without a suitable permanent dock, the *City of Milwaukee* relocated to Manistee in January 2000. Low water levels on Lake Michigan required that the area around the ship be dredged to allow towing. Fortunately, Luedtke Engineering was based nearby and used its outstanding historic steam dredge (shown here) to remove the mud from around the ferry's hull. (CofM.)

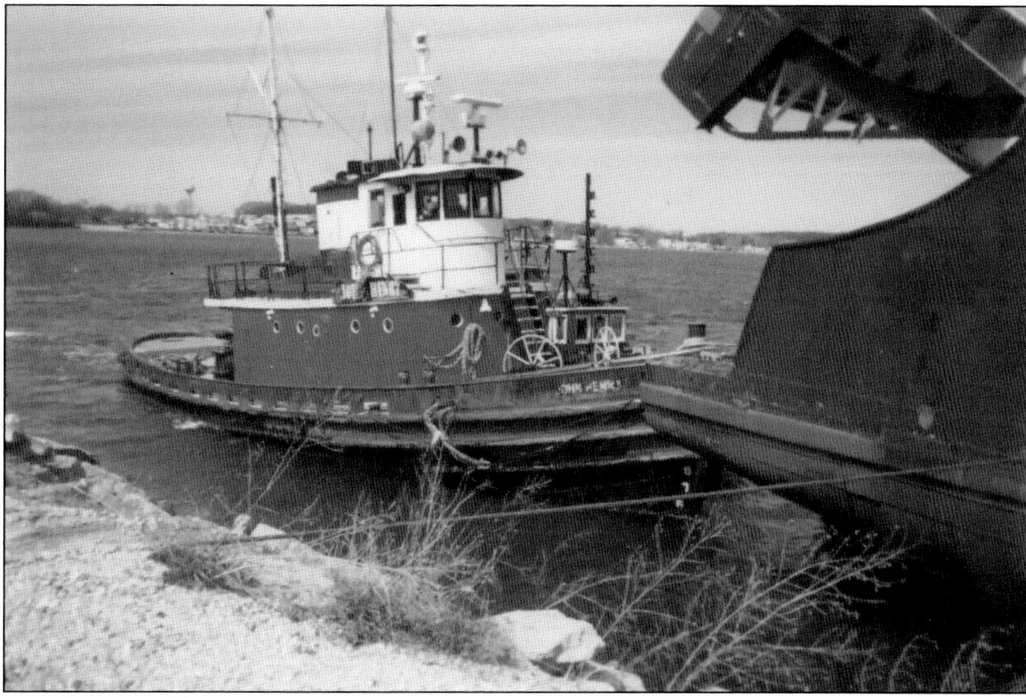

Tugs from Luedtke Engineering ready their lines in the first attempt to move the ferry; the tugs worked hard to move the *City of Milwaukee* from the Lake Betsie mud. The society was required to move the ship out of the harbor by February 14, 2000, or lose title. The Village of Elberta refused to negotiate with the society to establish a historical site at the former Ann Arbor docks and gave the society a "move it or lose it" ultimatum. (CofM.)

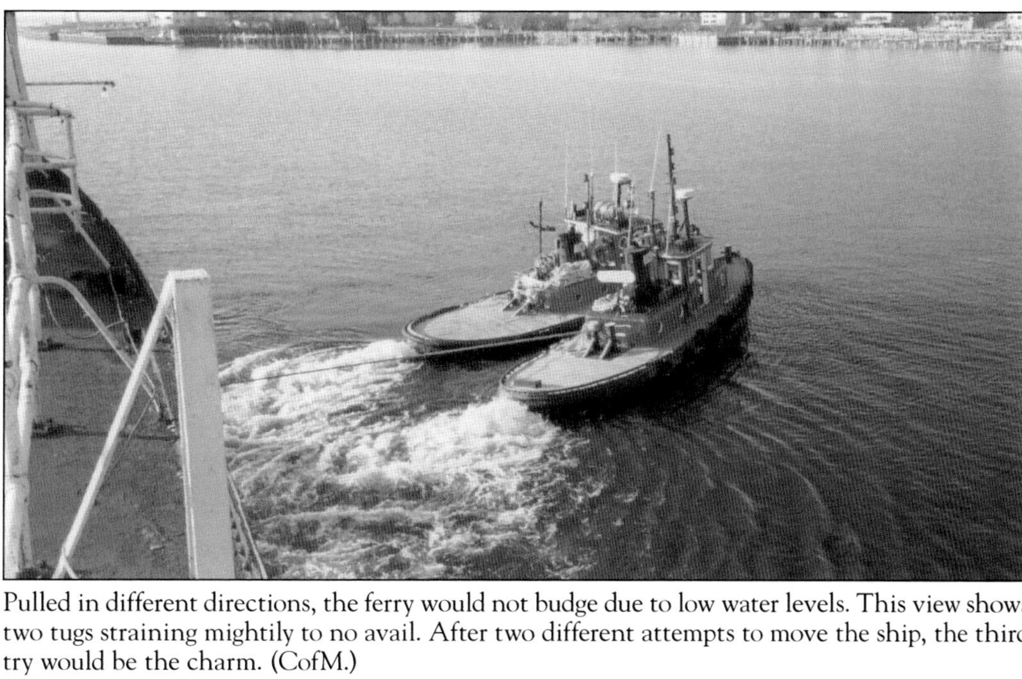

Pulled in different directions, the ferry would not budge due to low water levels. This view shows two tugs straining mightily to no avail. After two different attempts to move the ship, the third try would be the charm. (CofM.)

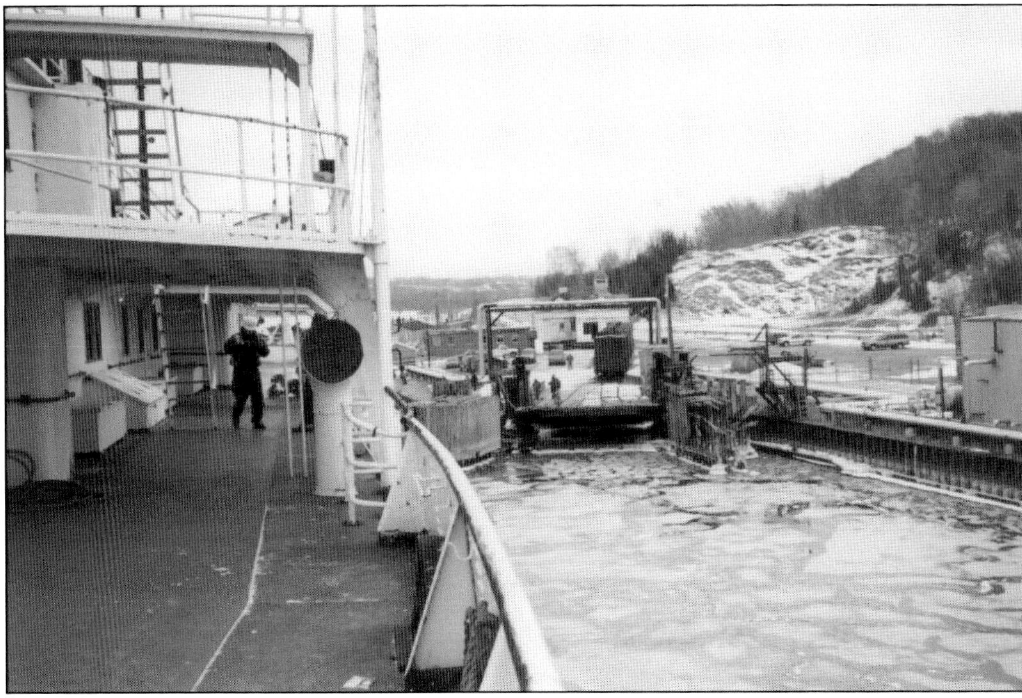

Tuesday, January 11, 2000—day three in the attempt to free the ship—was met with success, due to a high westerly wind that raised the water level on Betsie Bay. It was hoped that the boat could leave the harbor the next day, but the tow to Manistee was postponed by heavy weather. This allowed time to pick up three vintage Ann Arbor boxcars and an idler car at the west ferry slip. Two Andrie, Inc., tugs moved the ship into place while society officer Kirk Lorenz used his 4x4 pickup to pull the railcars aboard ship with a cable. (Photograph by Tom Read.)

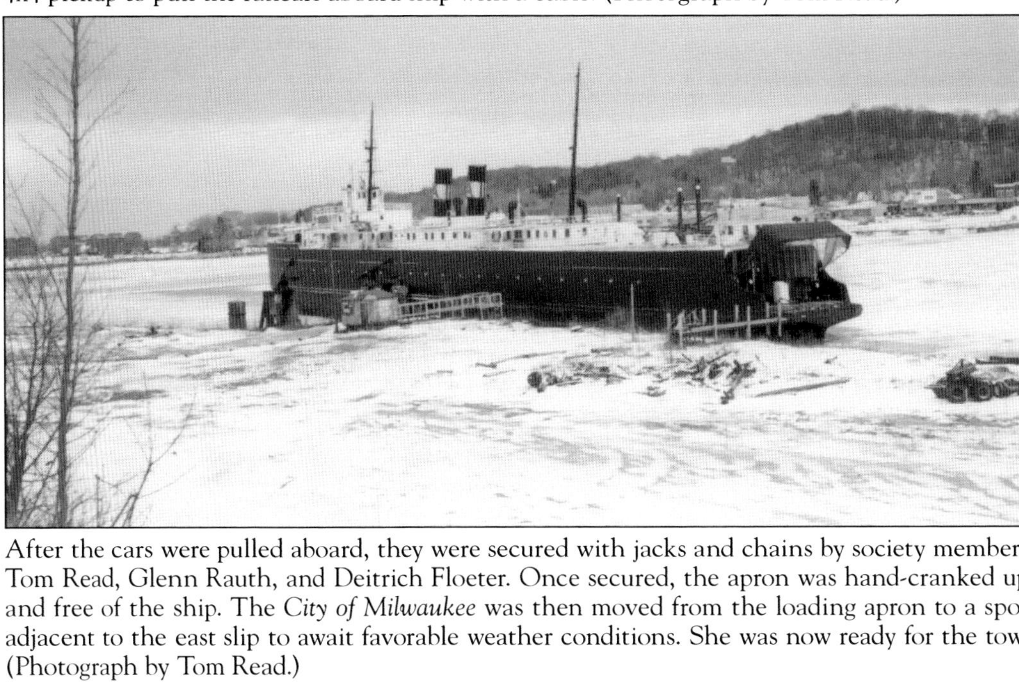

After the cars were pulled aboard, they were secured with jacks and chains by society members Tom Read, Glenn Rauth, and Deitrich Floeter. Once secured, the apron was hand-cranked up and free of the ship. The *City of Milwaukee* was then moved from the loading apron to a spot adjacent to the east slip to await favorable weather conditions. She was now ready for the tow. (Photograph by Tom Read.)

Society member Tom Read is shown getting the deck gear ready for the tow. Thirteen volunteers rode the ship down the shoreline. Since there was no heat aboard, save for a few small portable heaters and the galley stove, heavy winter clothing was in order for all those involved. The tow finally got underway at 3:15 a.m. on Friday, January 14, 2000. (CofM.)

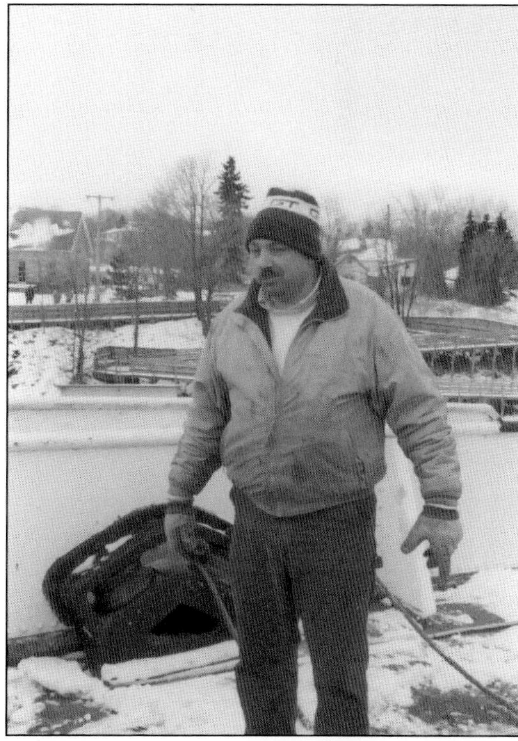

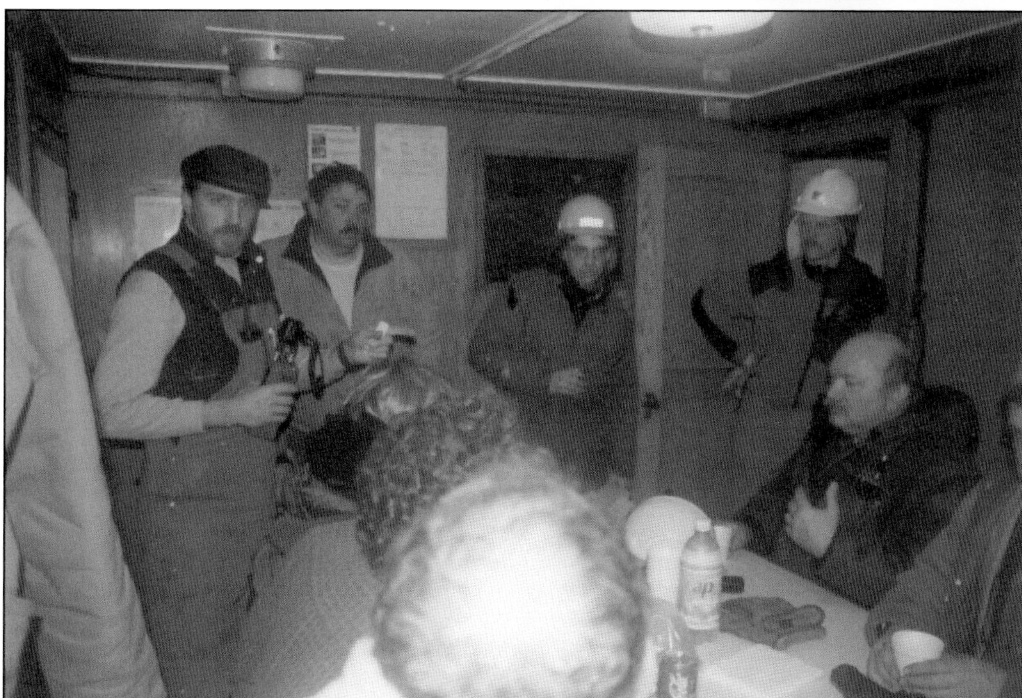

Facing the camera are, from left to right, safety and mooring line coordinator Jed Jaworski, deckhand and generator operator Tom Read, winch operator Tom Stoltmann, deckhand Paul Rauth, ground coordinator Kirk Lorenz, and electrician Jim Baker. (CofM.)

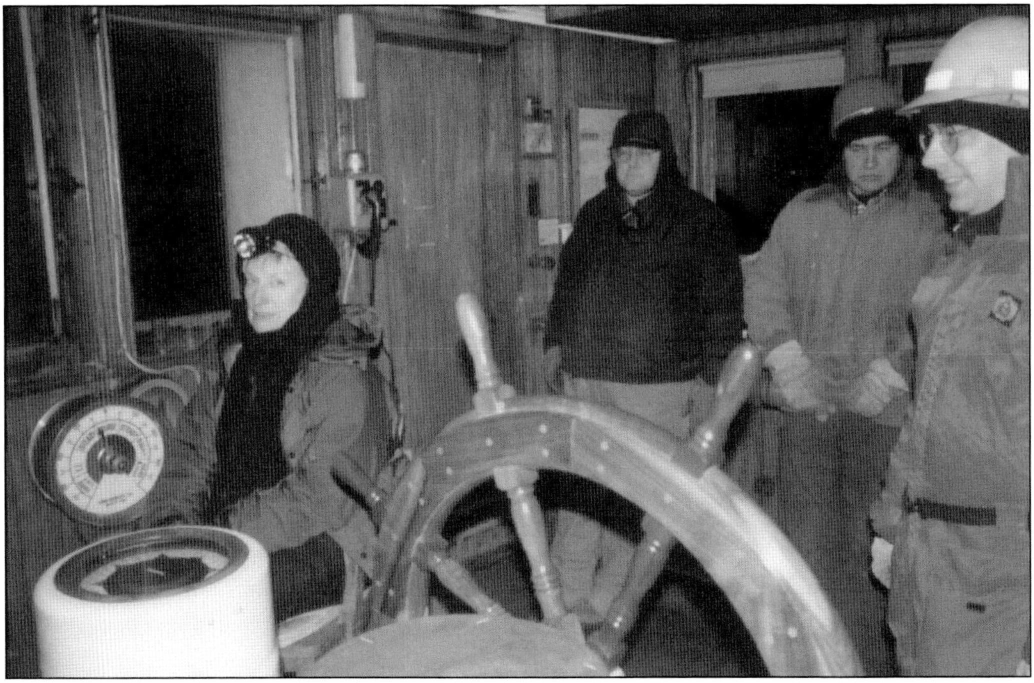

On watch in the *City of Milwaukee*'s pilothouse during the predawn tow are, from left to right, Mayor Pro Tem Jan Gavlinski; Capt. Dean Hobbs, master of the SS *Badger*; electrician Jim Baker; and mooring winch operator Tom Stoltmann. Captain Hobbs served as pilot of the tow and coordinated the communication between the Andrie tugs, the ship's crew, and the ground crew. (CofM.)

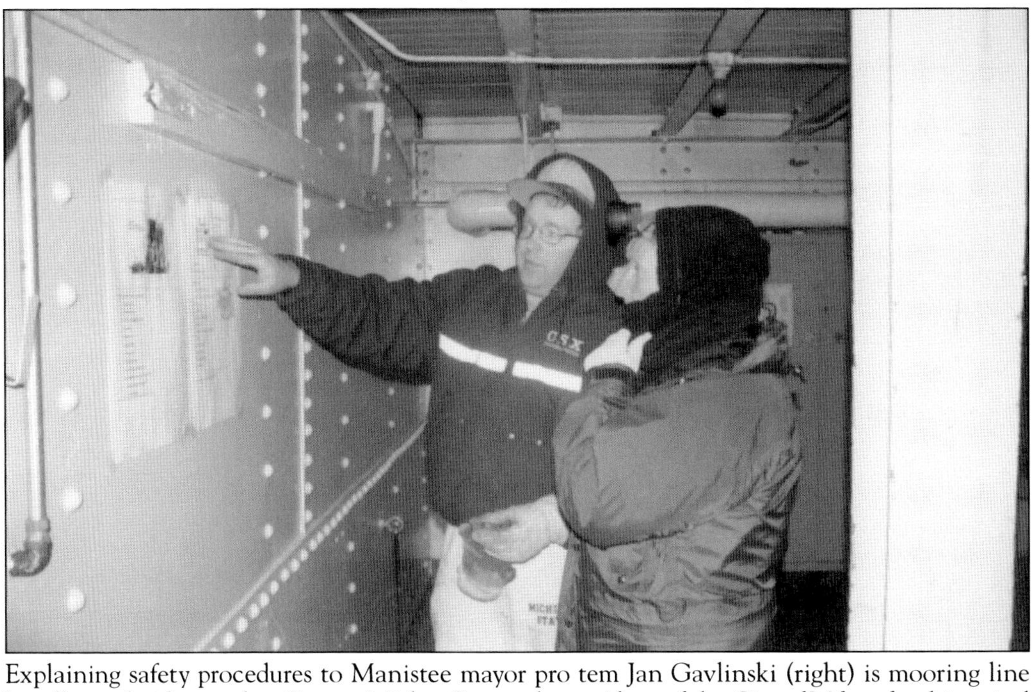


Explaining safety procedures to Manistee mayor pro tem Jan Gavlinski (right) is mooring line handler and videographer George Micka. Currently president of the *City of Milwaukee* historical organization, Micka has held the position longer than any other person. (CofM.)

This view from the *City of Milwaukee*'s crow's nest shows the Andrie, Inc., tug *Maribeth Andrie* leading the tow through the narrow, winding channel entrance to Manistee harbor. During the tow in the open lake, the towline is played out to great length to provide slack in the event that the car ferry should overtake the tug while the towing operation is at full speed. In the restricted waters of a harbor, the line is shortened considerably for reduced speeds and tight maneuvering in the Manistee River. The Andrie tug *Seneca Queen* is guiding the aft end of the *City of Milwaukee*. (CofM.)

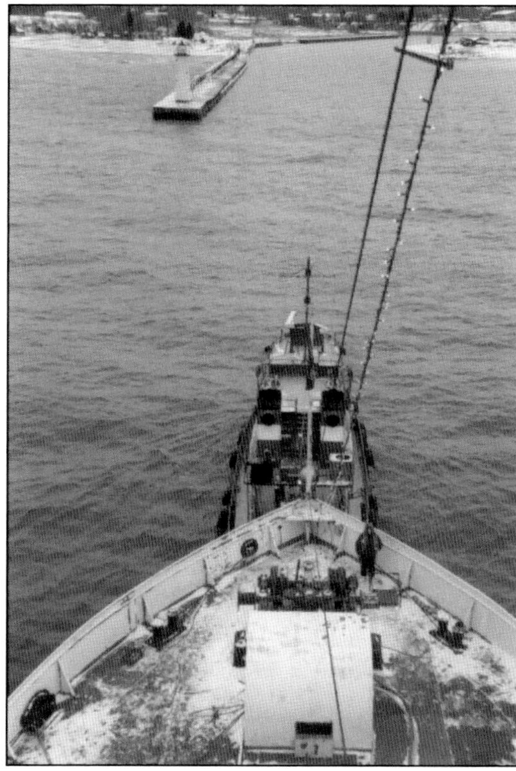

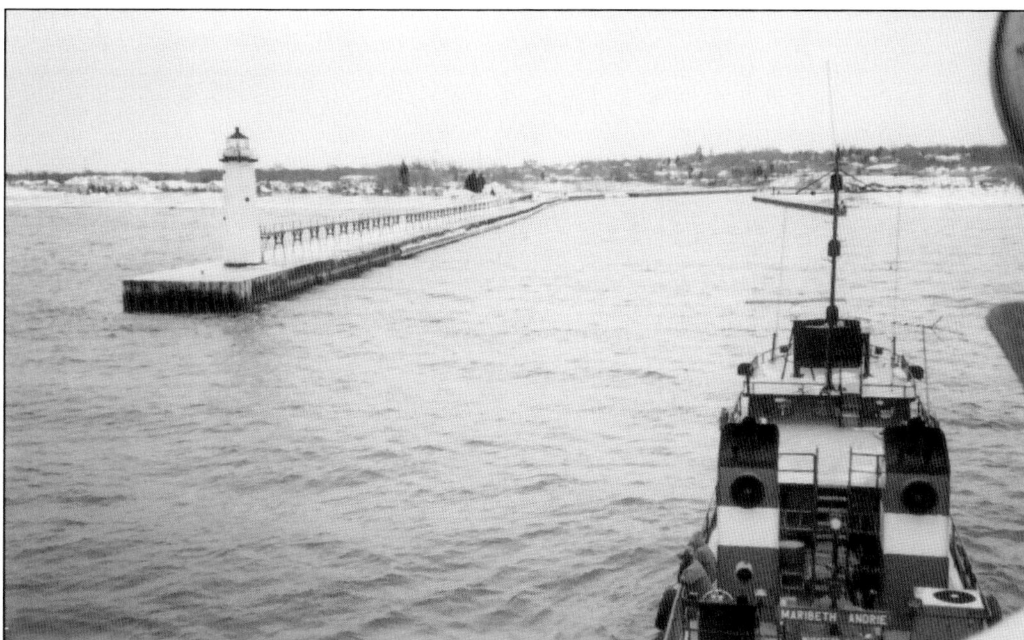


Entering the channel and about to pass Manistee's north pier-head light, the *Maribeth Andrie* faces the most challenging aspect of the tow. The *Maribeth* is 80 feet long and 24 feet wide, with a hull depth of 11 feet. With two Detroit Diesel 12V-149 engines, the twin-screw tug has an indicated horsepower rating of 2,200. (Photograph by Tom Read.)

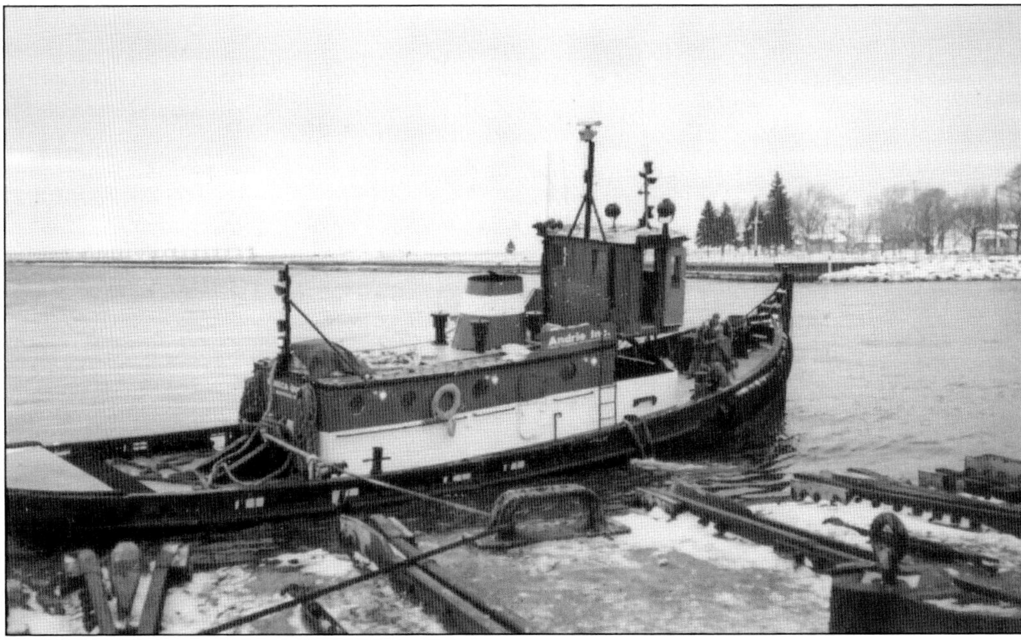

The Andrie tug *Seneca Queen* pulls hard to keep the stern of the *City of Milwaukee* aligned with the lead tug *Maribeth Andrie* as they prepare to make the first turn in the Manistee River. The *Seneca Queen* was built at Ferrysburg, Michigan, in 1903 and has since been reconditioned. The single-screw tug is powered by one Detroit Diesel 16V-149 engine that is rated at 1,100 horsepower. (CofM.)

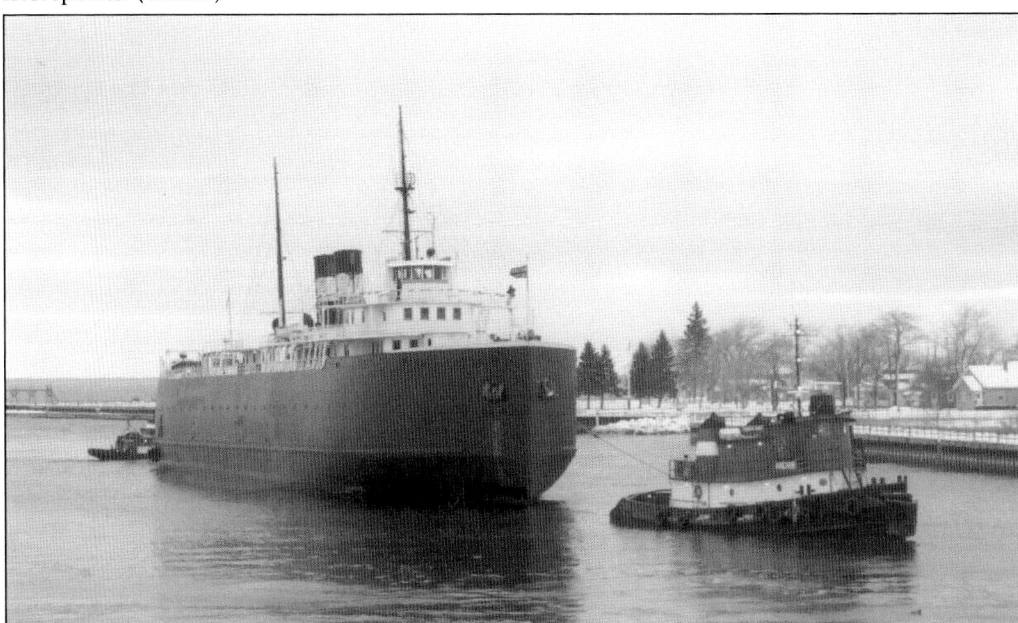

Arriving for the first time in her new home port of Manistee, Michigan, the *City of Milwaukee* is led into the harbor on Friday morning, January 14, 2000. Normally not a car ferry port, Manistee has had car ferries visit in the distant past for repair and boiler work. These were ships of the Ann Arbor and Mackinac Transportation Company fleets. (CofM.)

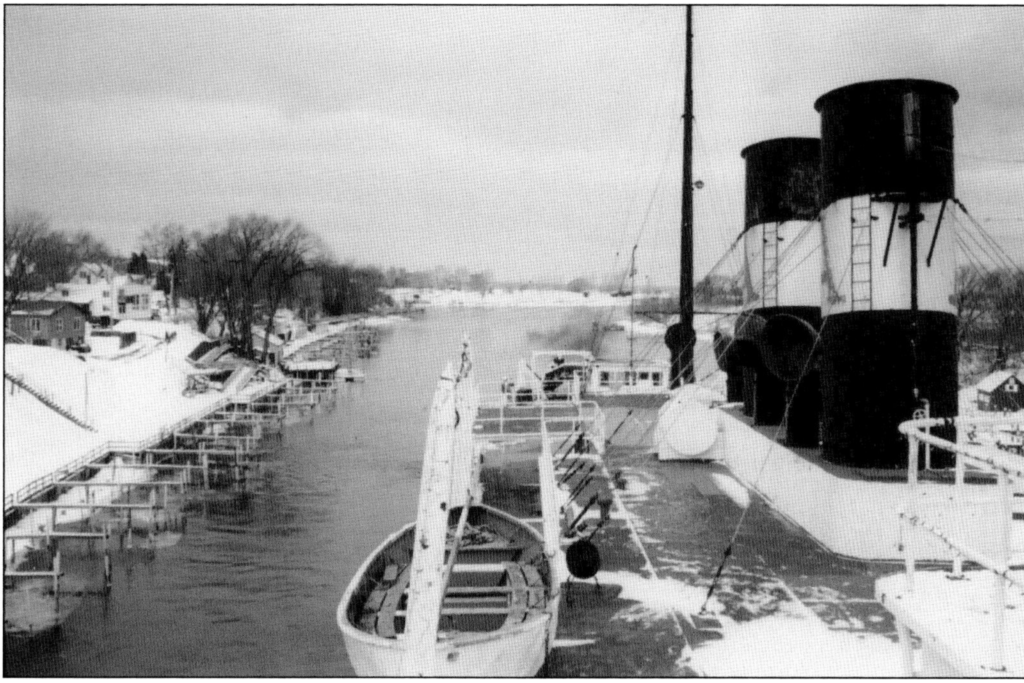

Looking aft on the *City of Milwaukee*'s starboard side, mooring slips for the large Manistee charter boat fishing fleet jut out from the south bank of the river. The winds had moderated to permit the tow to negotiate the narrow channel. (Photograph by Tom Read.)

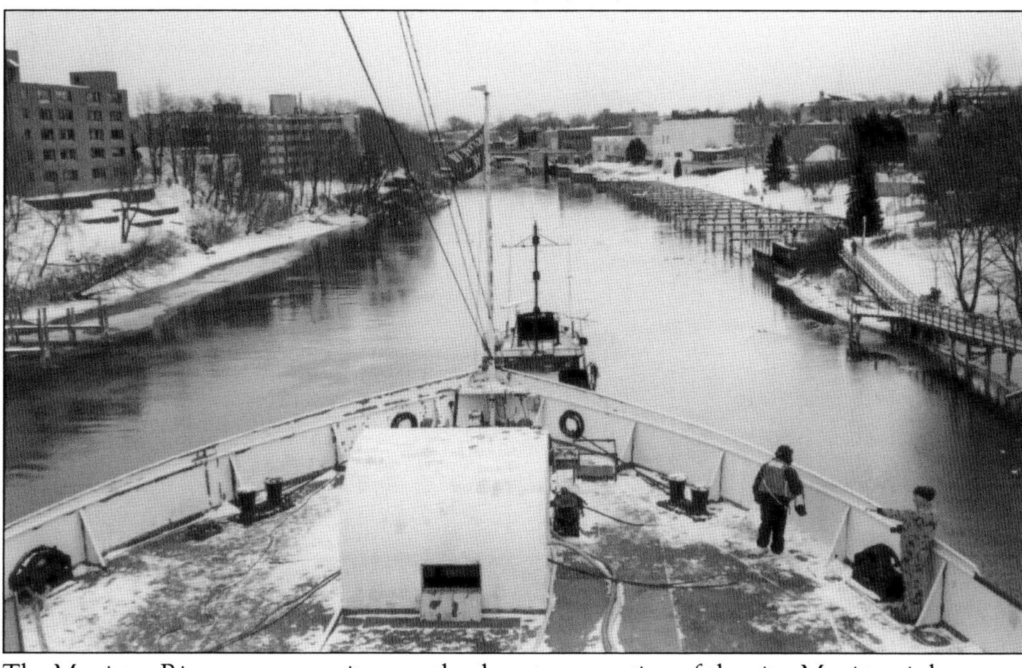

The Manistee River narrows as it nears the downtown section of the city. Manistee is known as the Victorian Port City, and the main street along the riverfront is lined with historic buildings, restaurants, shops, and motels. Here, the ship's deck crew gets ready to transfer lines as the tug nears the end of the trip. (Photograph by Tom Read.)

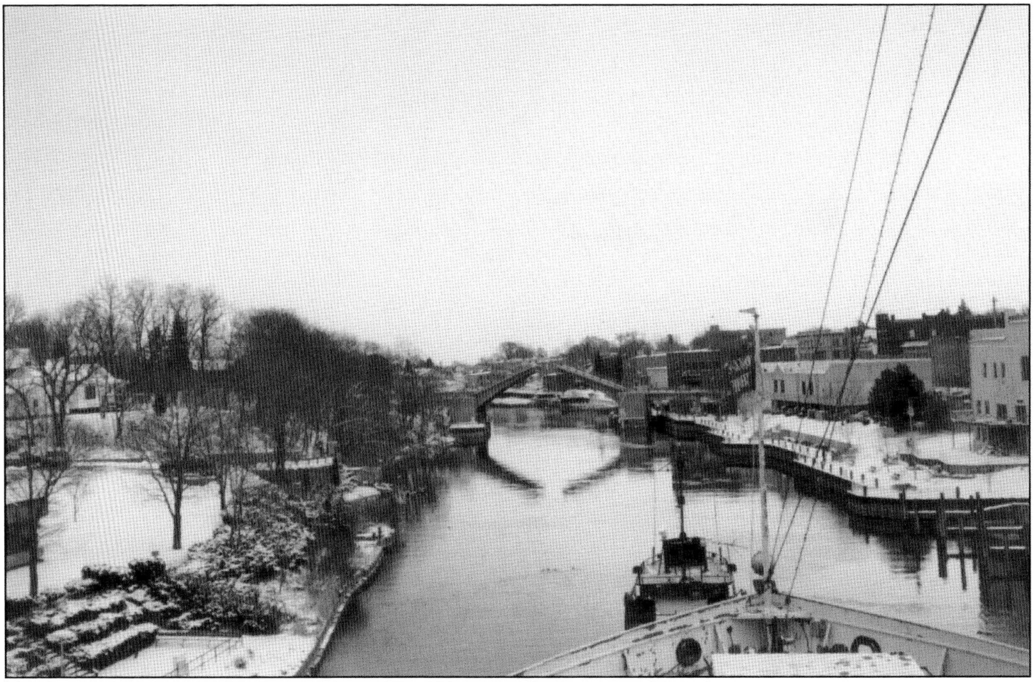

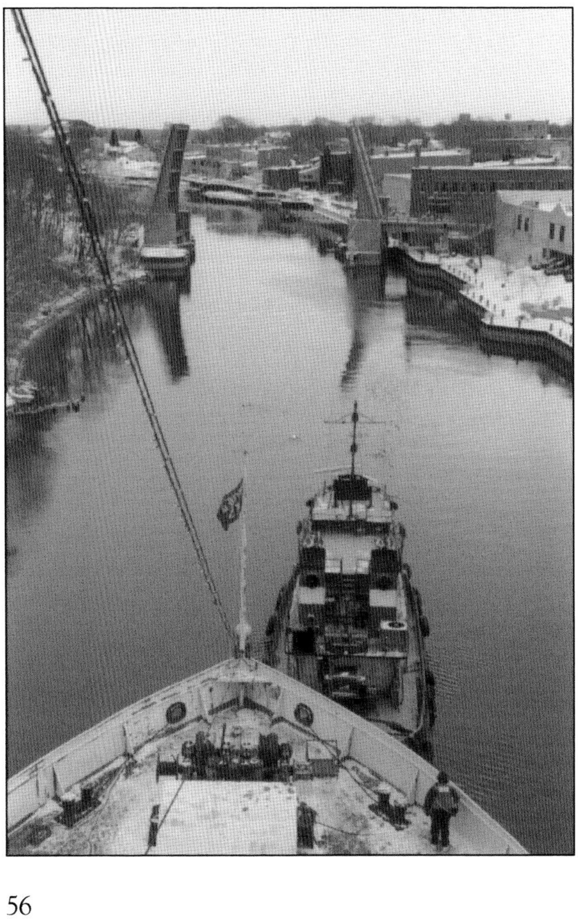

The Manistee River narrows even further as the tow gets ready to pass through the Maple Street Bridge, the first of three narrow spans that must be passed on the way to Manistee Lake. (Photograph by Tom Read.)

The tug *Maribeth Andrie* aims for the gap in the Maple Street Bridge as the tow reaches the home stretch. High winds would have postponed this leg of the trip due to the extremely tight quarters in which to maneuver. (CofM.)

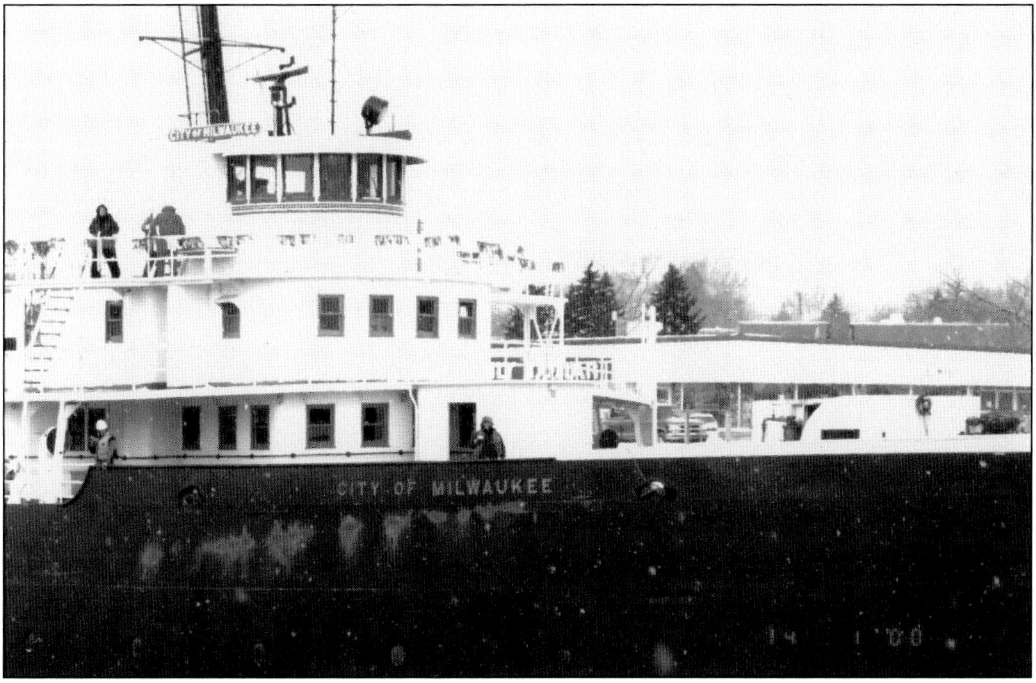


Manistee mayor pro tem Jan Gavlinski (in dark clothing to the left of the pilothouse) observes the tow as the *City of Milwaukee* glides past her city's downtown. As the first ship of the year to enter the port of Manistee, Gavlinski presented the *City of Milwaukee* with the customary top hat and wooden cane, fashioned from a tree harvested along the Manistee River. (CofM.)

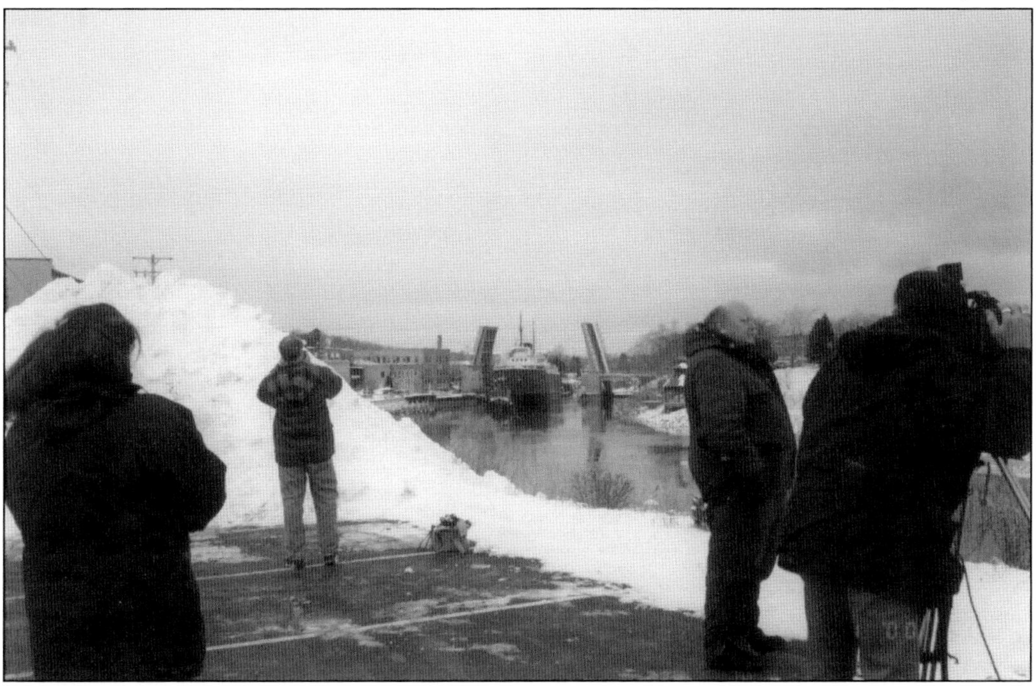

Members of the local media outlets and city residents await passage of the *City of Milwaukee* as she begins to make the bend in the river to line up with the US Highway 31 Bridge. (CofM.)

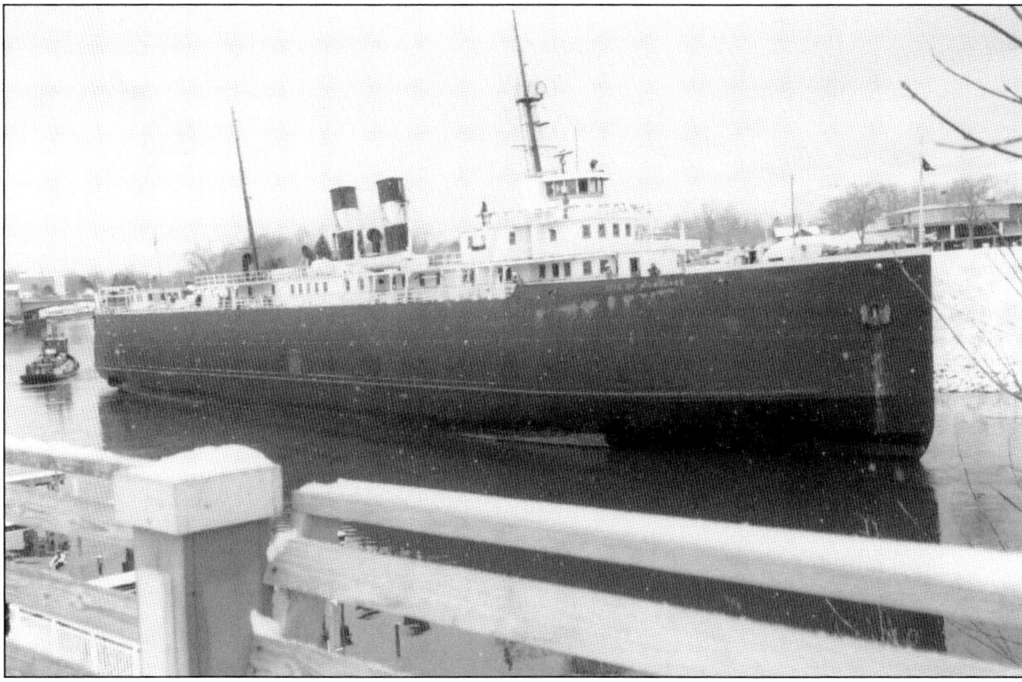

The *City of Milwaukee* straightens out for the next open bridge span with the aid of the tug *Seneca Queen*, visible holding the aft end of the ship in place. (CofM.)

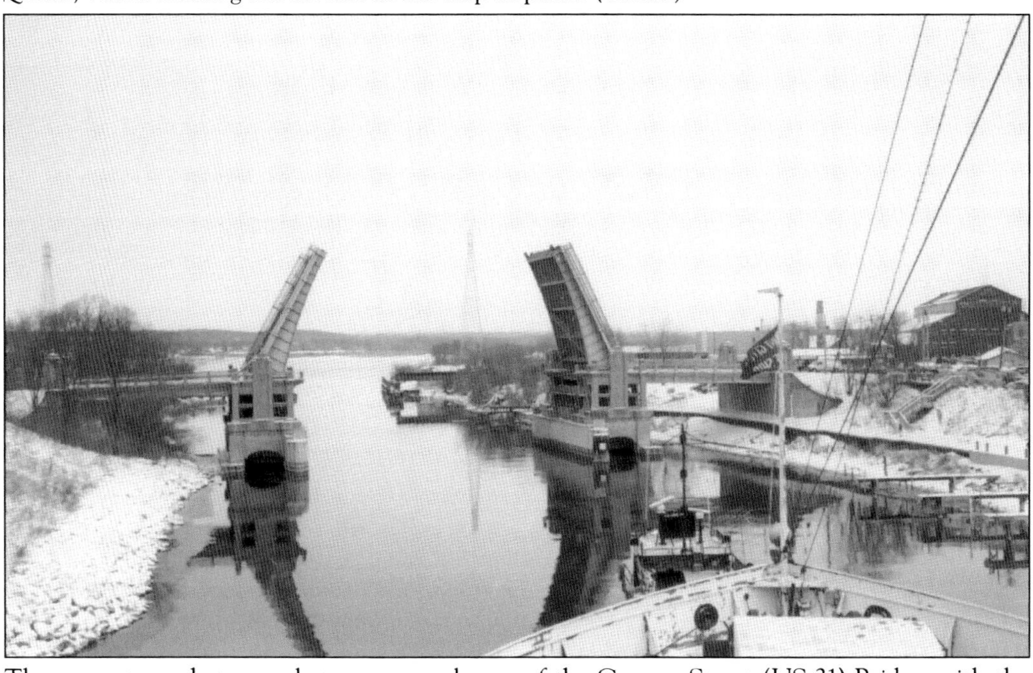

The tow gets ready to pass between open leaves of the Cypress Street (US 31) Bridge, with the wide-open expanse of Manistee Lake visible in the distance. The Society for the Preservation of the SS *City of Milwaukee* was given favorable terms on a temporary mooring site on Manistee Lake by the Ed Seng family. Numerous individuals and organizations offered support for the expensive move from Elberta. (CofM.)

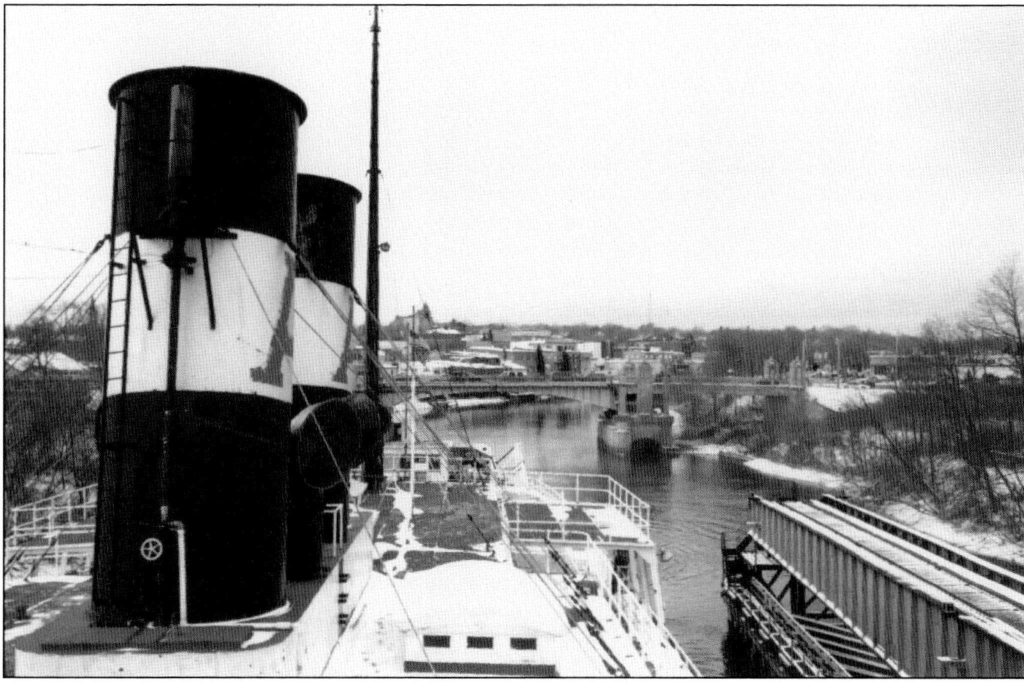

Looking aft from the bridge of the *City of Milwaukee*, the ship's port side glides by the CSX Railroad's swing bridge, the third and final span through which the tow had to pass. (Photograph by Tom Read.)

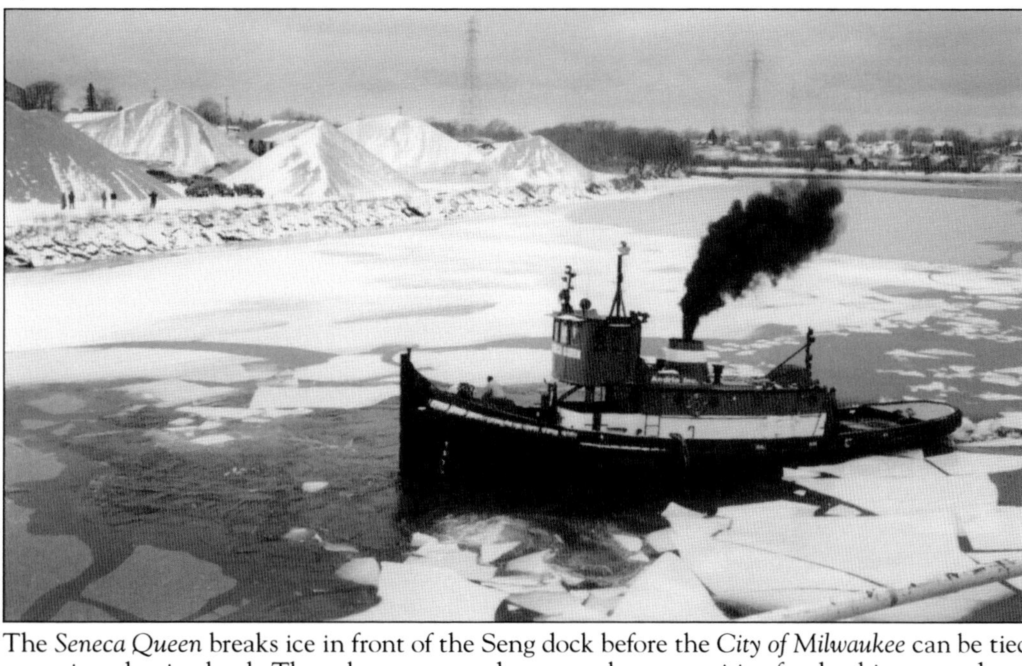

The *Seneca Queen* breaks ice in front of the Seng dock before the *City of Milwaukee* can be tied up against the riverbank. The volunteer ground crew can be seen waiting for the ship to cast down lines for the mooring procedure. The ship would eventually be moved twice more on Manistee Lake, where she now rests at her permanent home at Arthur Street, just north of downtown Manistee on US 31. (Photograph by Tom Read.)

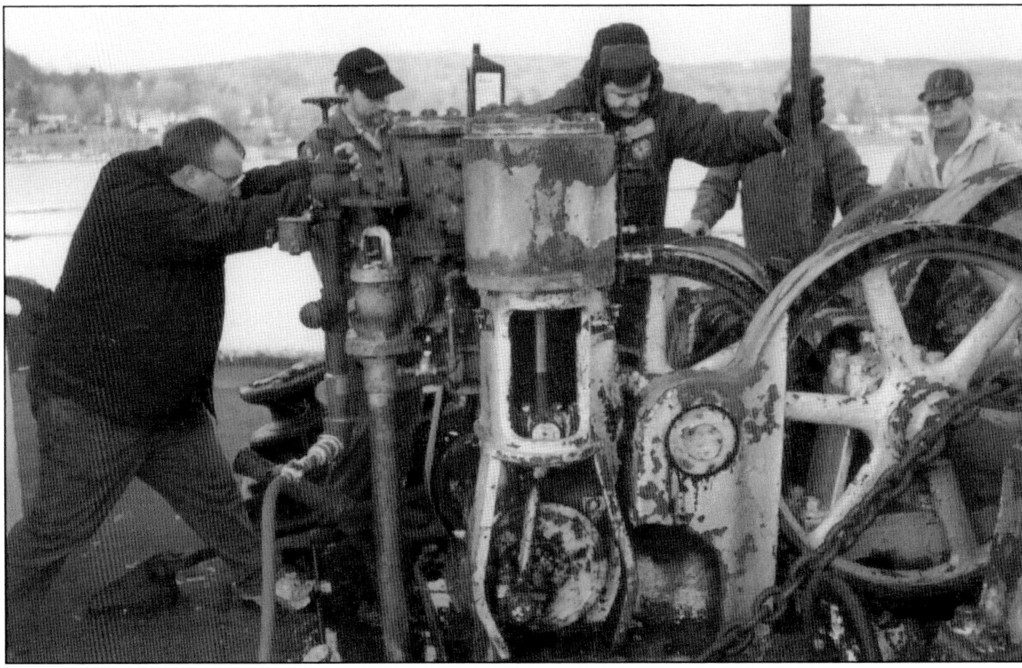

Capt. Dean Hobbs (left) leads the deck crew in attempt to get the *City of Milwaukee*'s anchor windlass to function after nearly two decades of inactivity. An air compressor was used to power the machine, which was normally steam-actuated. The air hose is visible entering the left side of the windlass. (CofM.)

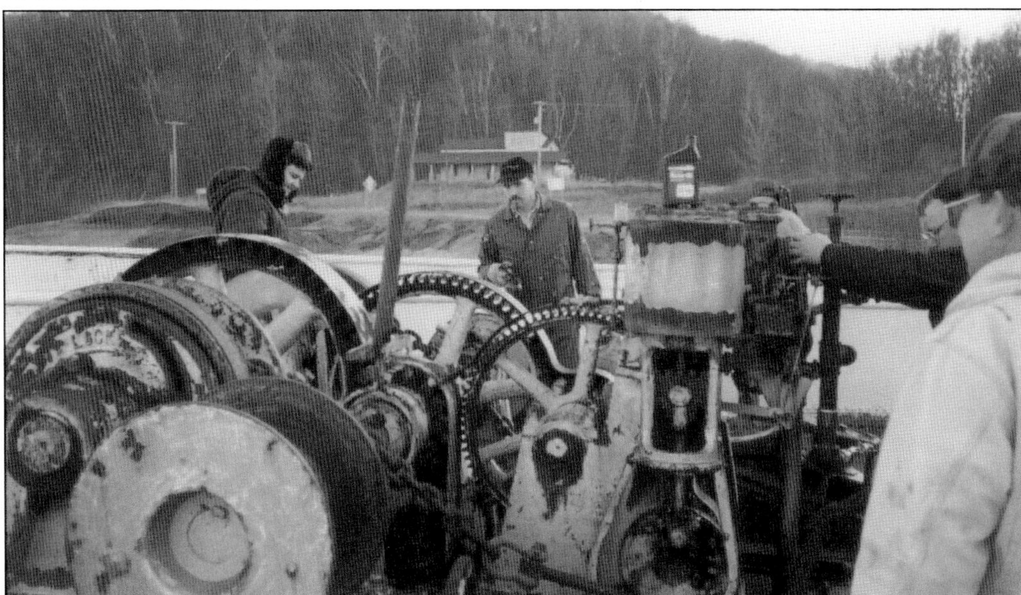

The windlass (shown here) is used to raise and lower the ship's two anchors. The air compressor, purchased from Ed Seng, was also used to power the mooring winches, sea gate engine, and ship's whistle. The volunteer crew stated that this equipment was brought back into use with limited repair work needed, due to the thorough job done by the Ann Arbor Railroad in laying up the ship in 1982. (CofM.)

# *Six*

# Lights, Camera, Action!

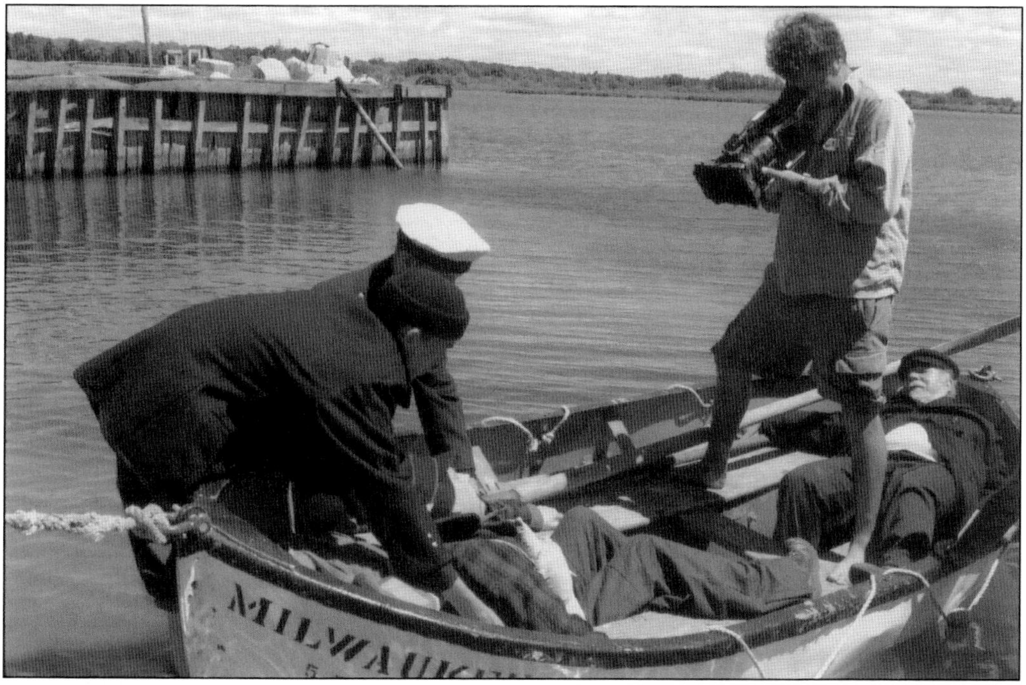

Vintage ships like the *City of Milwaukee* provide a unique backdrop for the visual arts. Over the years, numerous artists have used the vessel for a variety of activities, but the most exciting to nearly everyone involved is the action surrounding film crews on-site to work aboard and around the ship. Here, a film crew from the History Channel's *Deep Sea Detectives* television series films a reenactment in 2005 of a recovered lifeboat from the wreck of the car ferry *Milwaukee*. Assisted by members of the Manistee Coast Guard Station, Tom Stoltmann (left) and Bob Newcomb portray shipwreck victims found lying in the lifeboat. (Photograph by Debra Townsend.)

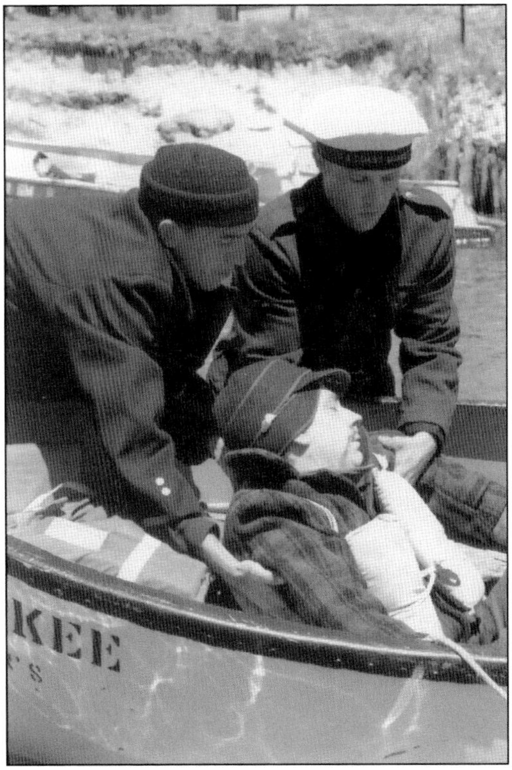

Manistee Coast Guard station crew, dressed in period clothing provided by Jed Jaworski, former *City of Milwaukee* curator, act out a shipwreck recovery scene with society member Tom Stoltmann in the lifeboat. One week in July 2005, a film crew from Lone Wolf Documentary Group, producers of History Channel's *Deep Sea Detectives*, was researching and filming for a one-hour television show focusing on the 1929 sinking of the *Milwaukee*, predecessor to the *City of Milwaukee*. (Photograph by Debra Townsend.)

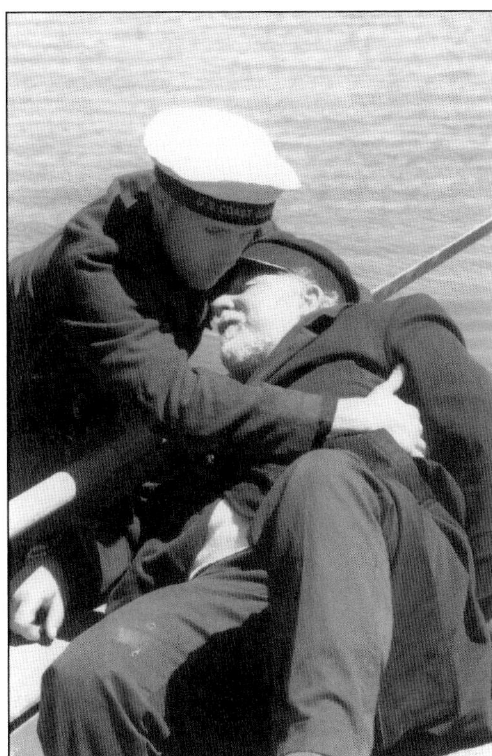

Society member Bob Newcomb portrays one of four *Milwaukee* crew members found dead from exposure in October 1929. A workboat from the *City of Milwaukee* was used for filming, though it is smaller than the actual lifeboat from the *Milwaukee*. Only two men could lie comfortably inside, but tight camera shots and black-and-white filming added realism to the reenacted scenes. (Photograph by Debra Townsend.)

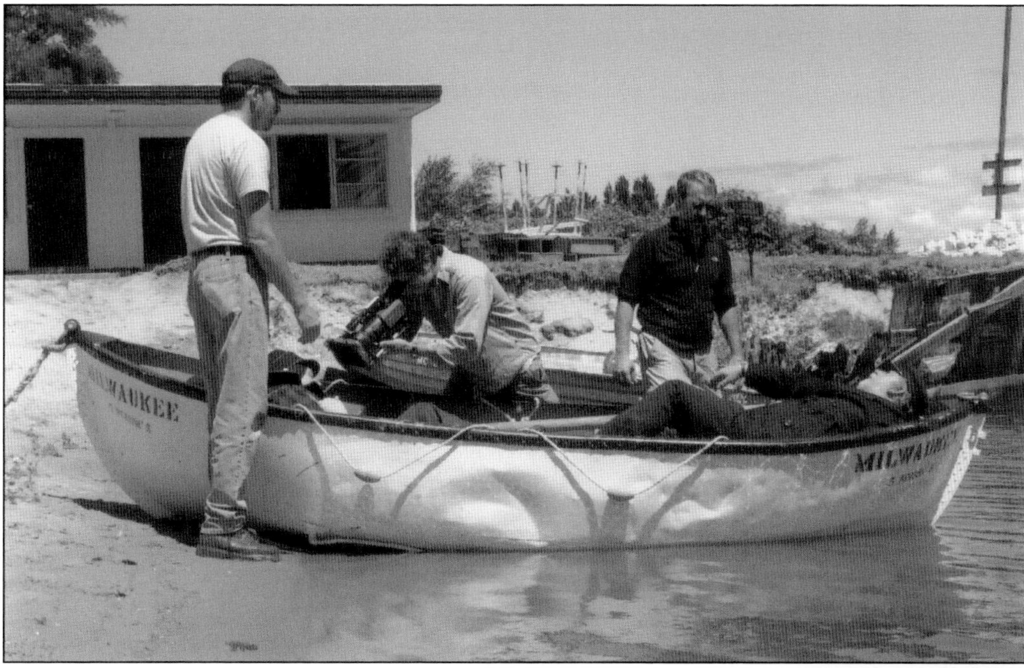

Jed Jaworski (standing left) was instrumental in working with Lone Wolf Documentary Group in staging the *Deep Sea Detectives* reenactment scenes. Jaworski repainted the name *Milwaukee* over the *City of Milwaukee* lettering on the workboat, provided props and period outfits for the participants, and added other details for a successful two days of shooting. (Photograph by Debra Townsend.)

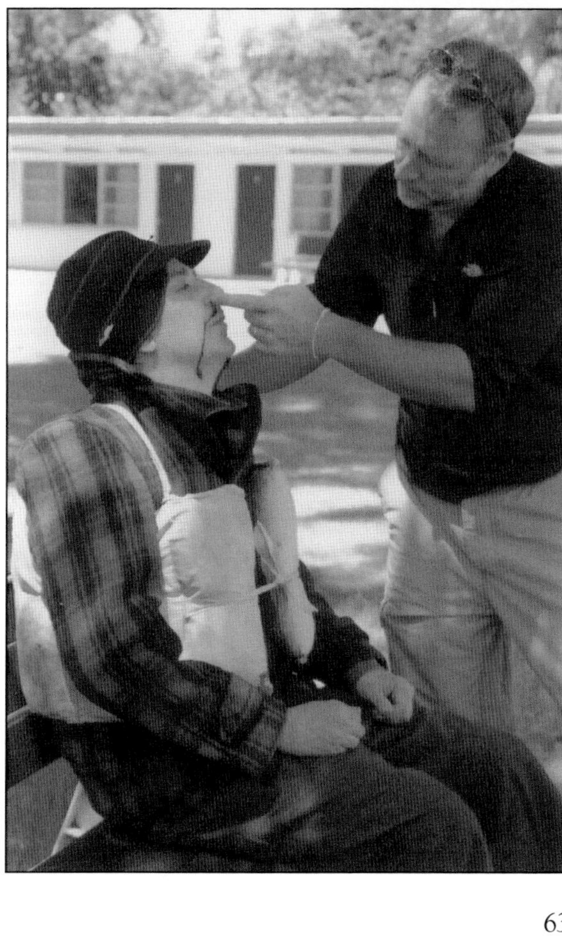

Kirk Wolfinger, producer/director and one of the principals of Lone Wolf Documentary Group, applies theatrical blood to Tom Stoltmann's nose. Standing in as a victim of the *Milwaukee* disaster, Stoltmann portrays the last of four men found in one of the *Milwaukee*'s open lifeboats to succumb to hypothermia. Coast Guardsmen reported the victim's body was still responsive and his nose bled when his rescuers accidentally bumped him. It is believed he may have survived if he had been rescued several hours earlier and that he would have been able to tell the story of his ship's plight. (Photograph by Debra Townsend.)

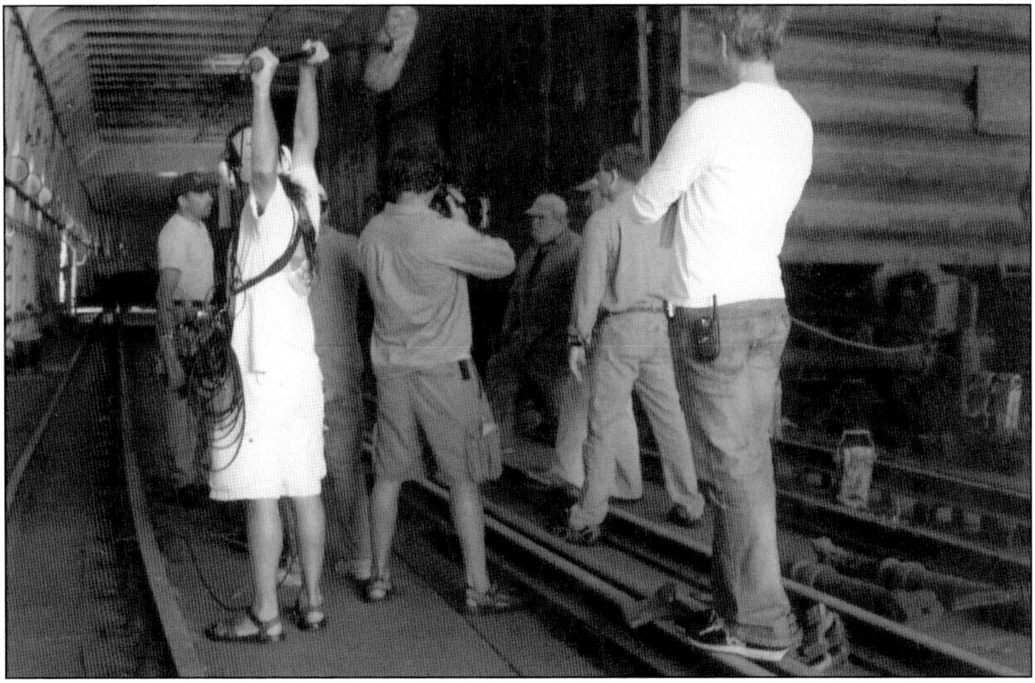

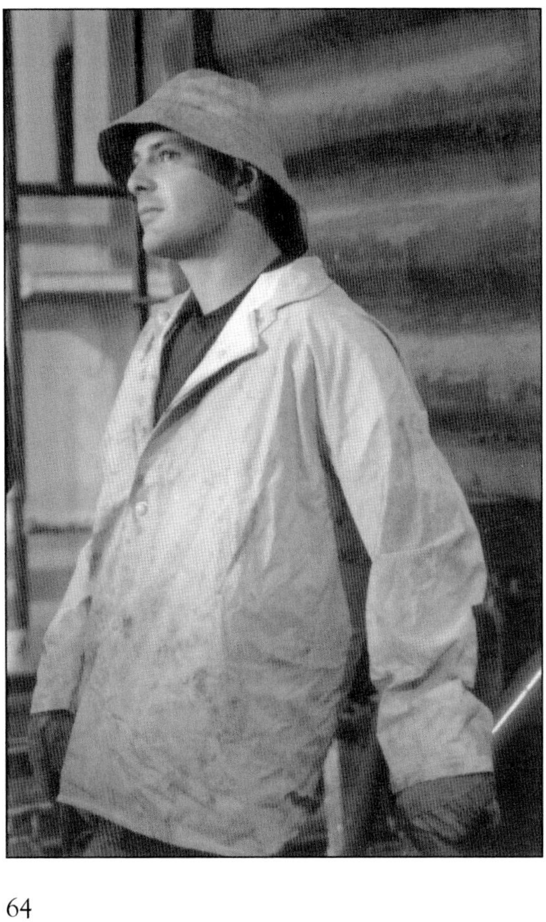

Lone Wolf's director, Rocky Collins, watches as *Deep Sea Detectives* hosts John Chatterton and Richie Kohler interview former car ferry deckhand and society member Pat Brandon. Both Brandon and Jaworski demonstrated how railcars were secured during a heavy Great Lakes storm. (Photograph by Debra Townsend.)

A young seaman from the Manistee Coast Guard Station stands in as a deckhand working the car deck of the foundering *Milwaukee*. Within the hour, he would be doused with a water hose as he reenacted the struggle to resecure jacks and clamps beneath the railcars that were breaking free of their restraints. It is surmised that some of the railcars broke loose and were running freely on the *Milwaukee*'s car deck, playing a major factor in the ship's sinking. (Photograph by Debra Townsend.)

Bob Newcomb portrays the role of chief engineer Ray Dickey at the engine throttles in his last hours alive aboard the sinking car ferry *Milwaukee*. The gloomy lighting added to the atmosphere of dread and chaos during the filming. Shaking cameras and fast, blurred scenes added to the drama of the finished product, entitled "Train Wreck on Lake Michigan," an episode of the television show *Deep Sea Detectives*. (Photograph by Debra Townsend.)

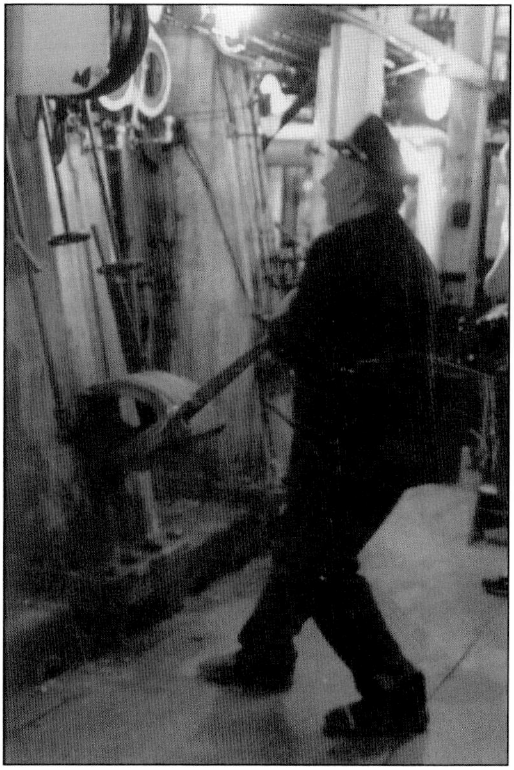

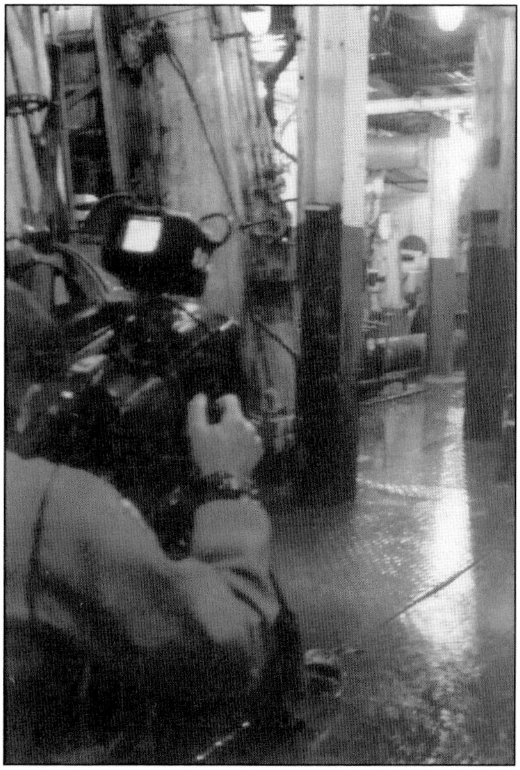

A cameraman filming in the *City of Milwaukee*'s engine room wears a dry suit to keep from being soaked with water during a historical flashback segment of the struggle to keep the car ferry *Milwaukee* afloat during the 1929 storm. It appears that everyone escaped from the engine compartment during the actual sinking, as the extensively explored shipwreck has not revealed a trace of human remains. (Photograph by Debra Townsend.)

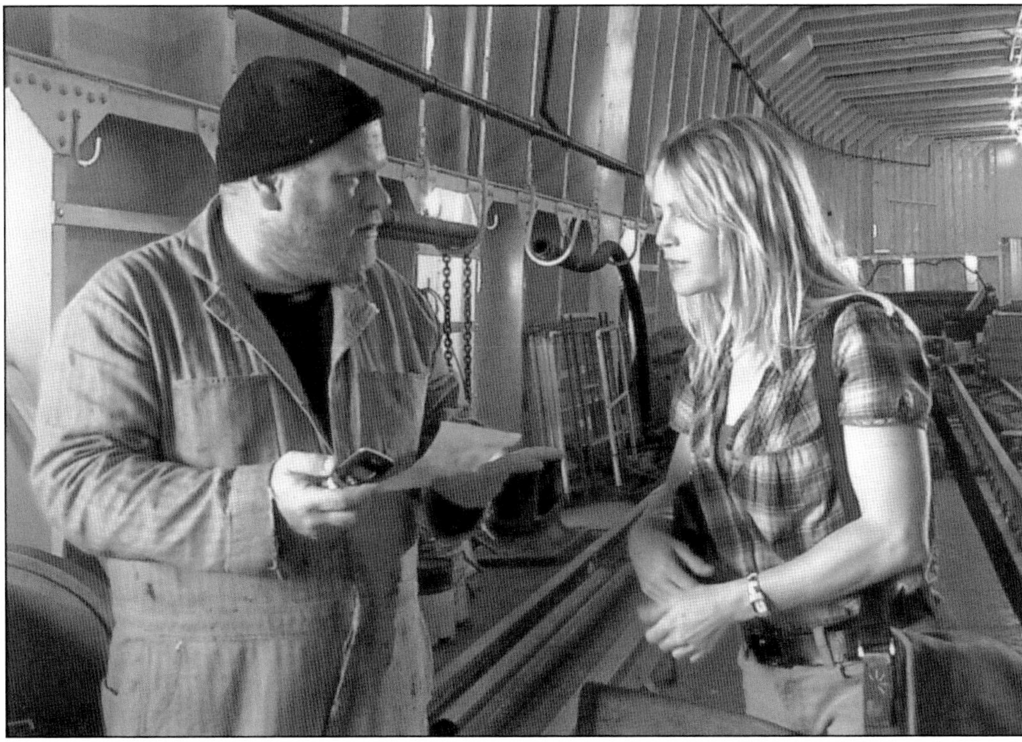

In summer 2009, Brauer Productions of Traverse City, Michigan, produced *Fitful*, filmed entirely aboard the *City of Milwaukee*. Starring Renée O'Connor (Gabrielle in *Xena: Warrior Princess*) and Larry Joe Campbell (the Best Man in *Wedding Crashers* and Andy in *According to Jim*), the 95-minute film took advantage of the atmospheric surroundings of the interior. In this scene, Historic Trust representative Paula (O'Connor) meets ship's caretaker Vigs (Campbell) shortly after her car comes to a tragic end while on a visit to the ship. (Brauer Productions, Inc.)

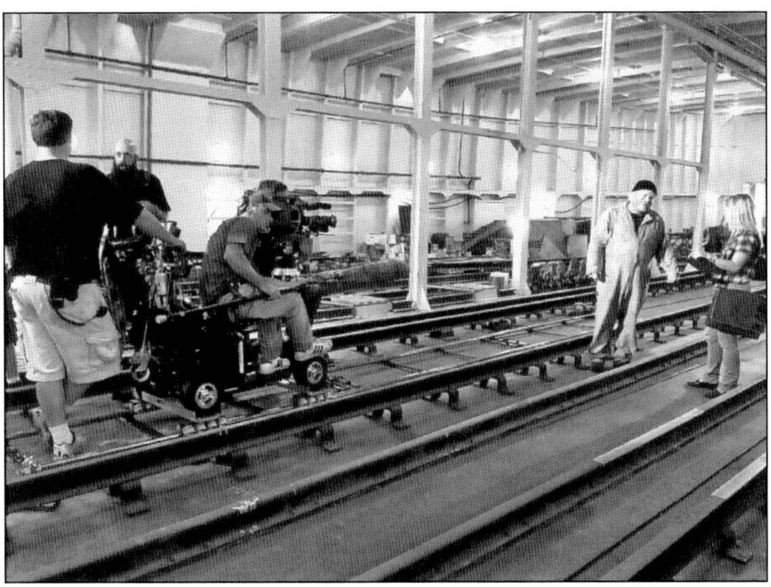

A camera films the action on the *City of Milwaukee*'s car deck during an early scene in *Fitful*. Here, Vigs tells Paula the history of the railroad ferry he has chosen to caretake in an effort to obtain a grant for the ship's restoration. A remote location and lack of transportation add a twist to the film's plot. (Brauer Productions, Inc.)

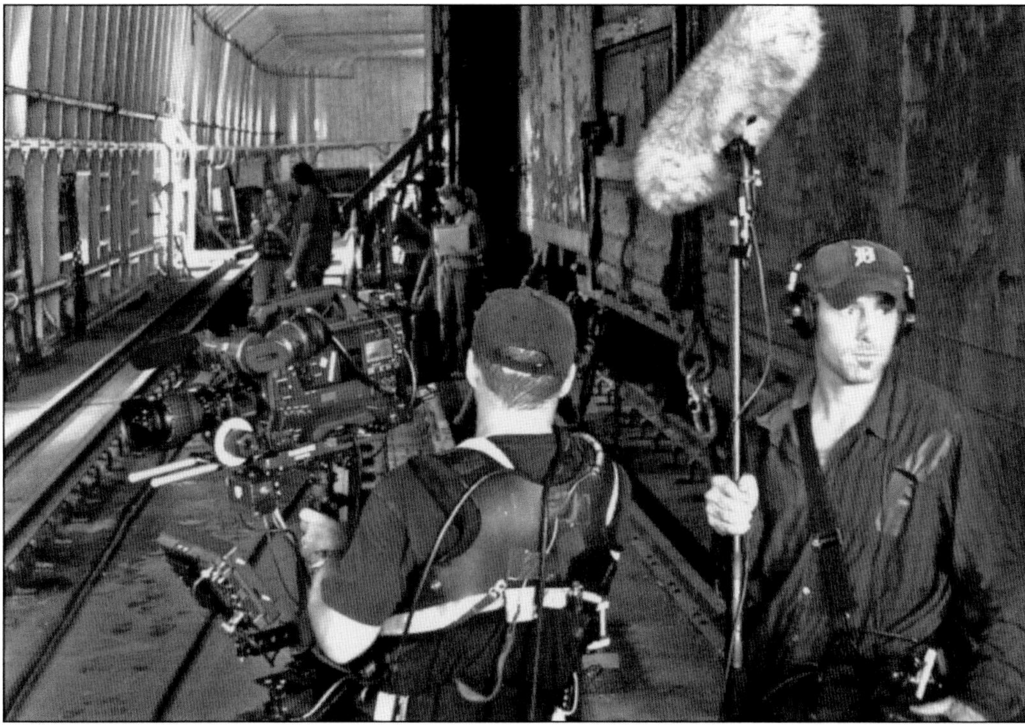

A cameraman and soundman await the set-up of a scene from the independent film *Fitful* on the car deck of the *City of Milwaukee*. The ship, already in good condition, benefitted from additional painting of certain areas in preparation for film scenes. Executive producer Rich Brauer made extensive use of the ship's vintage woodwork in lighting and setting the mood in key scenes of the movie. Brauer's intent was to make the ship a character of the film just as much as a human actor would be. (Brauer Productions, Inc.)

The main saloon, which is the public area into which the staterooms open up, was one of the primary locations for filming dark and eerie segments of the movie. Script supervisor Sheryl Hayward (center left) discusses a scene with first assistant director Laura Anderson Burnell (center) and executive producer and director Rich Brauer (center right). (Brauer Productions, Inc.)

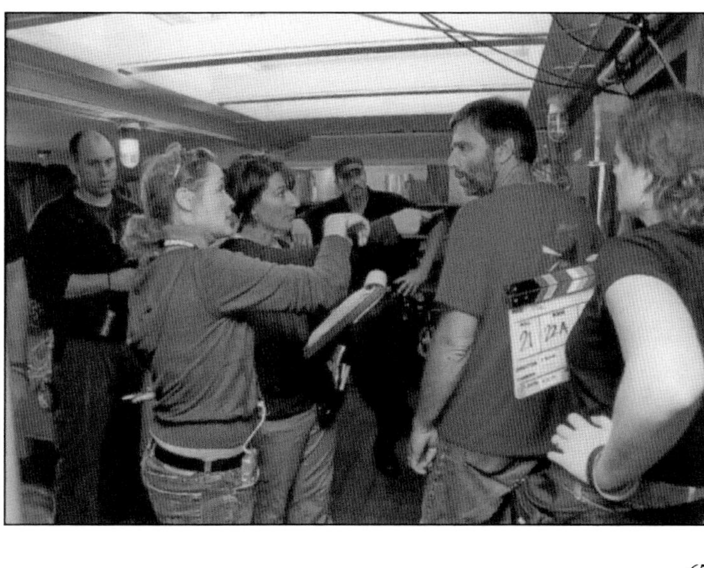

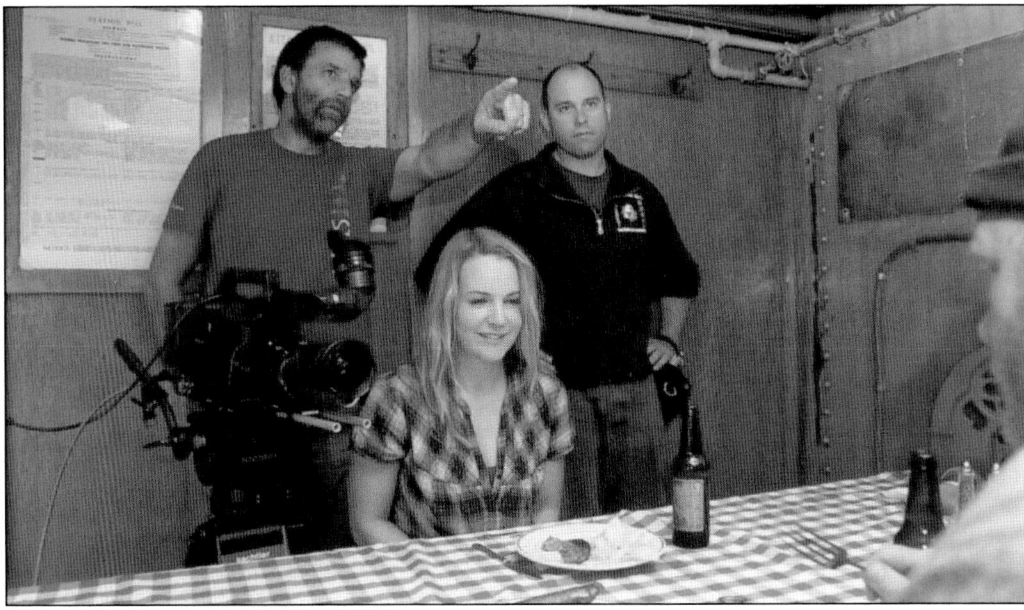

*Fitful* executive producer/director Rich Brauer (standing left) discusses a scene with first assistant cameraman Matt Lamphere in the crew's mess hall aboard the *City of Milwaukee*. Seated at the table are the film's stars, Renee O'Connor and Larry Joe Campbell, during the "Mess Hall/ Bratwurst" scene. (Brauer Productions, Inc.)

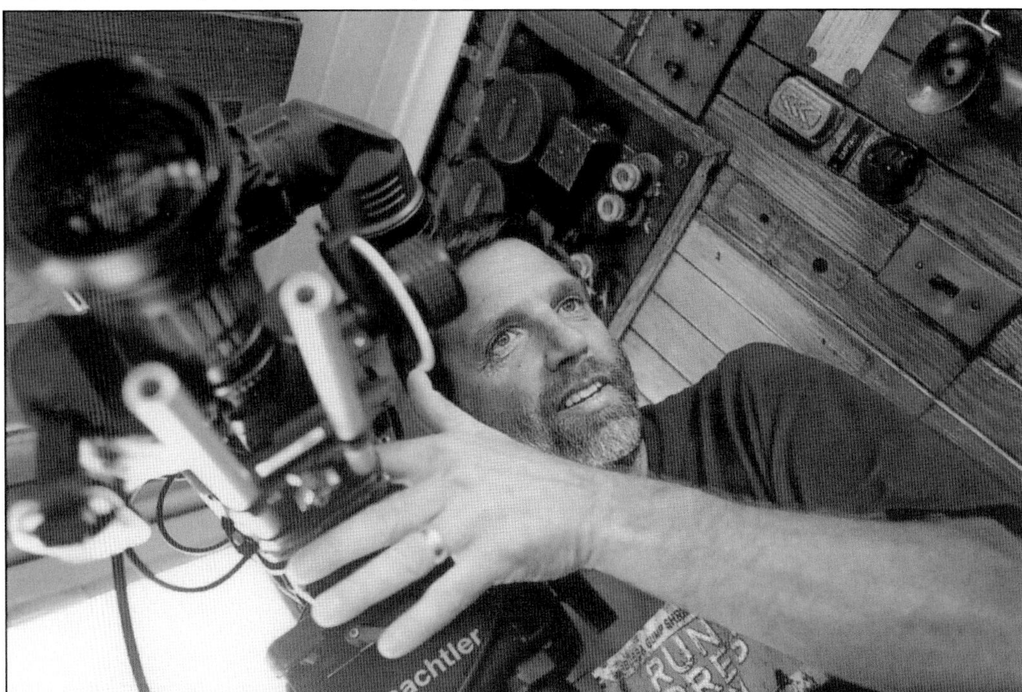


Prior to setting up a scene, *Fitful* director Rich Brauer sets up a Sachtler motion picture camera in the cramped, archaic, 1931-era pilothouse of the *City of Milwaukee*. The contrast between the old ship's electronics and modern film technology is striking. (Brauer Productions, Inc.)

# *Seven*

# Restoration, Preservation, and Display

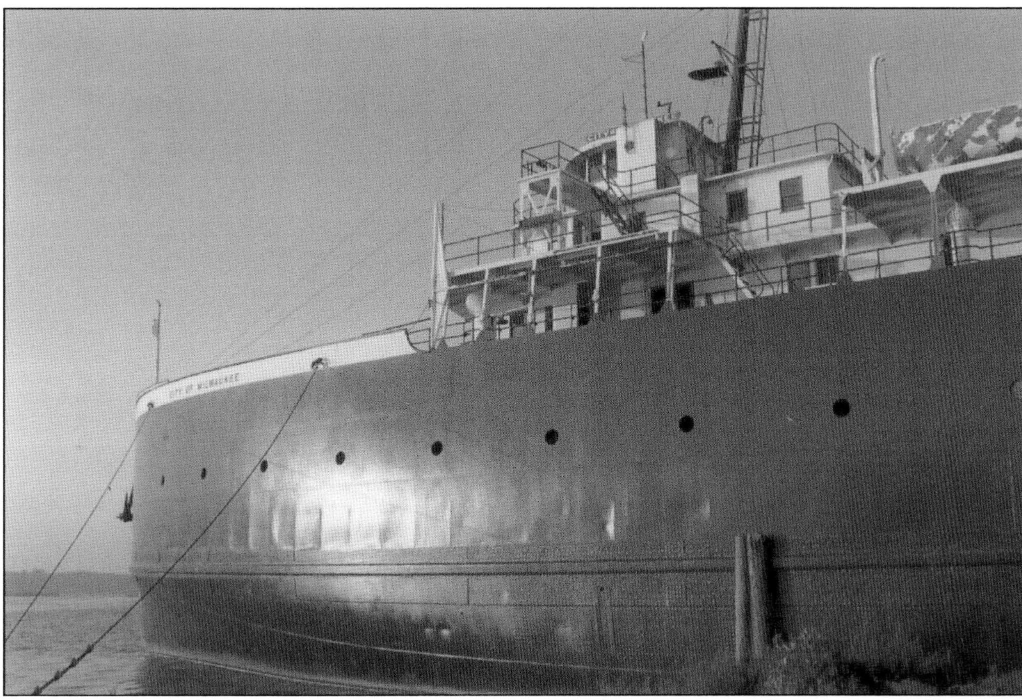

The *City of Milwaukee* sailed under her own steam for the last time on August 9, 1981. Following the cessation of the Ann Arbor operations in April 1982, the boat was sold by the State of Michigan to the City of Frankfort in 1983 for the sum of $2, and area residents formed the Society for the Preservation of the *City of Milwaukee*. After initial efforts to establish the ferry as a museum in Frankfort stumbled in 1986, a reorganized society purchased the ship from Frankfort for $2 in 1988. After a suitable site on the Frankfort side of Lake Betsie could not be obtained due to low water depths, and efforts to utilize the ferry slips at Elberta were rebuffed, the boat was moved to Manistee in 2000, where preservation and restoration—continuous and ongoing since the late 1980s—continues. (CofM.)

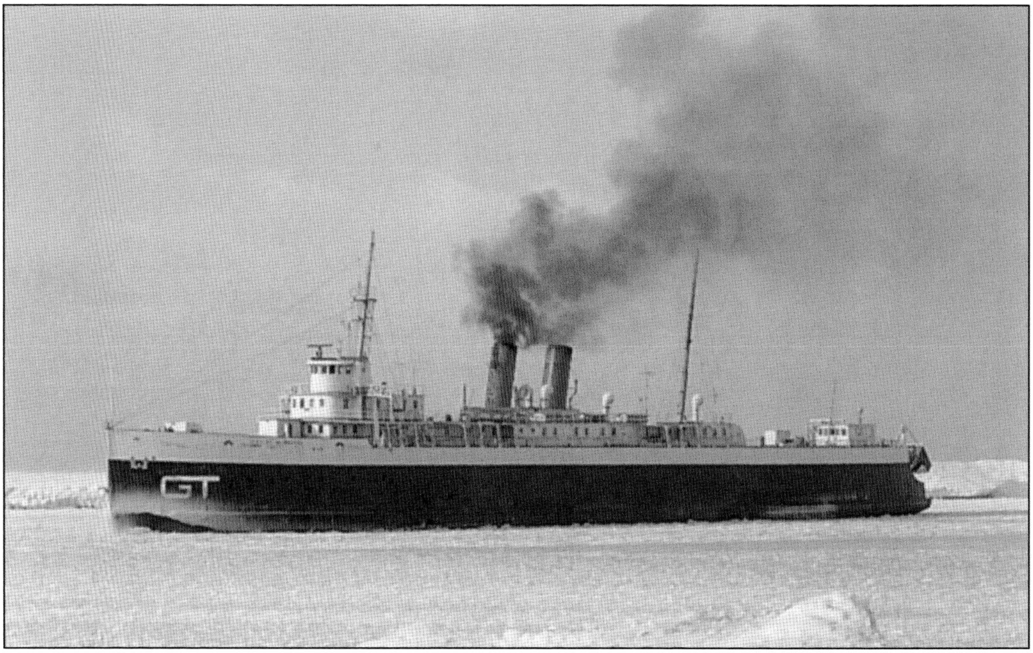

This March 1979 postcard view sees the *City of Milwaukee* entering the harbor at Elberta. Then owned by the State of Michigan, she still shows her Grand Trunk livery of a black hull with a broad white band, white superstructure, and blue stacks capped with red. Soon, the wet-noodle GT logo would be painted over, her stacks painted black, and she will finish her career leased to the Ann Arbor fleet. (Bob Strauss, C.T. Publishing; photograph by Joe McMillan.)

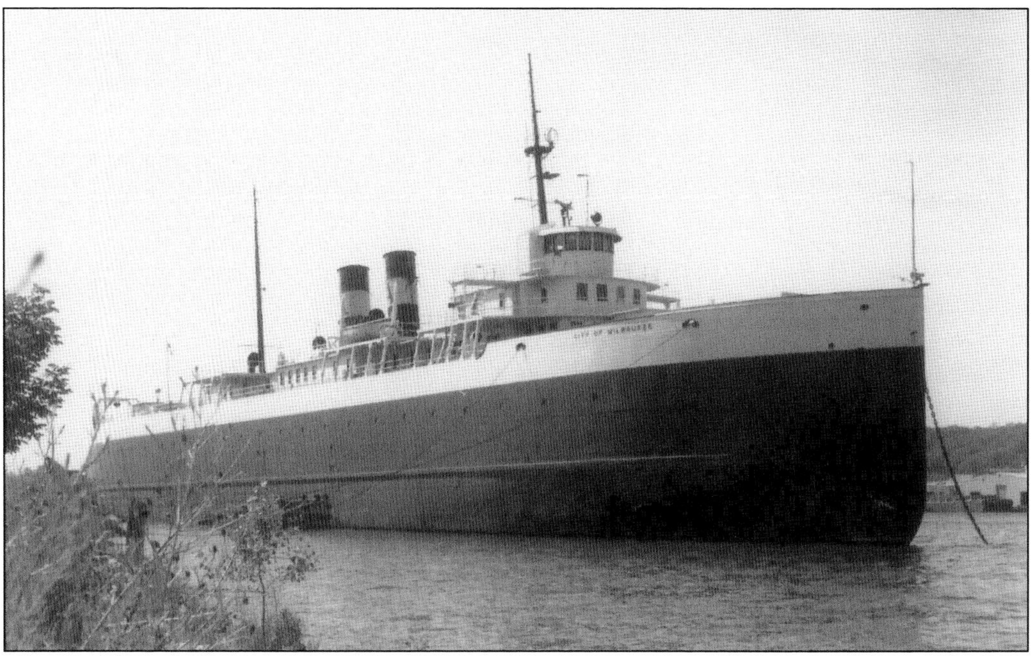

Still facing an uncertain future, the *City of Milwaukee* languishes in retirement at her berth in Elberta. Still retaining the broad white band from her GT days, the ferry enters her museum period sporting stacks painted in the Ann Arbor colors. (CofM.)

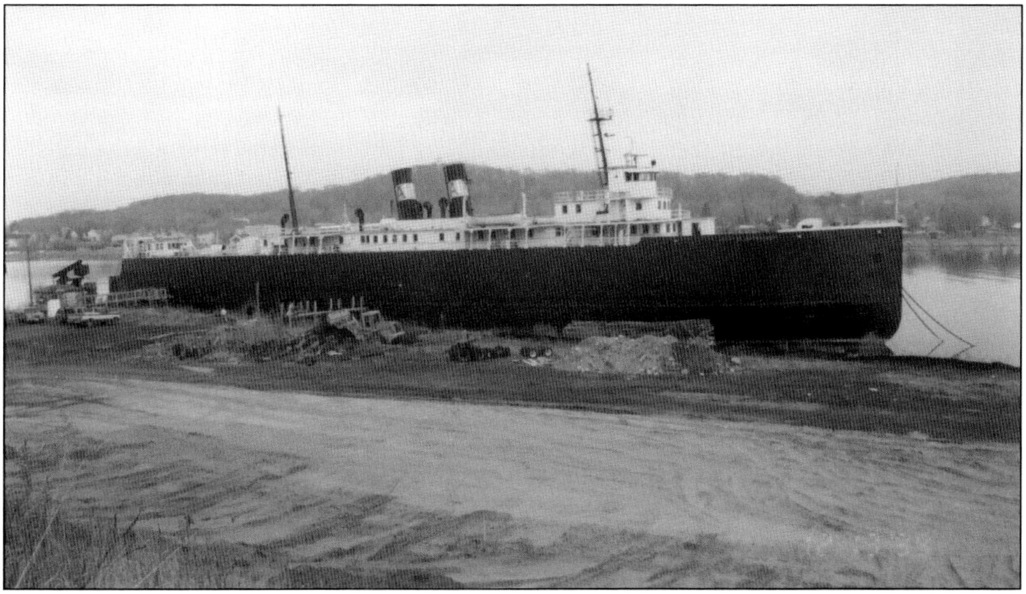

The *City of Milwaukee* rests at her mooring at Elberta. Though fully painted in the Ann Arbor fleet colors—all black hull, white superstructure, and black and silver stacks with red As (to pay homage to her sister ship, the *Ann Arbor No. 7*), *City of Milwaukee* never sailed in this configuration. Where locomotives engines once shunted thousands of railcars on and off the ferries, a single bulldozer goes about its solitary affairs. (CofM.)

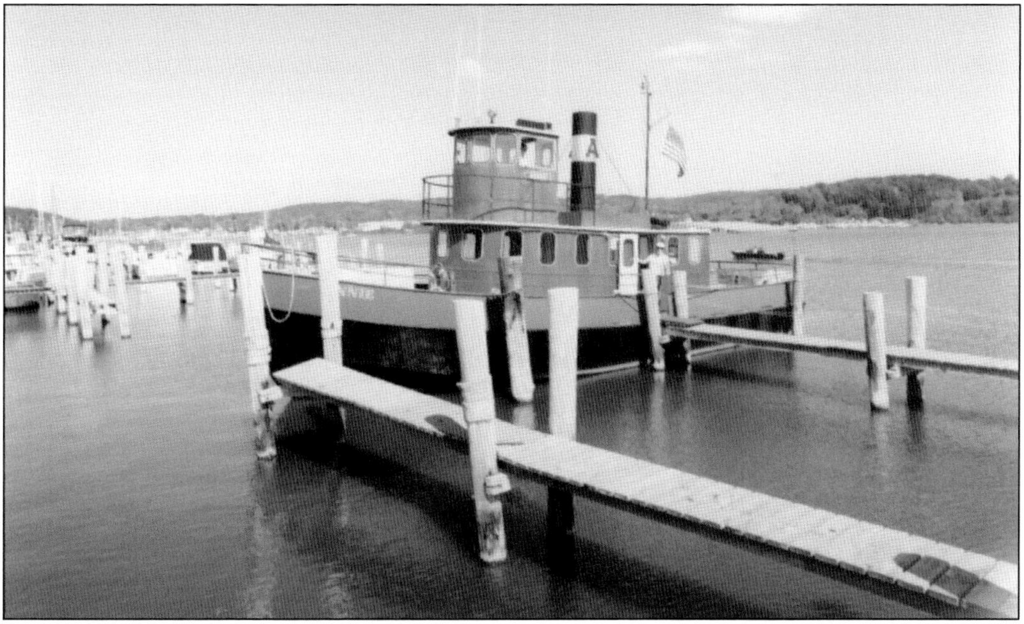

For two years in the 1980s, the Michigan Department of Transportation (MDOT) restricted the society from crossing the former Ann Arbor rail yard at Elberta to access the ferry. Founding members Kirk Lorenz and Jed Jaworski leased a vessel, which they named *Annie*; working from a Frankfort dock, they offered a 45-minute harbor tour, including a stop at the *City of Milwaukee*, accessing the ferry from the water. To help defray operating costs, a sunset cruise was also offered. Eventually, things were settled with MDOT, and the society could access the ferry from land. (CofM.)

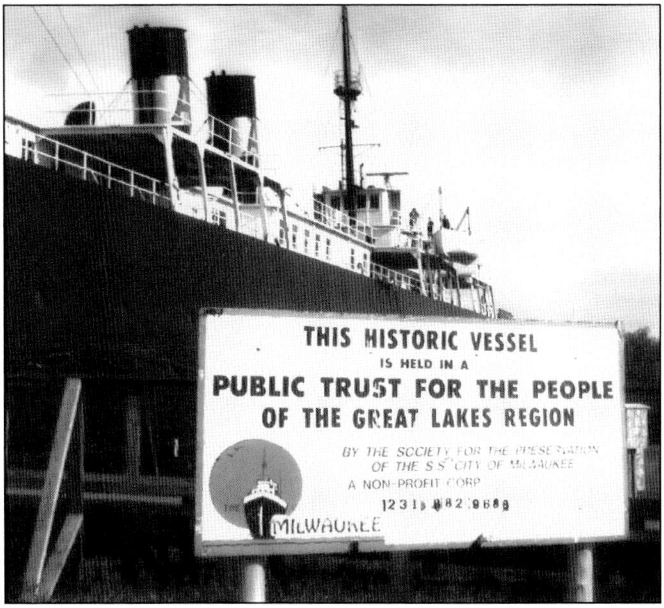


After the voyage from Elberta and a short stay at the Seng's Excavation River Street dock, the *City of Milwaukee* is ensconced at a rented location on Manistee Lake, at the foot of Ninth Street. The generosity of the Seng family, who allowed the temporary dockage and also owned the Ninth Street site, was key in the move. A wooden sign before the gangplank describes the intent of the society: to find a permanent home for the ship. Though many welcomed the boat to Manistee, a handful of people did not care for the ferry occupying this site. (CofM.)

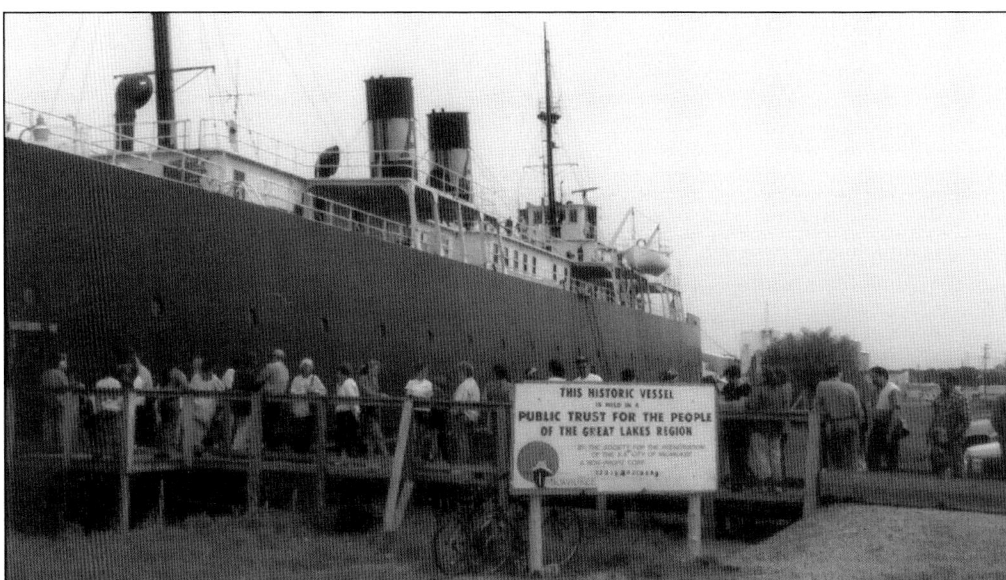


In spite of the grumbling of a few, a line of people winds its way on board the *City of Milwaukee* during one of the initial opening tours. Many of these visitors were impressed with the state of preservation on board the boat and were appreciative of the efforts of the staff and volunteers in maintaining it as a historic landmark. The boat also became favored by many of the neighborhood kids, who in those early days in Manistee enjoyed being on board and helping out as they could. (CofM.)

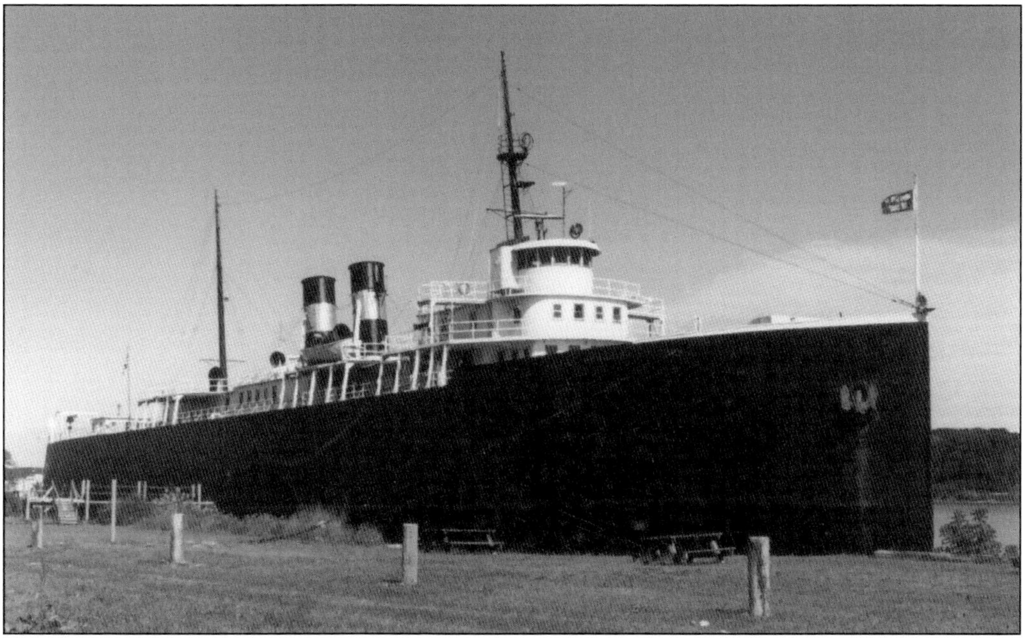

The *City of Milwaukee* lies at her Ninth Street berth in Manistee. Still in Ann Arbor colors, she flies a flag bearing the motto adopted by the society, "Don't Give Up The Ship." The Ninth Street site was the former home of the Century Boat Works, a manufacturer of small recreational craft. Evidence of the long-gone factory came in the form of chunks of fiberglass, which was dug up during trenching operations for the installation of utilities. (Photograph by Bob Strauss.)

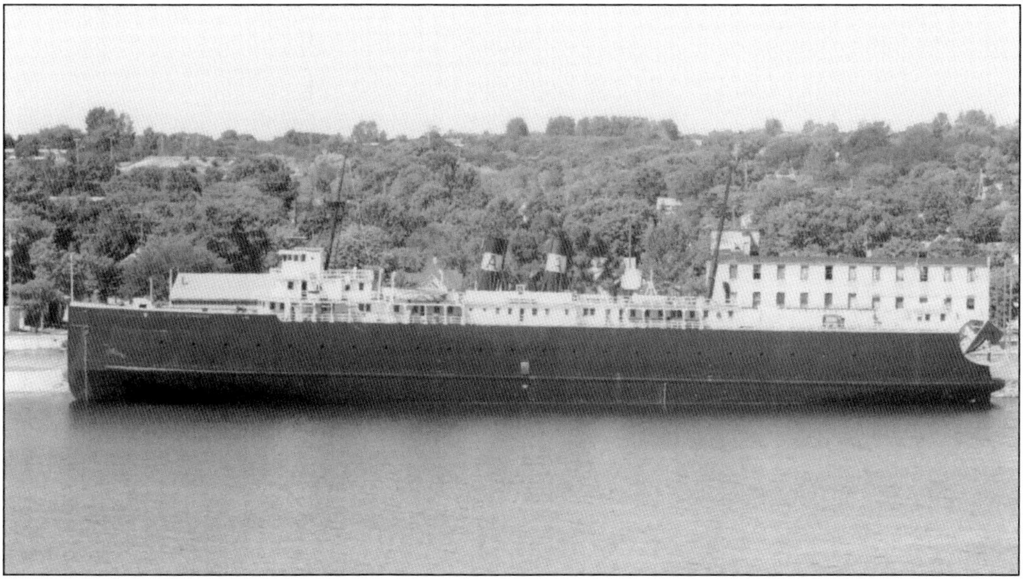

This view from across Manistee Lake shows the port side of the ferry at the Ninth Street site. Although the location was large and accommodating, it was somewhat remote, well off the main road that passed through the town, US 31. Although it was possible while traveling on US 31 to catch a brief glimpse of the ship's masts rising above houses and trees if one were looking in the right place at the right time, the lack of visibility prompted a move to a more prominent location near the northwest end of Manistee Lake. (CofM.)

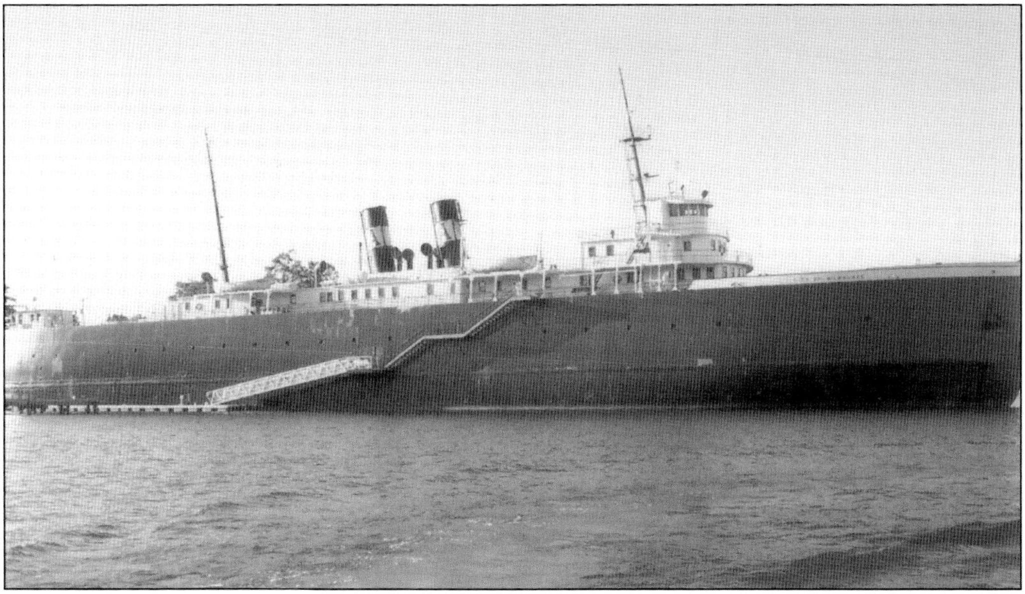

Now at her location along US 31 at the site of the Moonlight Motel and Marina, the *City of Milwaukee* shows off her new colors. With her stacks still painted in the familiar red double As, the rest of the boat has been restored to her original colors—a hunter green hull with a cream-colored superstructure. After chipping through multiple layers of paint, it was determined that these were her original hues. Also seen along the starboard side are the newly installed ramp and stairway to the upper deck. (CofM.)

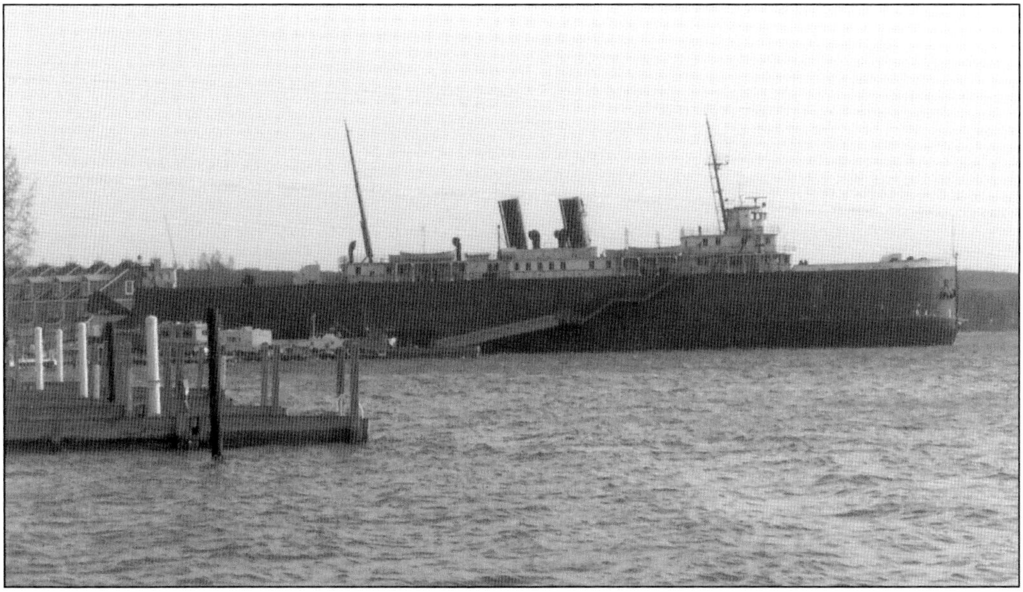

With her stacks painted black, the *City of Milwaukee*'s transformation back to her original colors is complete. It has taken the efforts of many to see the boat through this continuing restoration, just as it will take the efforts of many to continue the restoration and preservation. While much work has been done, there is still much left to do. It is the dedication and determination of the boat's staff, volunteers, and society members that will allow the *City of Milwaukee* to survive. (Photograph by Bob Strauss.)

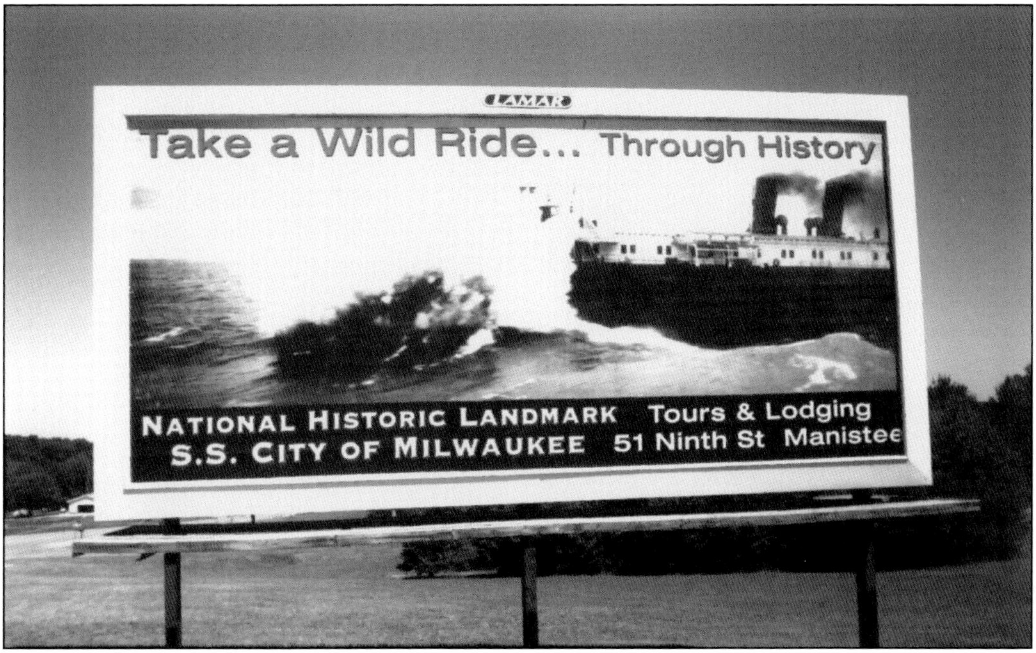


Shortly after the ship's move to Manistee, a series of billboards was erected around the area advertising the boat. This one shows a dramatic view of the *Pere Marquette 17* taking green water over her bow during a 1929 Lake Michigan storm. The *Pere Marquette 17* survived this, as well as many other storms, and was rebuilt in 1940 as the *City of Petoskey* for use as a Michigan State Ferry across the Straits of Mackinac. (Photograph by George Micka.)

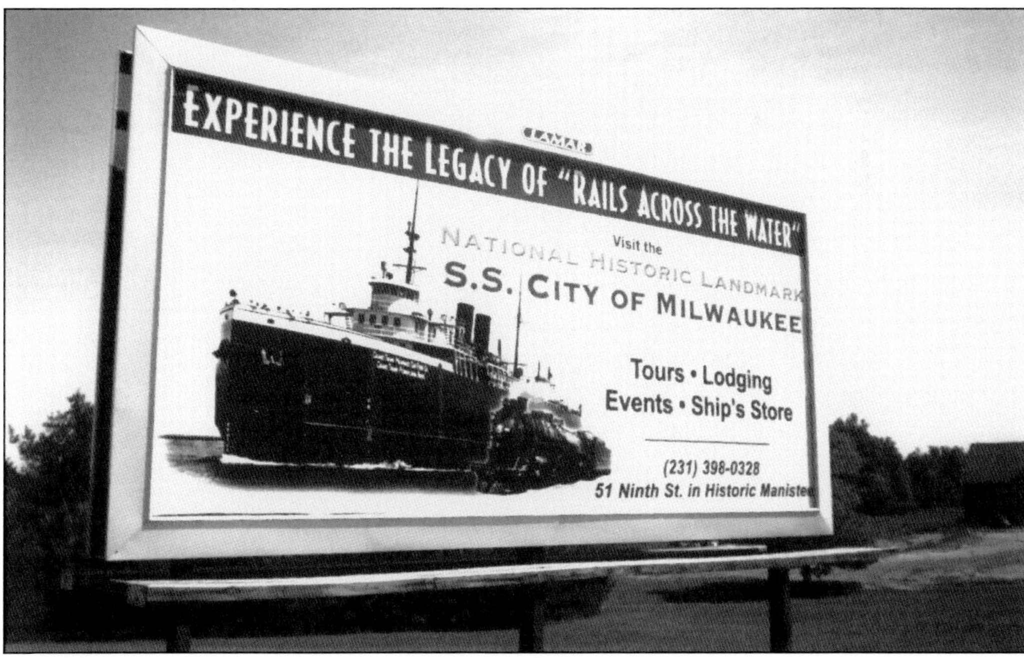


This billboard features a shot of the *City of Milwaukee* as she appeared shortly after her launching and maiden voyage in 1931. Promoting tours, lodging, special events, and the Ships Store, the sign advertises the fact that the ferry is now open for business. (Photograph by George Micka.)

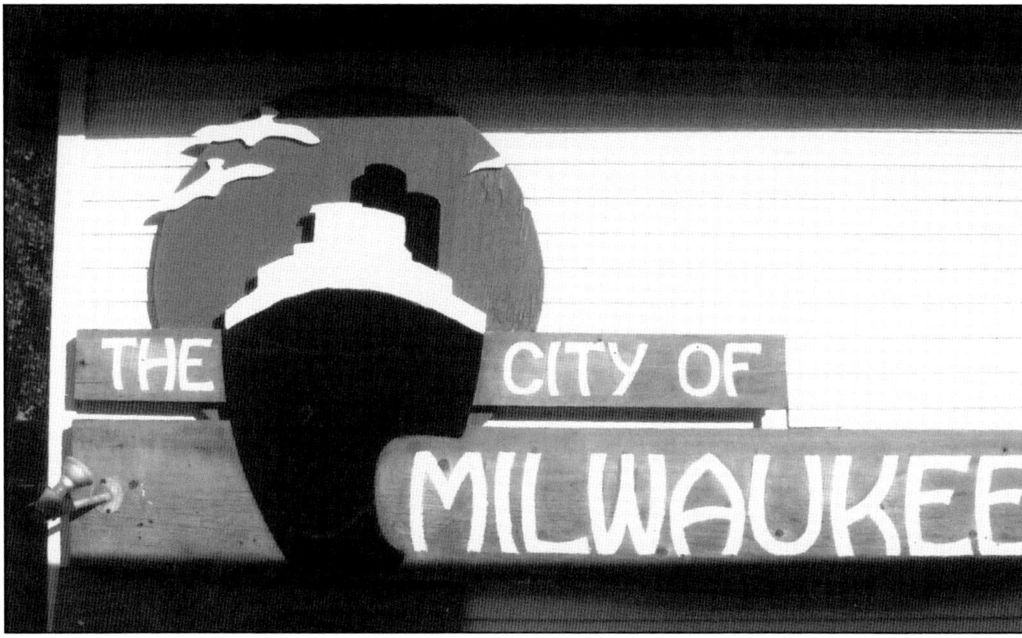


This attractive logo was designed by Frankfort resident Judith Brown during the early Elberta years. Used on the letterhead of the society's paperwork and on early newsletters, this logo helps to bridge the past with the present and the future of the society. (Photograph by Bob Strauss.)

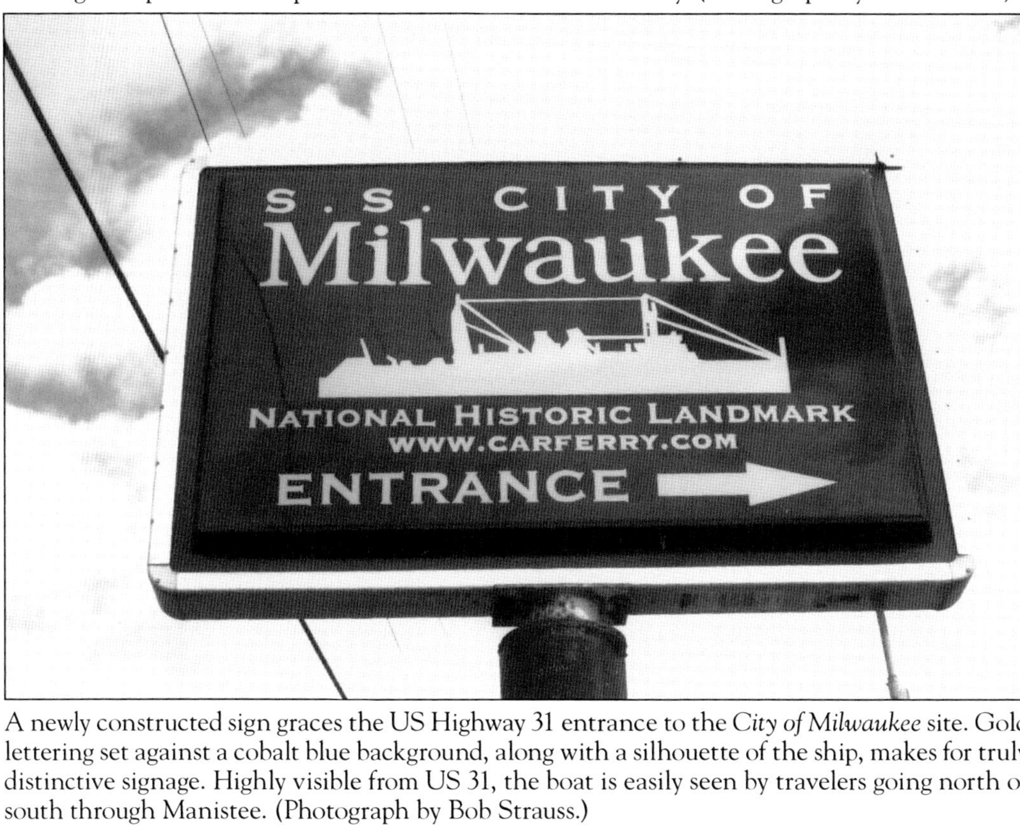


A newly constructed sign graces the US Highway 31 entrance to the *City of Milwaukee* site. Gold lettering set against a cobalt blue background, along with a silhouette of the ship, makes for truly distinctive signage. Highly visible from US 31, the boat is easily seen by travelers going north or south through Manistee. (Photograph by Bob Strauss.)

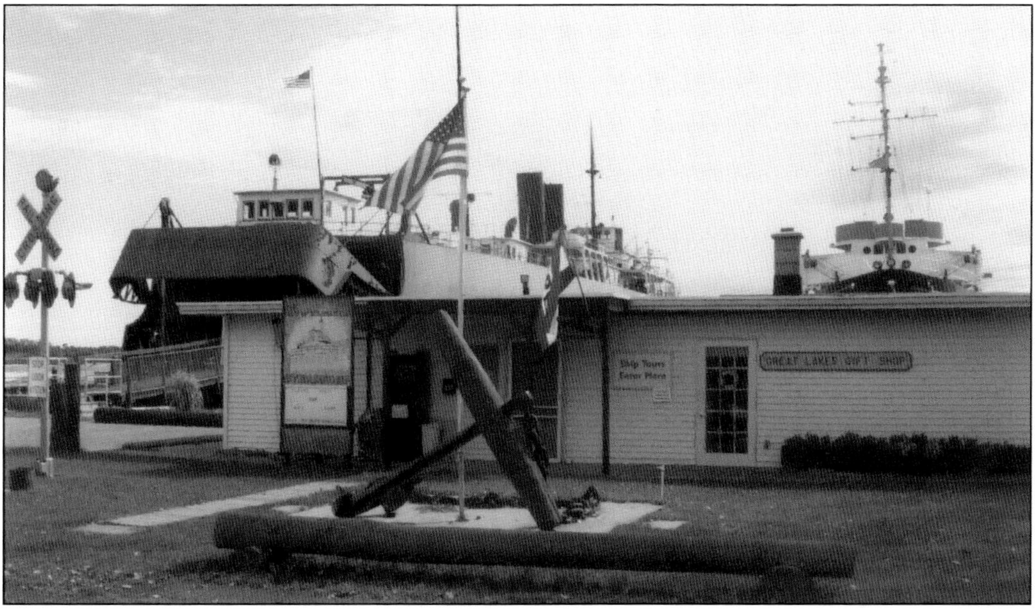


This is the headquarters of the *City of Milwaukee* historic site. An anchor and a railroad-crossing sign adorn the front yard of the building. The door to the right opens into a gift shop and reception area. The door below the flags enters into a common kitchen area. Public restrooms occupy the left end of the building. Peering over the roof of the gift shop is the society's October 2009 acquisition, the retired US Coast Guard cutter *Acacia*. (Photograph by Bob Strauss.)

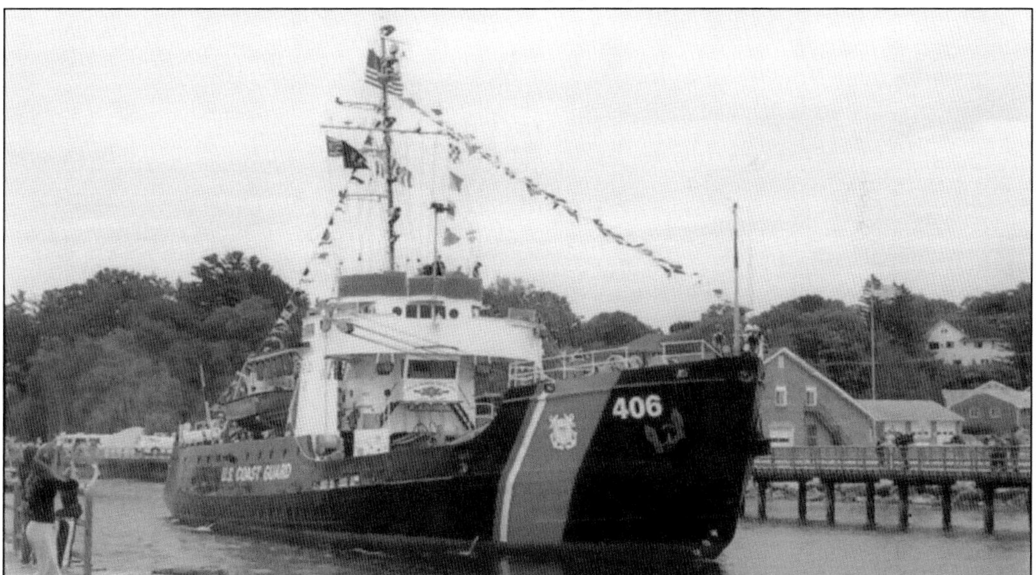


In the fall of 2009, the retired US Coat Guard cutter *Acacia* was acquired from a Chicago-based group in an endeavor spearheaded by board member Tom Read. Shown here on the Manistee River, it was sailed from Chicago to Manistee with a volunteer crew under the auspices of the crew of the SS *Badger*: Capt. Dean Hobbs, engineers Chuck Cart and Bill Kulka, and crew members Pat Lafreniere and Al Crank. It is hoped the fully operational *Acacia* can be used for short mini-cruises and overnight stays by interested groups. (CofM.)

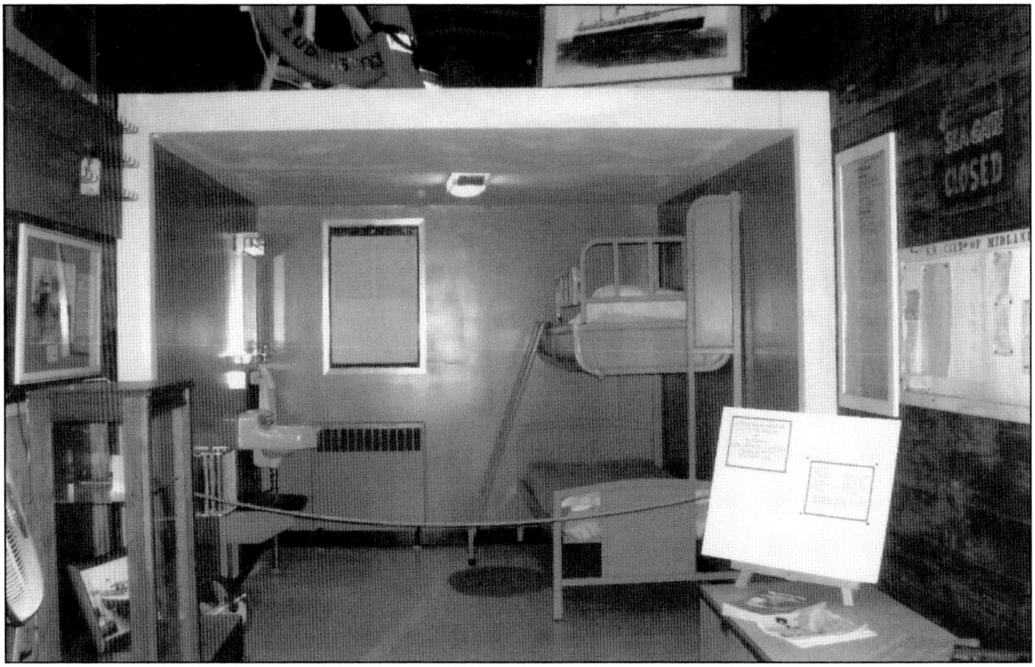


A re-creation of a stateroom from the former Pere Marquette/C&O car ferry *City of Midland 41* was built largely by society member Bob Newcomb. Items in the display were salvaged from the *Midland* when it was cut down to a barge in 1997. Also included are a *Midland* life ring and photographs and other items to commemorate what many buffs feel was the best designed, most popular car ferry to sail the Great Lakes. (Photograph by Bob Strauss.)

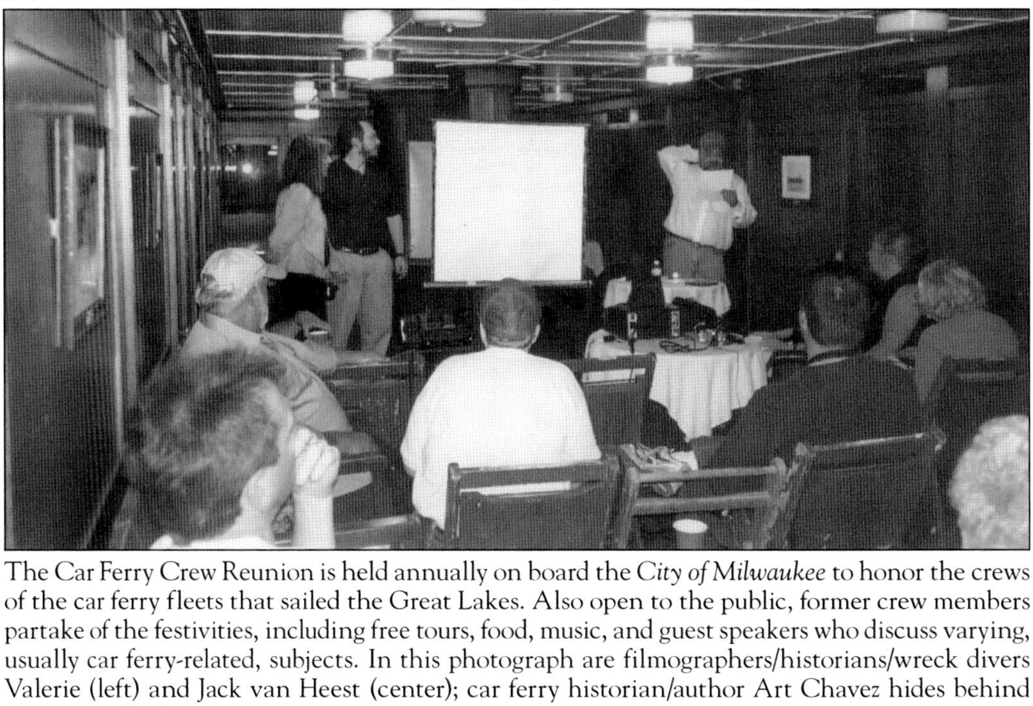

The Car Ferry Crew Reunion is held annually on board the *City of Milwaukee* to honor the crews of the car ferry fleets that sailed the Great Lakes. Also open to the public, former crew members partake of the festivities, including free tours, food, music, and guest speakers who discuss varying, usually car ferry-related, subjects. In this photograph are filmographers/historians/wreck divers Valerie (left) and Jack van Heest (center); car ferry historian/author Art Chavez hides behind his notes. (CofM.)

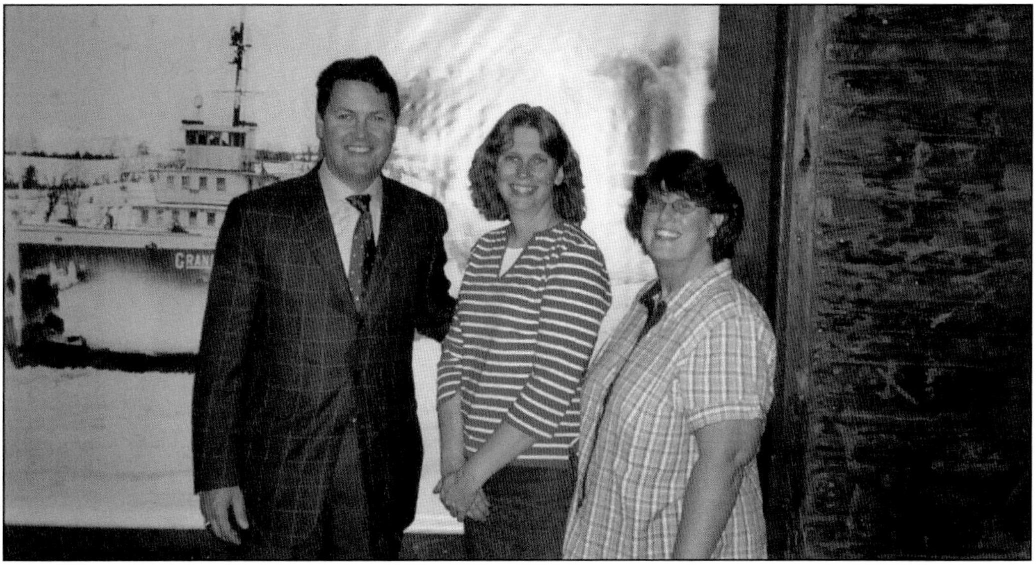

Michigan state representative David Palsrok, *City of Milwaukee* general manager Linda Spencer, and Manistee Middle School sixth-grade teacher Stephanie Oden were participants of the opening of a new Boxcar exhibit in 2008. Representative Palsrok participated in the ribbon-cutting for the new show, which featured displays designed by Oden's students. Also included in the exhibit is a Memorial Wall featuring photographs and short biographies of former Great Lakes car ferry crew members. (Photograph by Ed Andrews.)

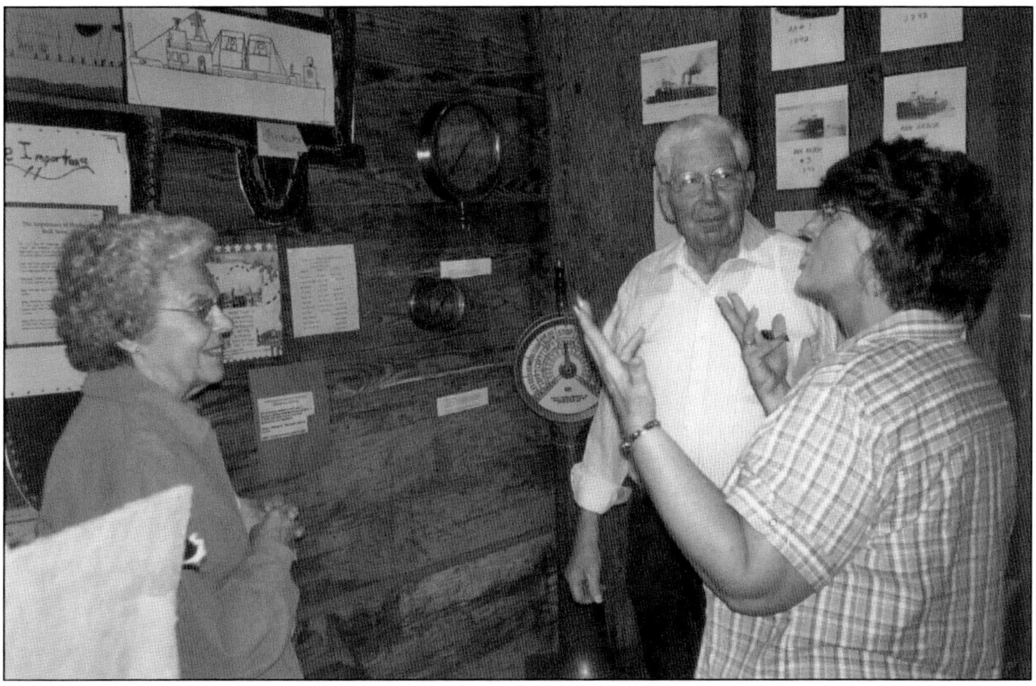

Stephanie Oden discusses her student's artwork with Capt. Bill Bacon and his wife, Olive. Captain Bacon was the superintendent of the Ann Arbor marine operations during the *City of Milwaukee*'s final operational years. Bacon has been an ardent supporter of and consultant to the preservation efforts and has also been a frequent visitor to the ferry. (Photograph by Ed Andrews.)

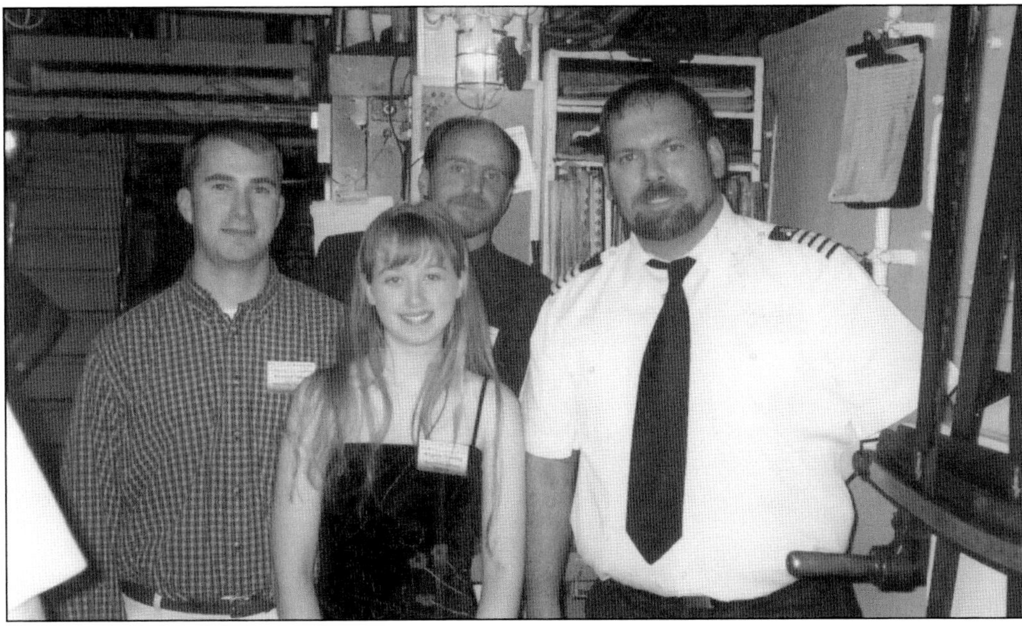

Standing alongside the SS *Badger*'s engine control throttles are, from left to right, Richard Tabor, Angela Diesing, Jed Jaworski, and *Badger* senior engineer Charles Cart. At the time, Richard and Jed worked as the *City of Milwaukee*'s marketing director and curator, respectively. Chief Cart and his employer, the Lake Michigan Carferry Company, have donated time and materials to the museum ship's restoration. (CofM.)

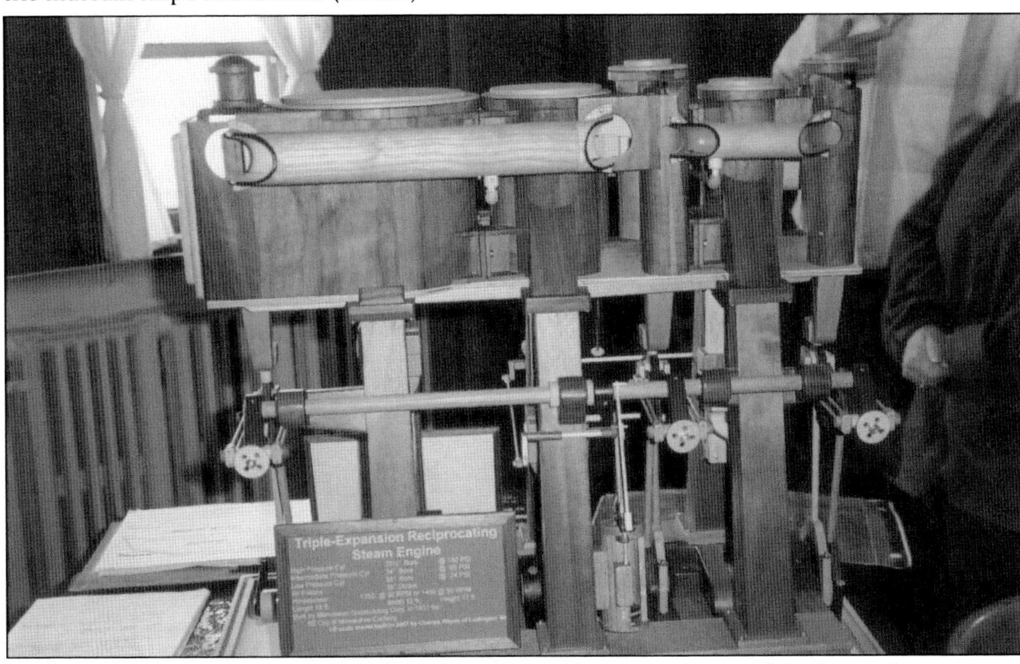


Another recent exhibit placed on board is this working wooden model of a triple-expansion steam engine crafted by Charles Hayes. A functional, hands-on model, it is used to demonstrate how steam is compressed in the engine cylinders to provide power to turn a ship's propeller. (Photograph by Bob Strauss.)

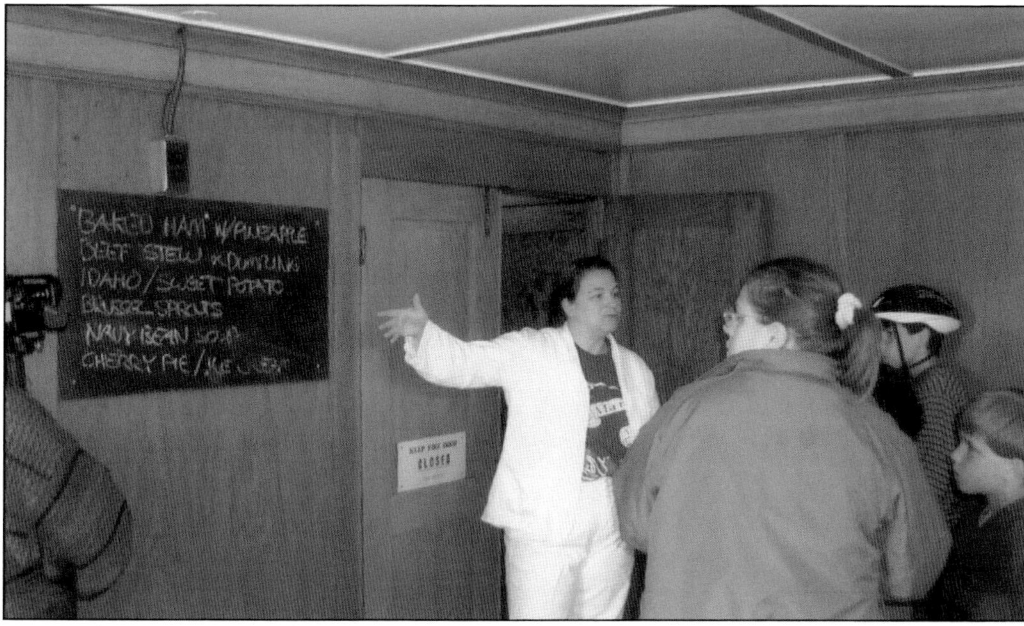

Tour guide JoLynn Hanley describes the passenger dining room, in which the wood has a green tint. In one apocryphal story, a relief captain had the room painted green in honor of the vacationing captain, who was Irish. When the Irish captain returned, he ordered the paint stripped. Allegedly, the green pigment stained the wood. This interesting tale is probably a sailor's yarn, as early newspaper accounts of the ship describe green-stained wood. (CofM.)

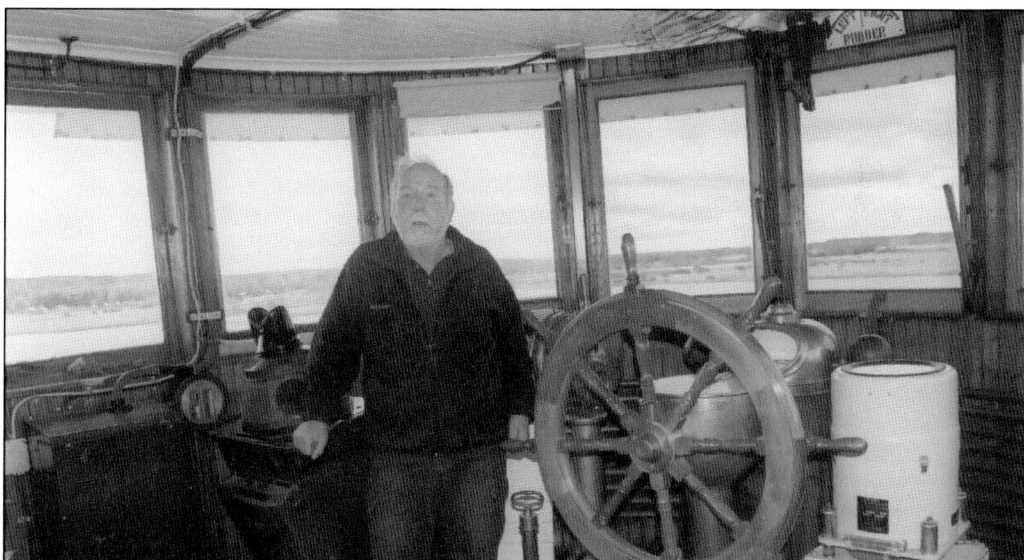

Tour guide Bob Newcomb stands at the ready in the pilothouse. The wooden ship's wheel and brass engine-order telegraphs (chadburns) are replacements; the original items went missing during the years the vessel was laid up in Elberta. Souvenir hunters and scavengers took numerous artifacts from the boat. The society has a "no questions asked" policy concerning the return of purloined items and encourages people to return them to their rightful place on board the *City of Milwaukee*. (CofM.)

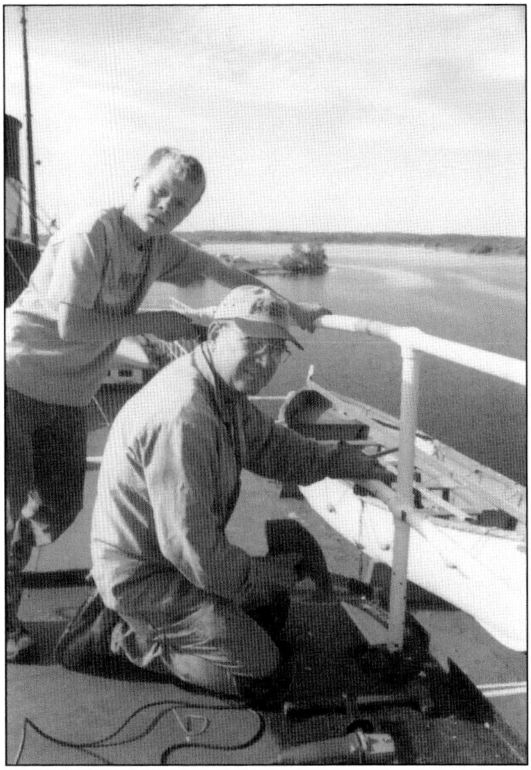

Two generations of volunteers work hard at scraping and painting deck railings. Volunteers are the lifeblood of the ship, and they are a critical component in the preservation effort. Whenever possible, the majority of the work done on board—from cleaning and painting to welding and other major work—is accomplished through the efforts of member volunteers. (CofM.)

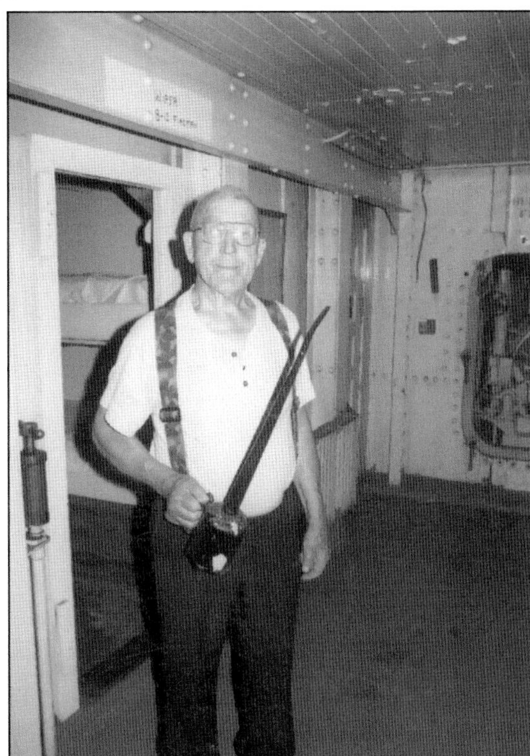

Here, an unidentified former oiler from the *City of Milwaukee* poses in the flicker with one of his tools of the trade. Former crewmen such as this often visit the boat during the tourist season to reminisce and commiserate with the current crew. Note the watertight door leading to the engine compartment. (CofM.)

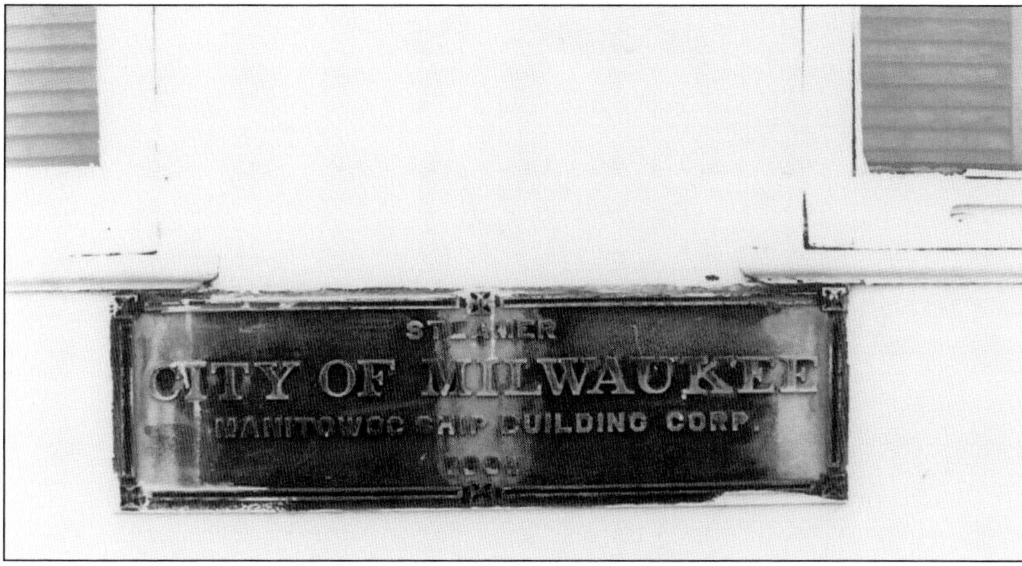


This undated photograph shows the *City of Milwaukee*'s weathered and paint-spattered builders plate as it looked during the ship's operational years. Located just below the pilothouse on the bulkhead outside of the captain's quarters, the plate disappeared in the early 1980s. A nearly identical plate, located in the engine room, was removed at the same time and remains missing. (Bruce Groeneveld.)

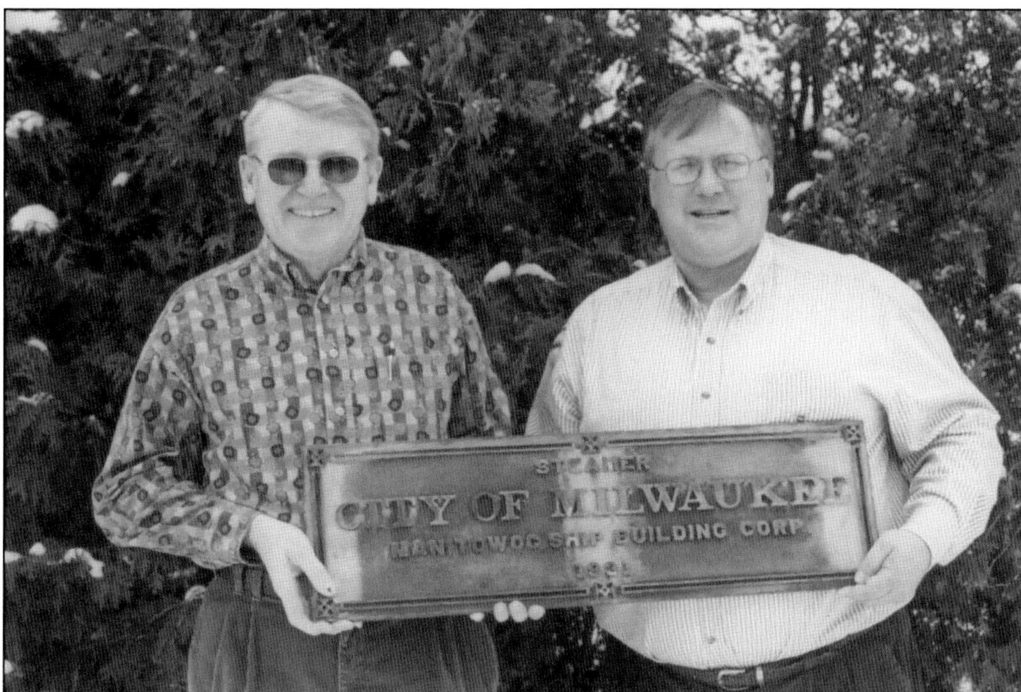


Society board president Duane Nugent (left) and Capt. Dean Hobbs, master of the car ferry SS *Badger*, hold the recovered builders plate of the *City of Milwaukee*. Captain Hobbs was instrumental in the recovery of the plate. Cleaned up, it would soon be restored to its original location on the front of the pilothouse. (CofM.)

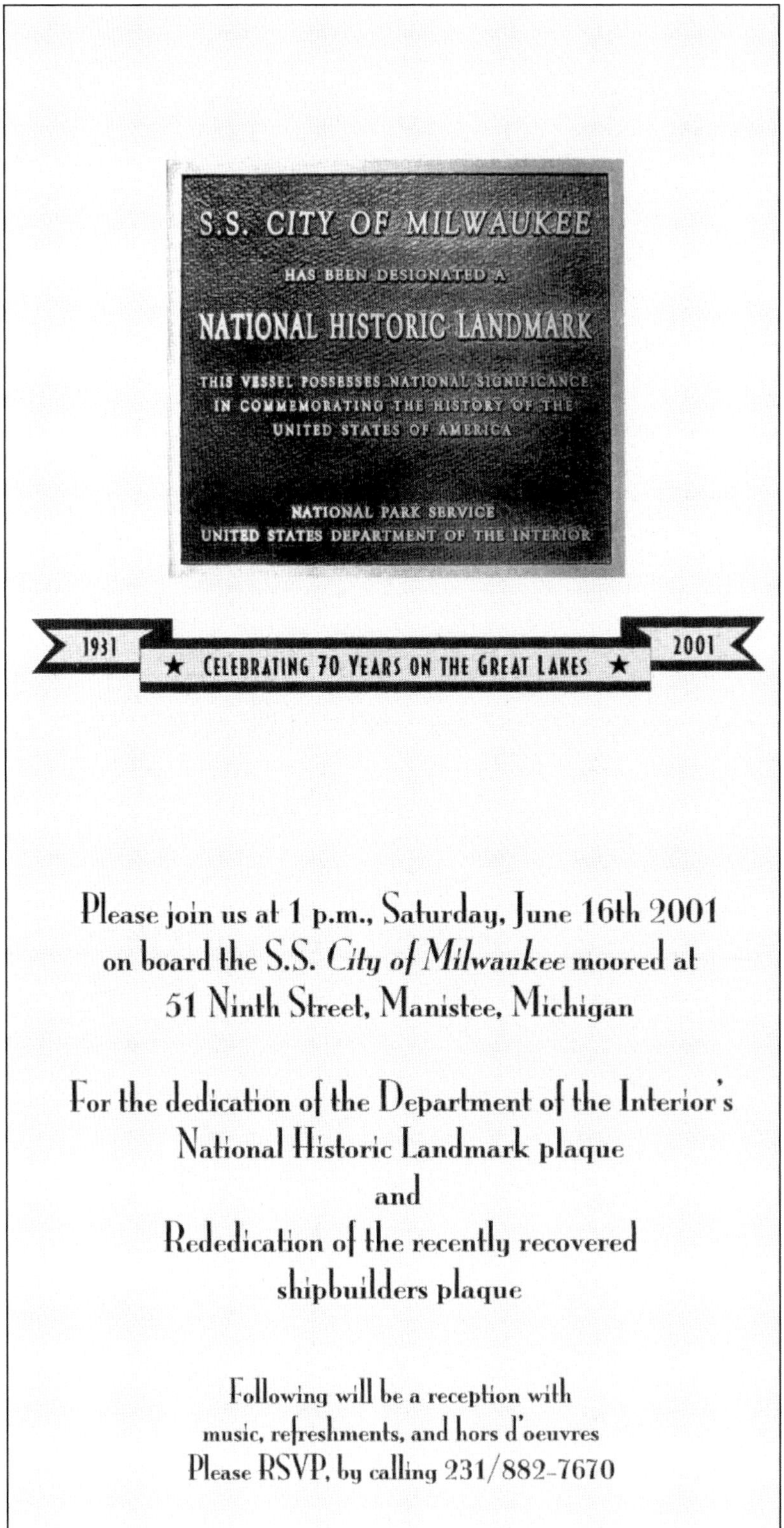
S.S. CITY OF MILWAUKEE
HAS BEEN DESIGNATED A
NATIONAL HISTORIC LANDMARK
THIS VESSEL POSSESSES NATIONAL SIGNIFICANCE IN COMMEMORATING THE HISTORY OF THE UNITED STATES OF AMERICA
NATIONAL PARK SERVICE
UNITED STATES DEPARTMENT OF THE INTERIOR

1931 ★ CELEBRATING 70 YEARS ON THE GREAT LAKES ★ 2001

Please join us at 1 p.m., Saturday, June 16th 2001
on board the S.S. *City of Milwaukee* moored at
51 Ninth Street, Manistee, Michigan

For the dedication of the Department of the Interior's
National Historic Landmark plaque
and
Rededication of the recently recovered
shipbuilders plaque

Following will be a reception with
music, refreshments, and hors d'oeuvres
Please RSVP, by calling 231/882-7670

This invitation invited the public to the rededication of the recovered builders plate and the dedication of the plaque designating the *City of Milwaukee* as a National Historic Landmark. Held on June 16, 2001, this event also helped commemorate the 70th anniversary of the launch of the *City of Milwaukee*. (CofM.)

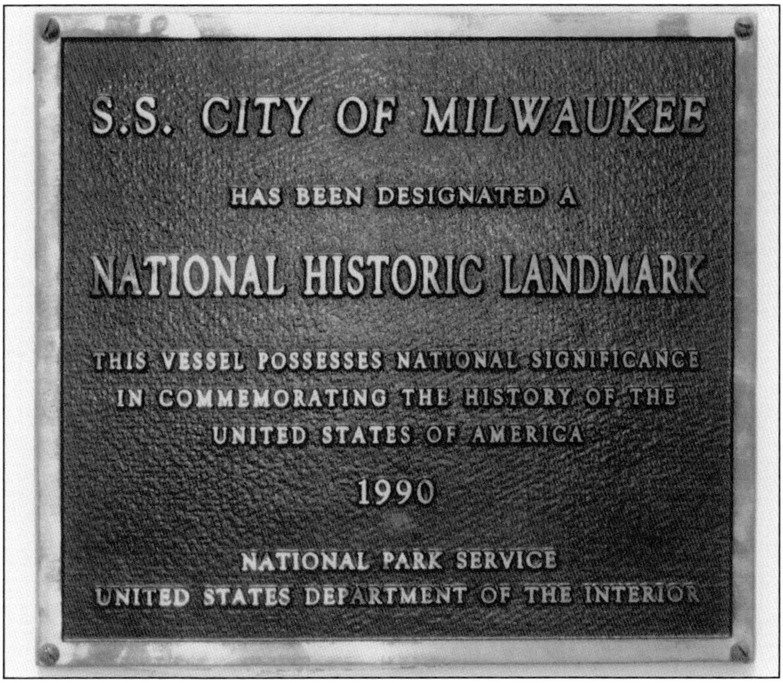


This bronze plaque officially designates the *City of Milwaukee* as a National Historic Landmark. This status is not an easily obtained classification. An organization must prove the historical and cultural relevance of a potential landmark's contribution to American history. (Bob Strauss.)

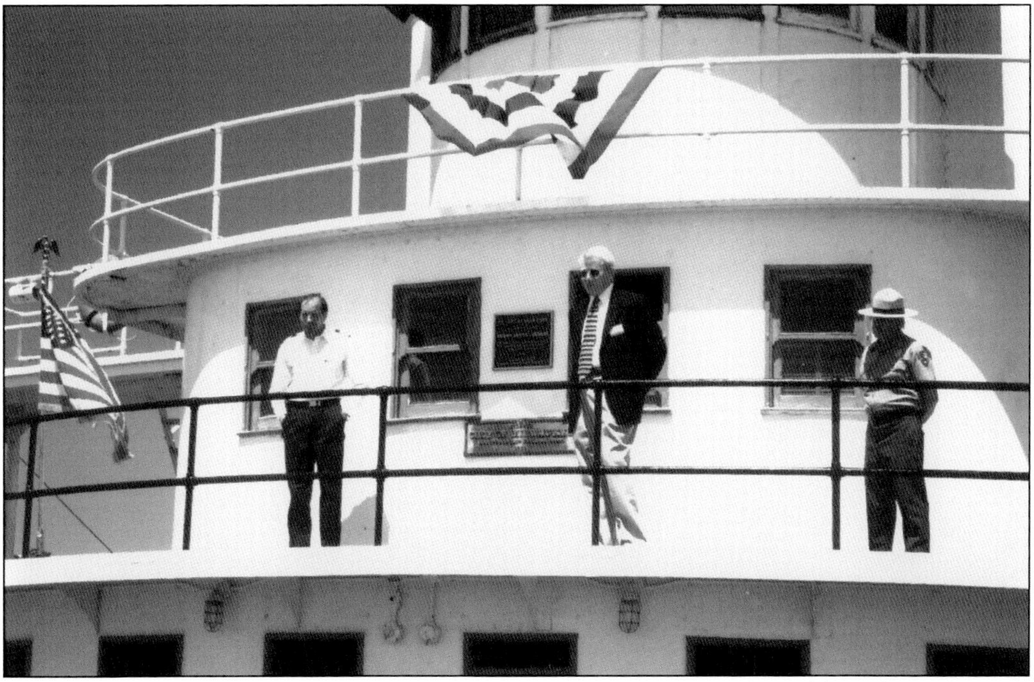

Curator Jed Jaworski (left), board president Duane Nugent (center), and board member Bill Herd pose after affixing plaques to the forward deckhouse during the 2001 festivities. Bill Herd represented the National Park Service during the ceremony. (CofM.)

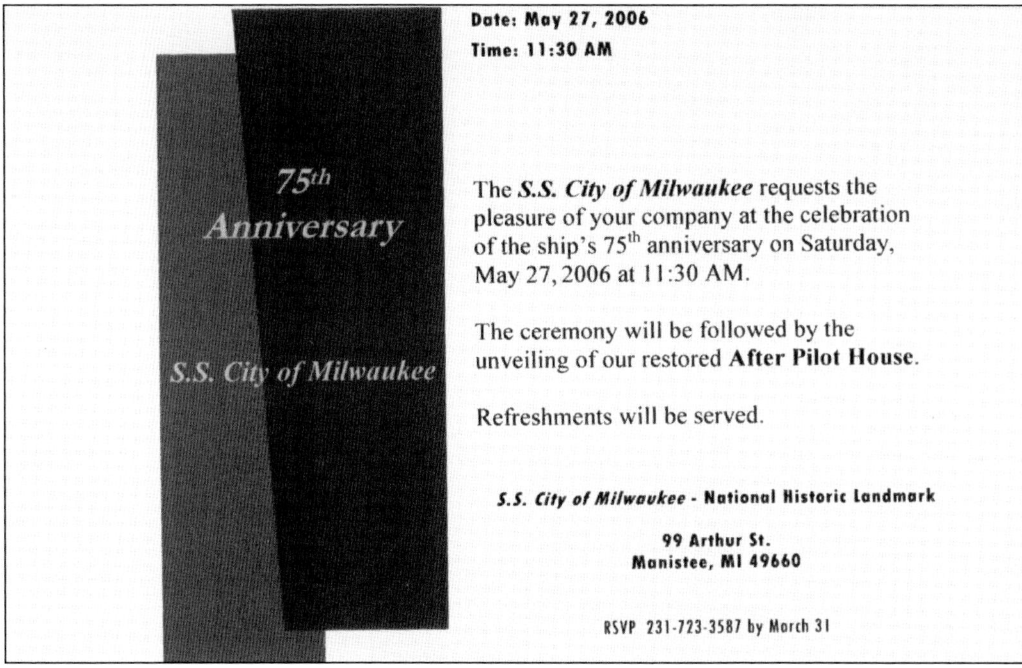

Date: May 27, 2006
Time: 11:30 AM

75th Anniversary

S.S. City of Milwaukee

The ***S.S. City of Milwaukee*** requests the pleasure of your company at the celebration of the ship's 75th anniversary on Saturday, May 27, 2006 at 11:30 AM.

The ceremony will be followed by the unveiling of our restored **After Pilot House**.

Refreshments will be served.

***S.S. City of Milwaukee*** - **National Historic Landmark**

**99 Arthur St.**
**Manistee, MI 49660**

RSVP 231-723-3587 by March 31

The 2006 crew member reunion festivities coincided with a celebration to commemorate the ferry's 75th anniversary. In conjunction with the anniversary celebration was the unveiling of the newly restored aft pilothouse. The years had taken their toll, as woodwork had rotted and metal plates rusted through. The wood flooring and some of the wooden window sashes were replaced in the restoration. (CofM.)

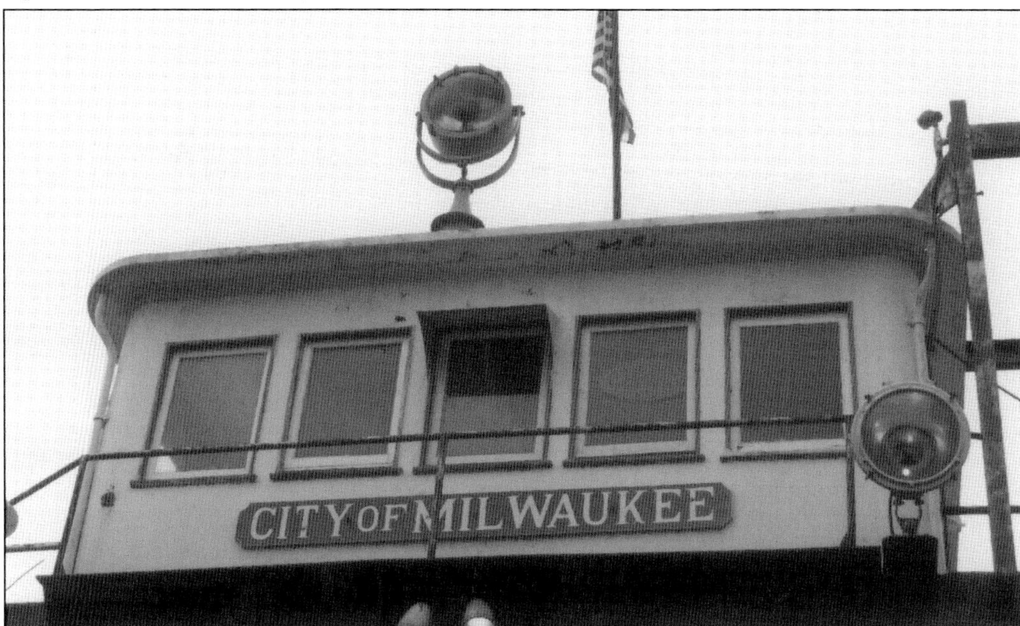


This view shows the aft pilothouse as seen from the car deck. Standing at the center window, the captain would maneuver the ferry, backing into the boat slip and lining up with the loading apron. The large spotlights were used for illumination when operating at night. (CofM.)

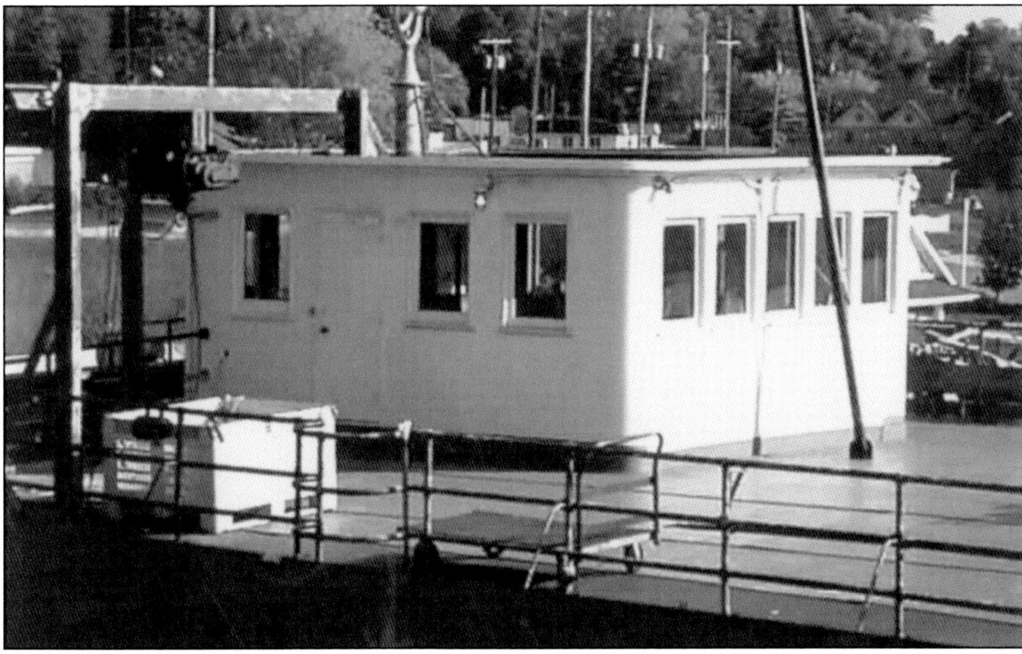

In this view of the starboard side of the aft pilothouse, doors on either side allowed access by the crew. To the left in the picture is a power hoist, added by the Ann Arbor, hanging from an I beam. The crew would use this hoist to lift supplies from the car deck to the upper deck. (Photograph by John Brandt.)

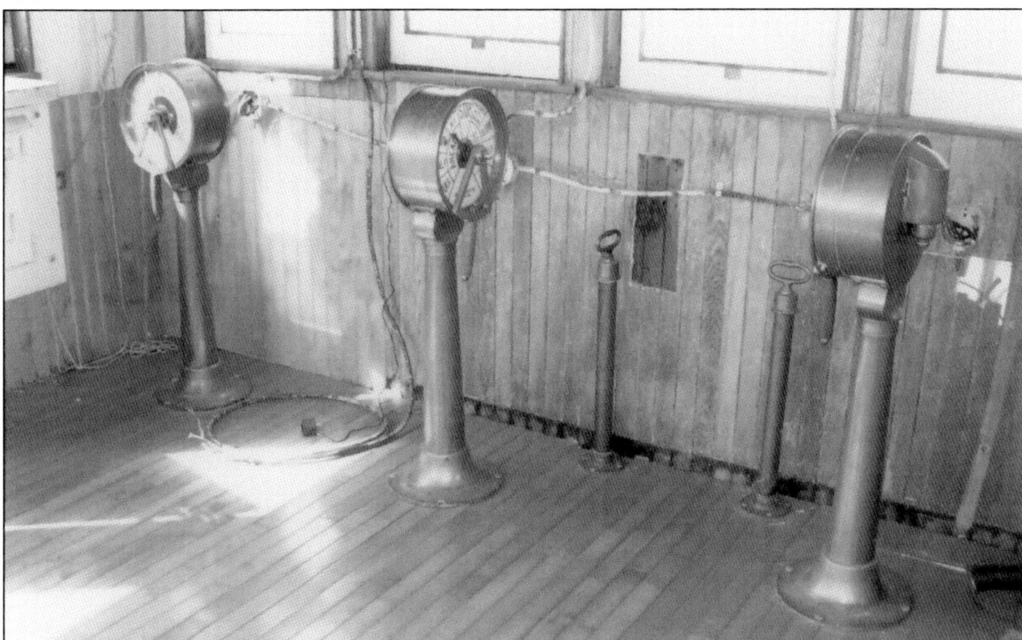

Lining the aft wall of the pilothouse are the chadburns used by the captain to dock the boat. The new flooring has been installed, with wood being donated by society member Steve Johnson. During the winter of 2005–2006, member Ron Yeo prepped for the new floor by welding in new floor plates to replace rusted ones. A flooring crew was hired to install the new boards. (CofM.)

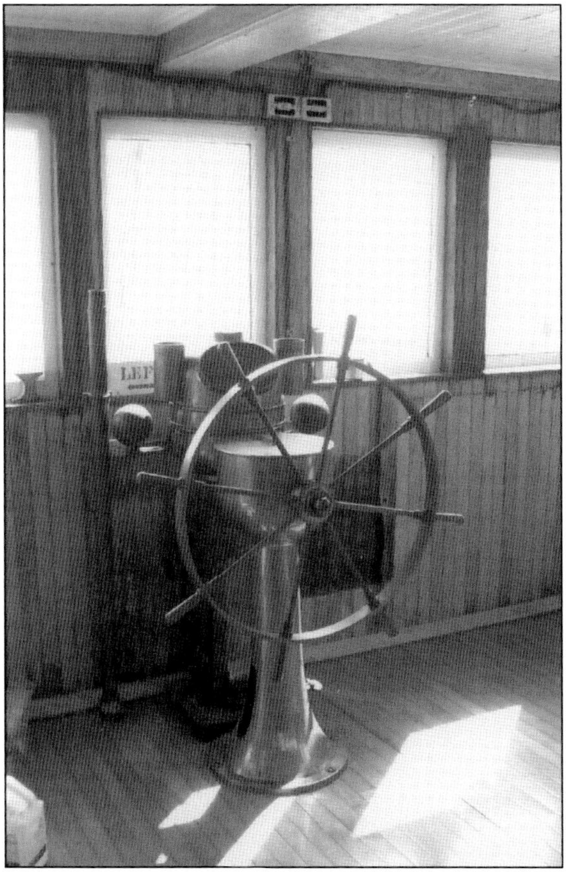

The restoration also included the recovery and reinstallation of the aft pilothouse wheel, which also had gone missing during the 1980s. It was, fortunately, returned in time for the restoration in 2006. The wheel is located at the forward wall of the aft pilothouse. As the ship's emergency wheel, it could be used to pilot the craft from this location, should the main wheel in the forward pilothouse be disabled for any reason. (CofM.)

Here is a view of the forward deckhouse. On top is the pilothouse; the next level down is the captain's quarters. The lower level is the passenger lounge. The black object in the foreground is the forward mooring winch. At one time, the Grand Trunk Railroad erected a metal structure around the winch, which somewhat marred the ship's appearance and also obstructed the view from the passenger lounge. This was removed in order to bring the boat back to her 1931 appearance. (Photograph by Bob Strauss.)

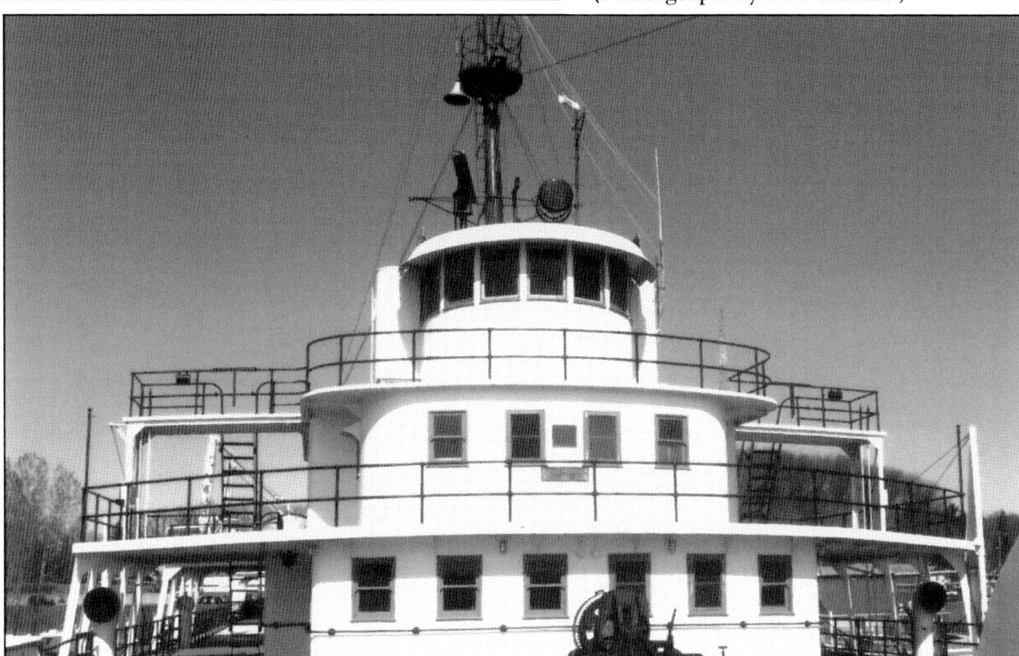

From this station, the wheelsman guided the ferry from port to port. On the left is the ship's radar, installed in the 1950s. Often, the captain would sit to the right of the wheelsman. The lever alongside the center window is the whistle pull. Windows wrap around the front half of the pilothouse, giving a nearly unobstructed view of the lake. (Photograph by Bob Strauss.)

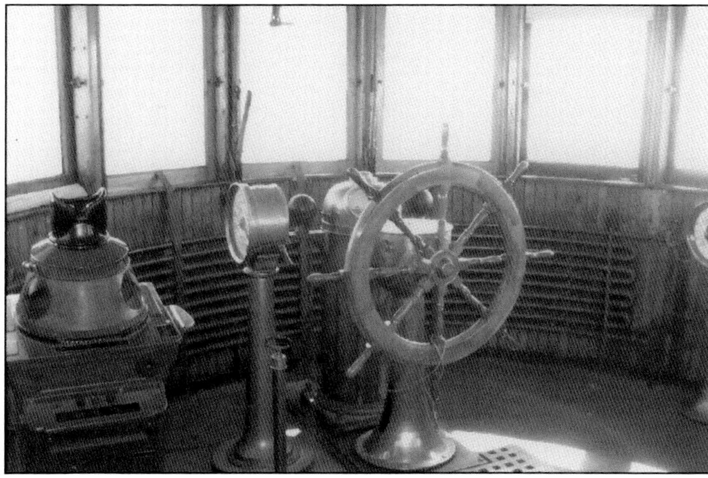

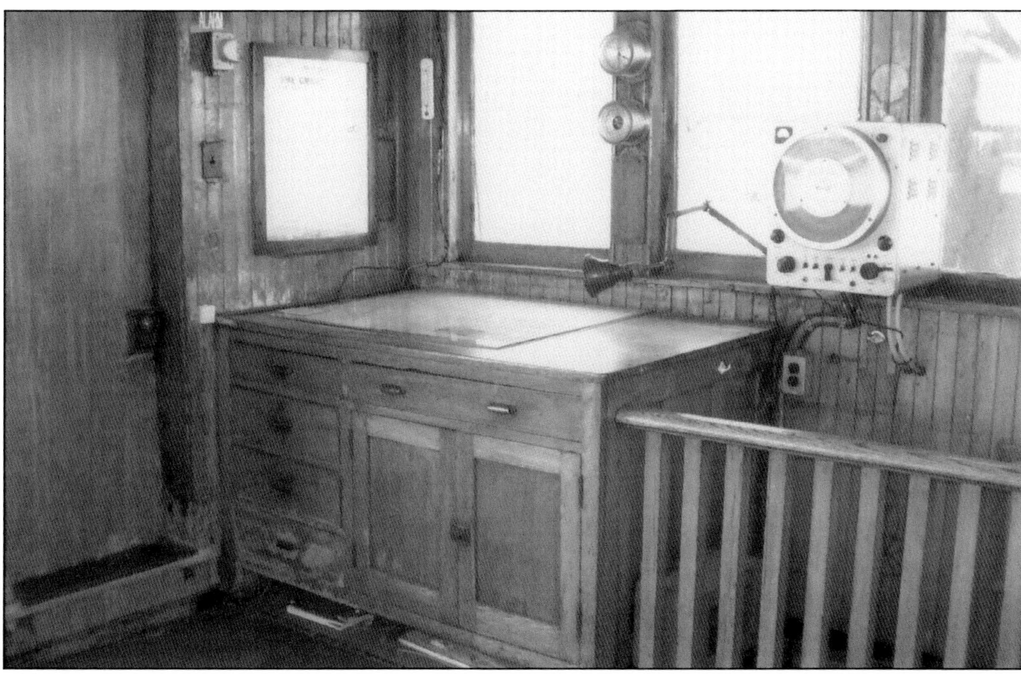

Located on the back wall of the pilothouse is the ship's chart table. Navigational charts were located in the drawers of the cabinet. On the tabletop, the captain and the mates would chart their course across the lake. The object between the windows to the right of the chart table is the ship's direction finder. The banister to the right is for the stairway leading down to the crew quarters. (Photograph by Bob Strauss.)

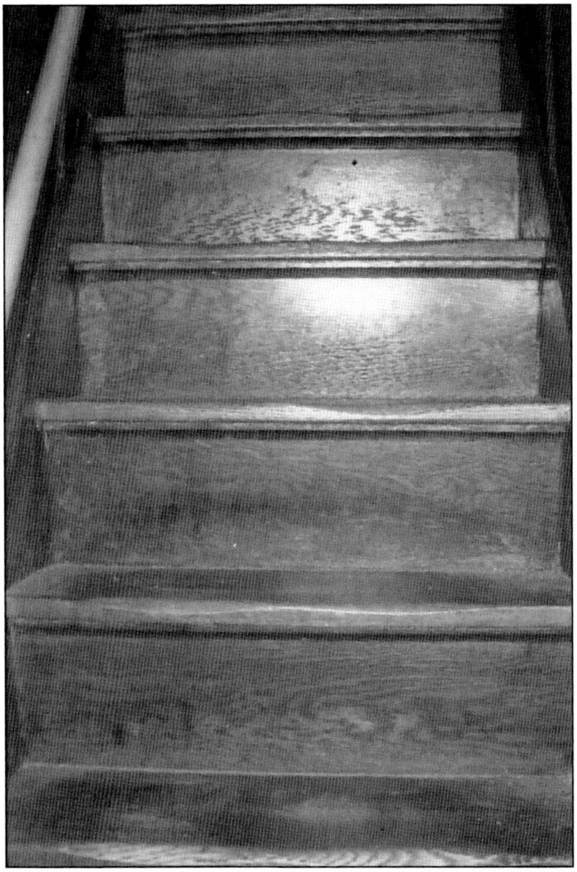

Showing the wear that comes from 50 years of service, these wooden steps lead from the pilothouse down to the crew quarters. The captain had an expansive room that spread across the front of the deckhouse; the mates had smaller rooms located just aft of the captain's quarters, with wheelsmen and lookouts sharing rooms at the aft end of the deckhouse. (Photograph by Bob Strauss.)

The captain's bed was known as a three-quarter bed, with a mattress larger than a twin-size but smaller than a double bed. As in the other quarters, the captain has his own washbasin; however, he had to share toilet and shower facilities with the rest of the forward crew. Capt. John Cavanaugh, the first captain of the *City of Milwaukee*, suffered a stroke in this bed in 1937. He died shortly thereafter in a Milwaukee hospital. There are some who say his spirit is still present, making sure things remain shipshape. (CofM.)

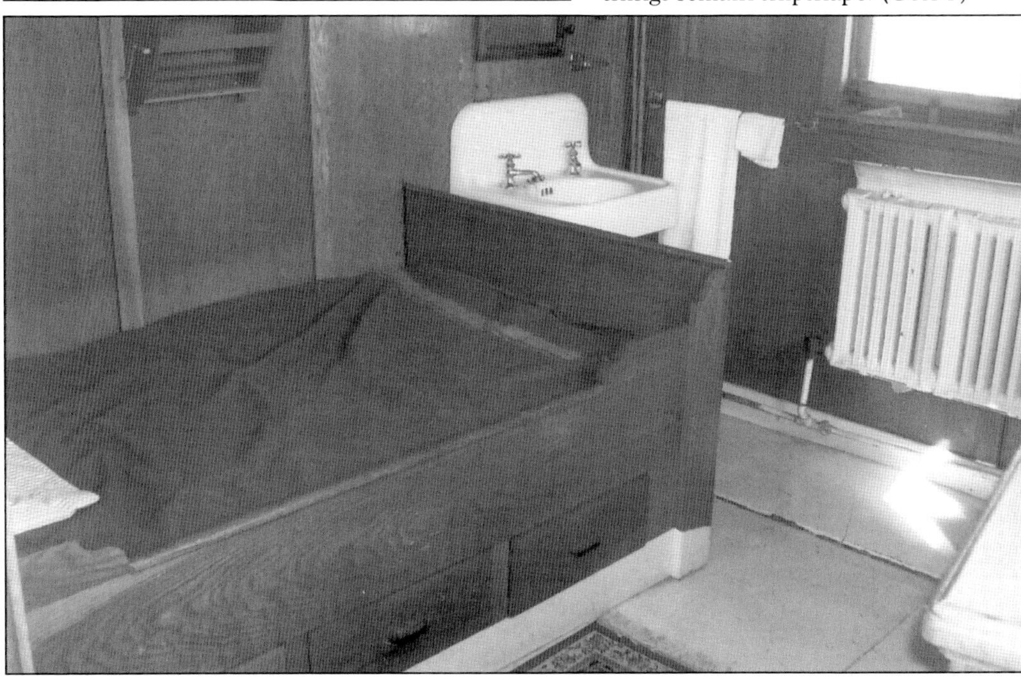

The fan on the bureau in the captain's room speaks to the fact that air-conditioning was practically unheard of in 1931. Ventilation was usually gained via an open window and an errant wind. Each window was fitted with a vented wooden shutter, which dropped down below the sill when not in use. When raised, the shutters allowed outside air to cool a room, while maintaining privacy for the room's occupants. Heat was never an issue on a steamboat. Boiler steam provided heat to the cast-iron radiator mounted next to the bureau. (CofM.)

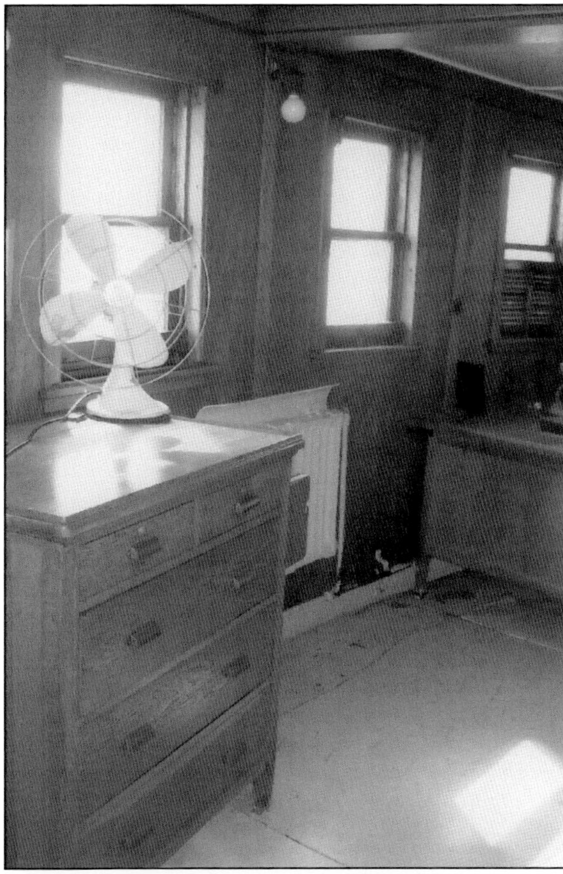

At this desk, the captain took care of all of the ship's important paperwork. All paperwork was taken care of with the use of a typewriter and lots of carbon paper. The captain was in charge of all aspects of the ship and as such was on call around the clock. One ship's captain, when asked what the first thing he planned on doing when he retired, replied, "Get a full night's sleep." (CofM.)

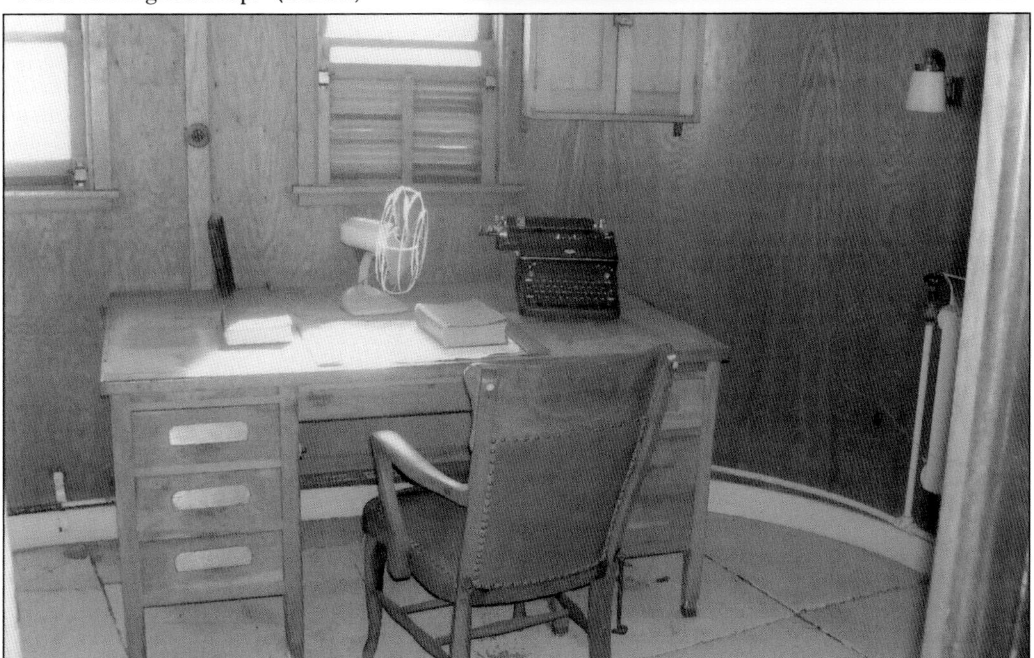

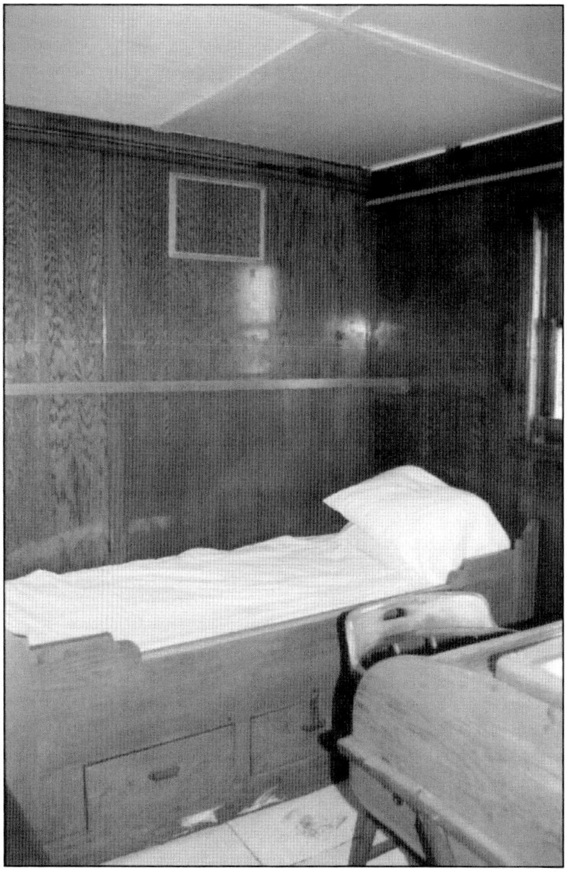

Somewhat less spacious than the captain's room but still accommodating is the first mate's quarters. The first mate had his own room, with the second and third mates sharing a single room. In later years, some of the mates made use of one of the larger, seldom used passenger cabins available below. (CofM.)

Bright and airy, the forward observation lounge was a place of refuge from cold Lake Michigan winds and afforded a generous view of the lake through numerous windows. A desk and chair in the corner of the room provided passengers a place to write family and friends. Much of the original wicker furniture remains in use. Woodwork throughout the ship is original from 1931. Designed in the Craftsman style, without Victorian ornamentation and unblemished by layers of paint, the wood adds soft warmth and quiet elegance to the ship's interior. (Photograph by Bob Strauss.)

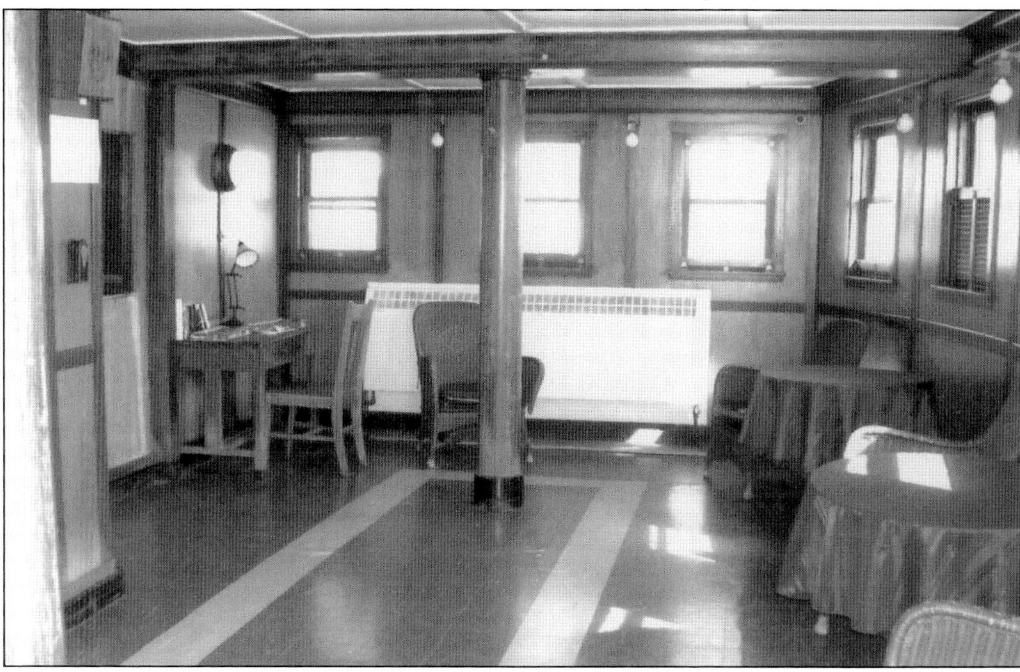

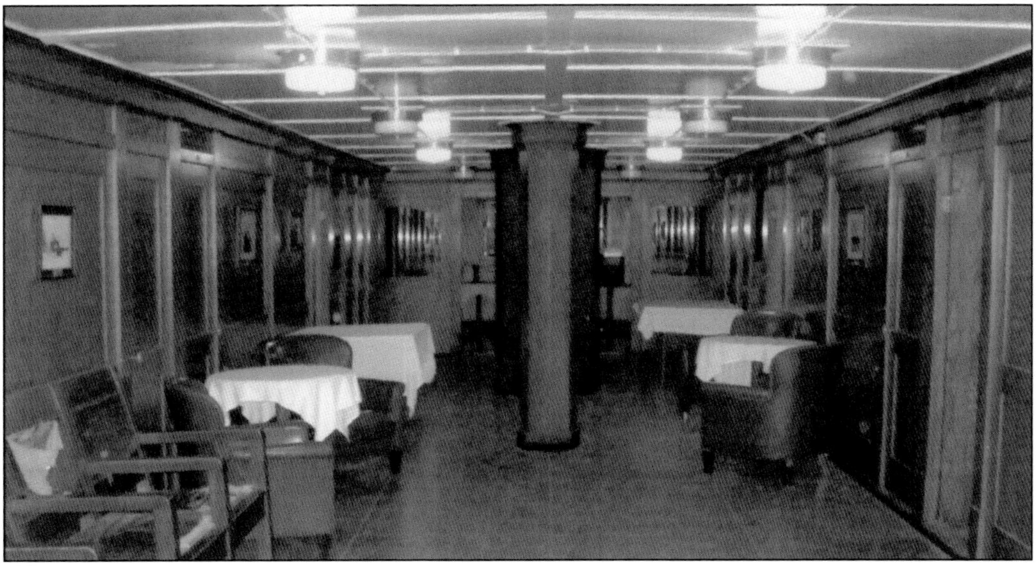

From the aft end of the passenger saloon, the forward observation room is through the doors at the far end. Six passenger cabins line each side of the saloon. A clerestory running the length of the ceiling provided natural light. It was removed, possibly around 1962, and the space was plated over and remodeled as seen today. Preservationists hope to restore the clerestory in the passenger saloon using a similar clerestory removed from a sister ship, the *Pere Marquette 22*, as a template. (Photograph by Bob Strauss.)

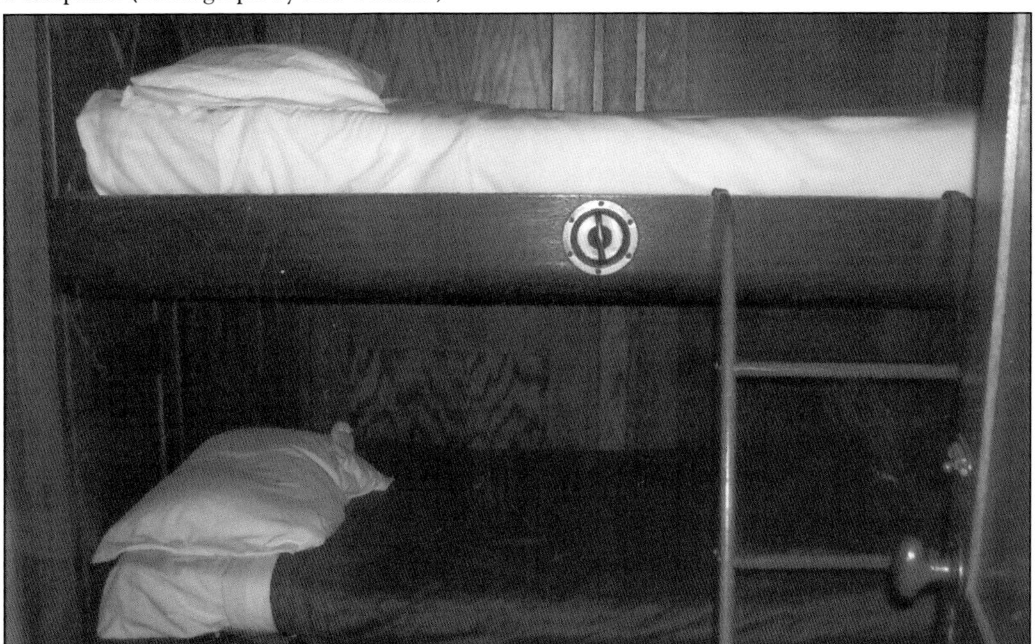

Two passenger cabins were equipped with Pullman-style bunks. The upper berth could be folded against the wall to provide additional headroom for the lower berth. The Pullman cabins have doors to the adjoining cabins, creating mini-suites. The 10 standard cabins are approximately five feet by seven feet, providing enough room for a single bed, a basin with hot and cold running water, and a small wooden seat attached to the wall. The Pullman cabins are somewhat larger. (CofM.)

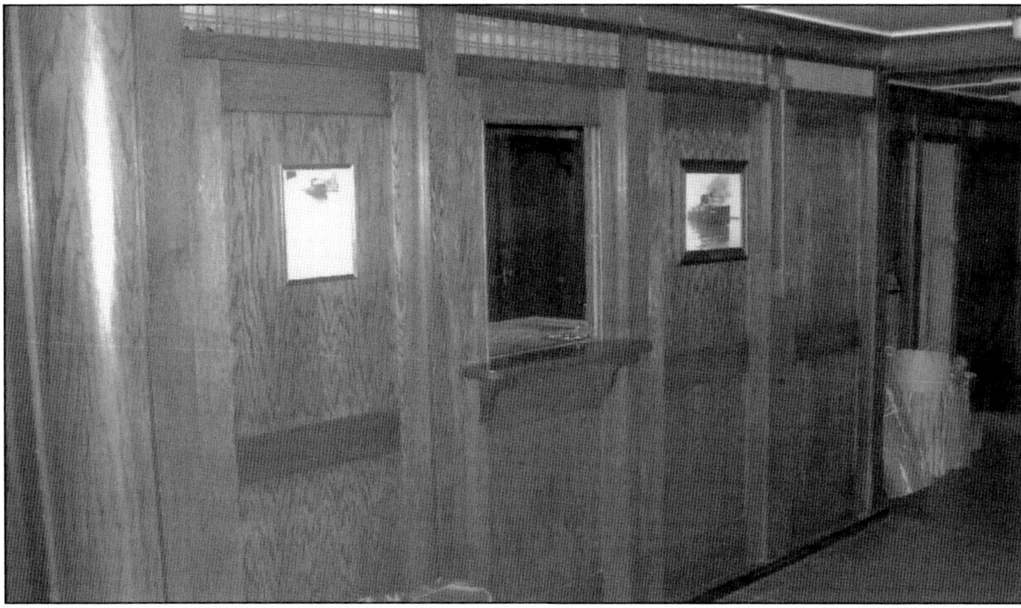

Located at the aft end of the passenger saloon on the starboard side is the purser's office. Through this window, passengers could purchase tickets and obtain keys to staterooms. A stateroom was a separate purchase, not included in the individual fare. The purser was responsible for storing valuables and any monetary transactions on the ship, and he kept track of the rail cargo hauled on board. (Photograph by Bob Strauss.)

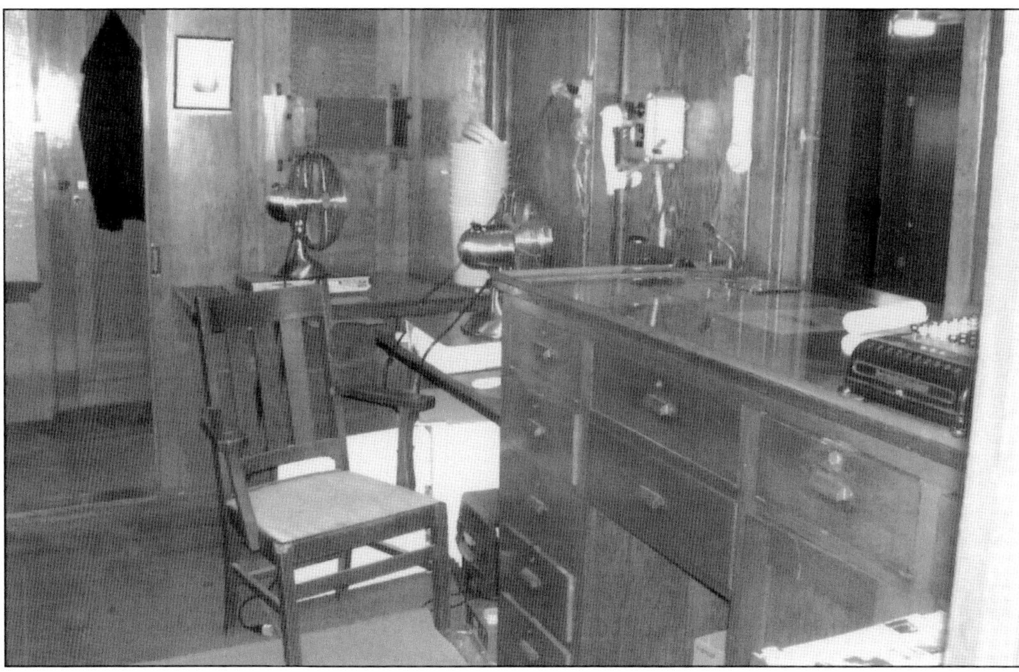

This view is inside the purser's office, looking aft. Located directly above the desk is a sound-powered phone with which the purser could call any part of the ship. On the right is the window through which the purser would conduct business with passengers. To the left is the entry into the purser's sleeping quarters. (Photograph by Bob Strauss.)

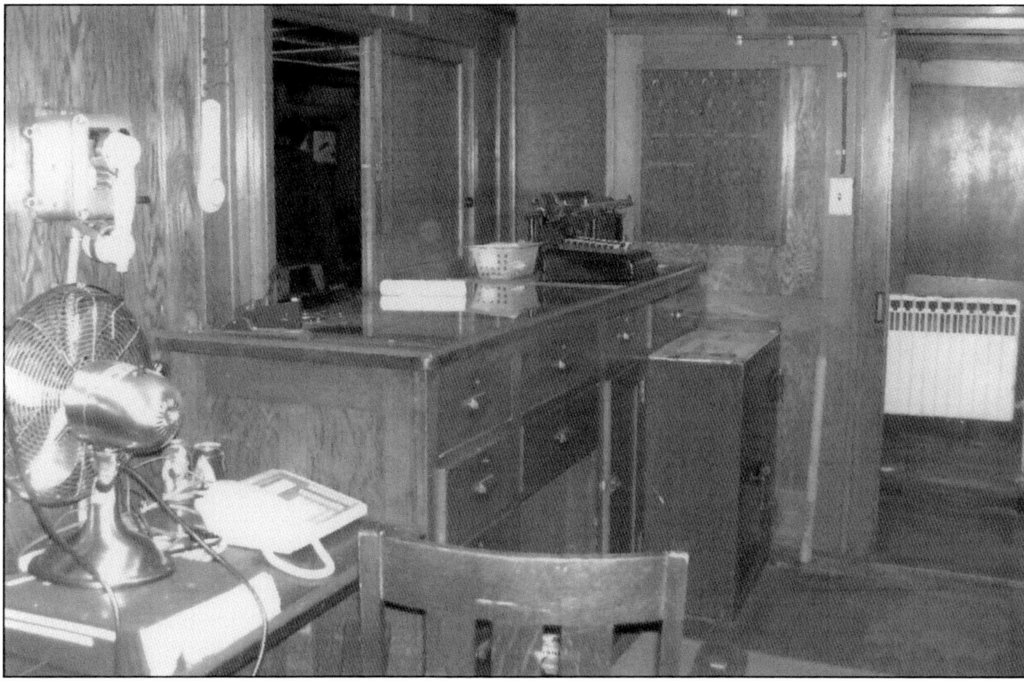

Looking forward in the purser's office, the large safe to the left of the doorway was used to safeguard passengers' and other valuables. Above the safe is the key rack, which held the stateroom keys; unfortunately, the keys are among the items that have "gone missing" over the years. Through the door to the right, the purser could either go left to enter the saloon or right through another door to the starboard deck. (Photograph by Bob Strauss.)

Across the saloon is the steward's room, used by railway officials. With the ship's only double bed, it is one of the largest rooms aboard. A settee is along the left wall. An aura of mystery surrounds this cabin, as many have reported unexplained phenomena. Here, a white mist seems to hover near the ceiling. It may just be a reflection from the flash, but no other image in the series shows this mist. (Photograph by Bob Strauss.)

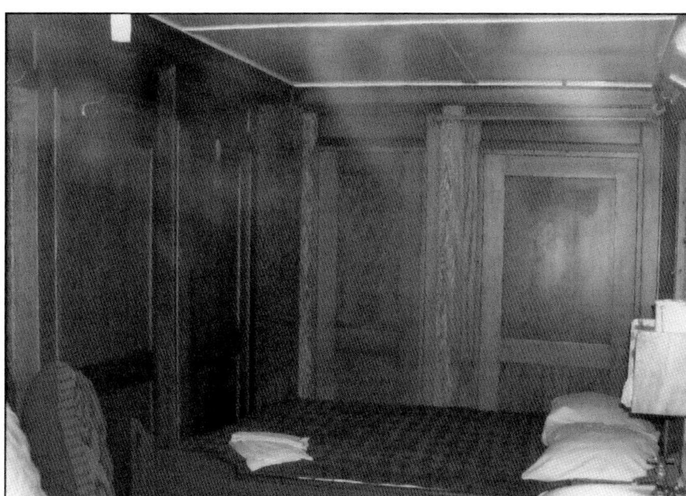

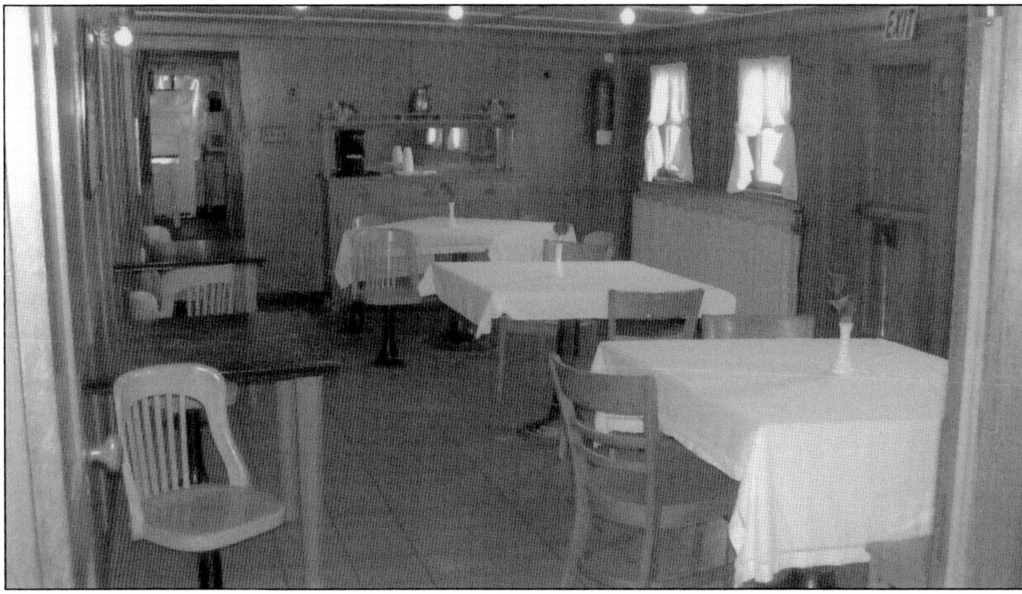

From the doorway to the main saloon, this view is looking to the rear of the passenger dining room. Although the Grand Trunk did not fully promote the ferry's passenger service, those who were carried did not go wanting. Passengers were offered a simple menu of hearty steamboat food. Tables and some chairs are bolted to the deck, and a door on the right provides easy access to the port spar deck. A buffet at the rear of the room provided a station for coffee and other items. (Photograph by Bob Strauss.)

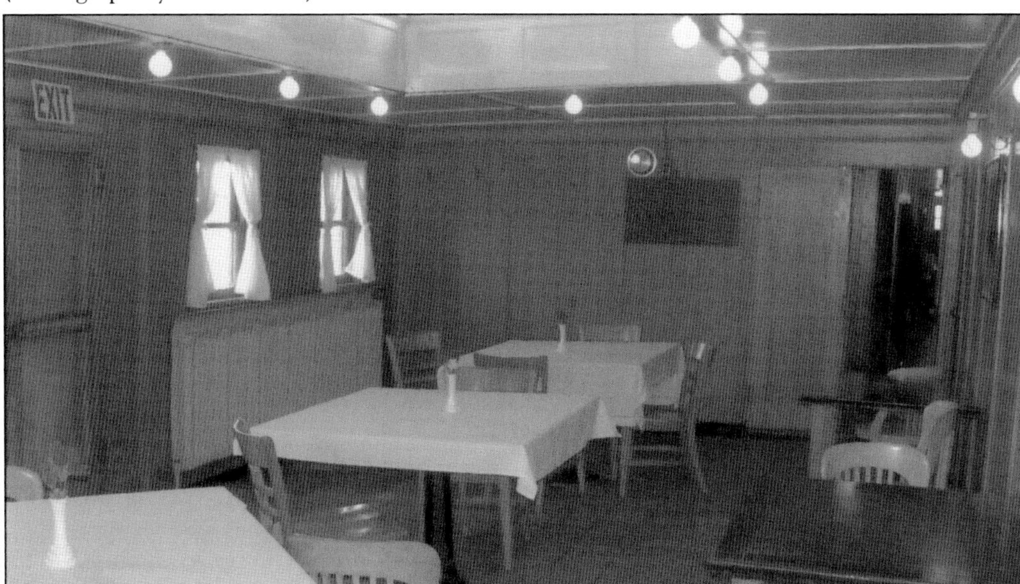

This view looks forward from the rear of the passenger dining room. On the forward wall is a chalkboard on which the menu of the day was written, and to the right is the doorway to the main saloon. Easily seen is the clerestory, which helped brighten the room with natural light. On rough days, water would be poured on the linen tablecloths; the water would create suction with the plate bottoms, preventing the dinnerware from sliding off the tables. (Photograph by Bob Strauss.)

With no automatic dishwasher, many a thousand cups, plates, and glasses, along with myriad pots and pans, were washed in this stainless steel sink. At least the dishwashers had a good view of the lake. Special shelving for plates was a necessity to prevent dishes from flying off during inclement weather. (Photograph by Bob Strauss.)

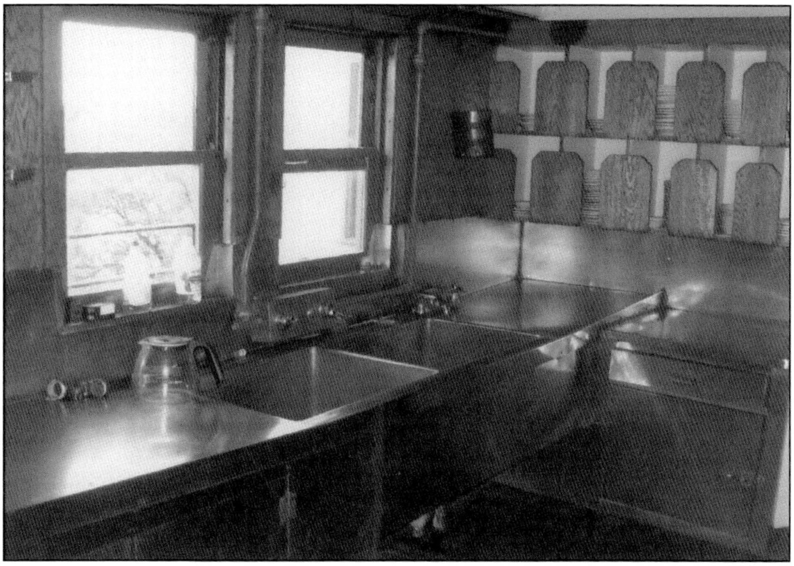

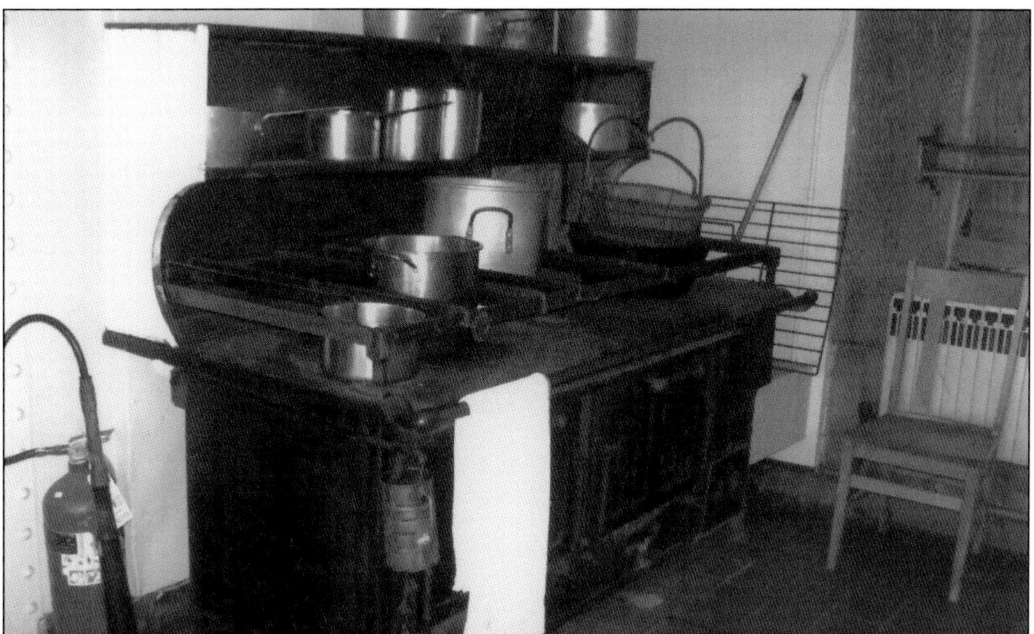

Countless meals were provided for both passengers and crew from this cast iron cookstove. Original to the 1931 build and originally coal-fired, the stove was converted to burn oil in 1947. Easily visible are the brackets around the stove-top burners, which prevented pots and pans from sliding off in bad weather. Weather be hanged; the crew brooked no excuse for lack of a hot meal. A good cook was worth his weight in gold; the culinary excellence of some cooks is famous in Great Lakes lore. (Photograph by Bob Strauss.)

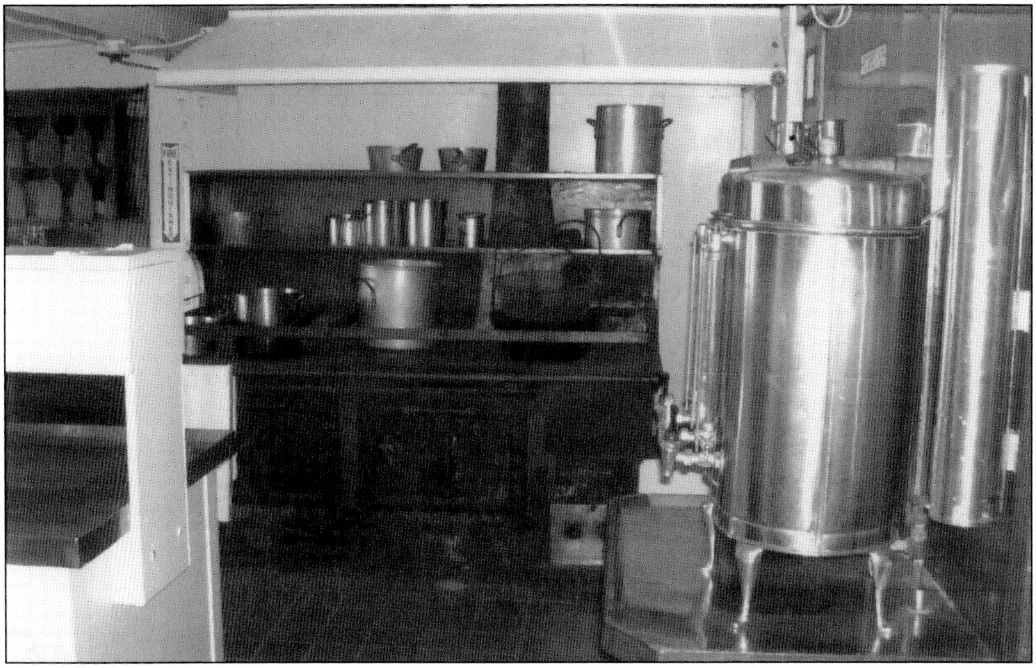

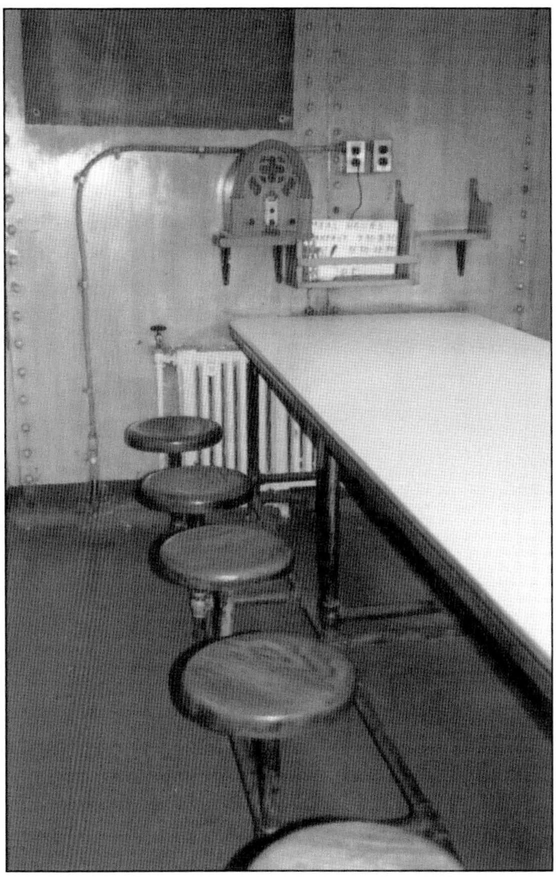

Another view shows the stove in the background, while on the right is an essential piece of equipment on any boat, the coffee urn. A happy boat was a well-fed boat, and the cook was an integral piece of the puzzle in maintaining good morale. Lake boats are well known for being generous with meals, and the railroad-car ferries were no exception. (Photograph by Bob Strauss.)

Next to the galley on the starboard side is the crew's mess. Seated on wooden stools attached to the floor at a long table, the crew took all their meals here. The radio was pretty much the extent of the entertainment available; in later years, a television found its way on board, but in an era before satellite dishes, antenna reception was spotty at best. Access to the crew's mess could be made either through the galley or through a door from the starboard deck. (CofM.)

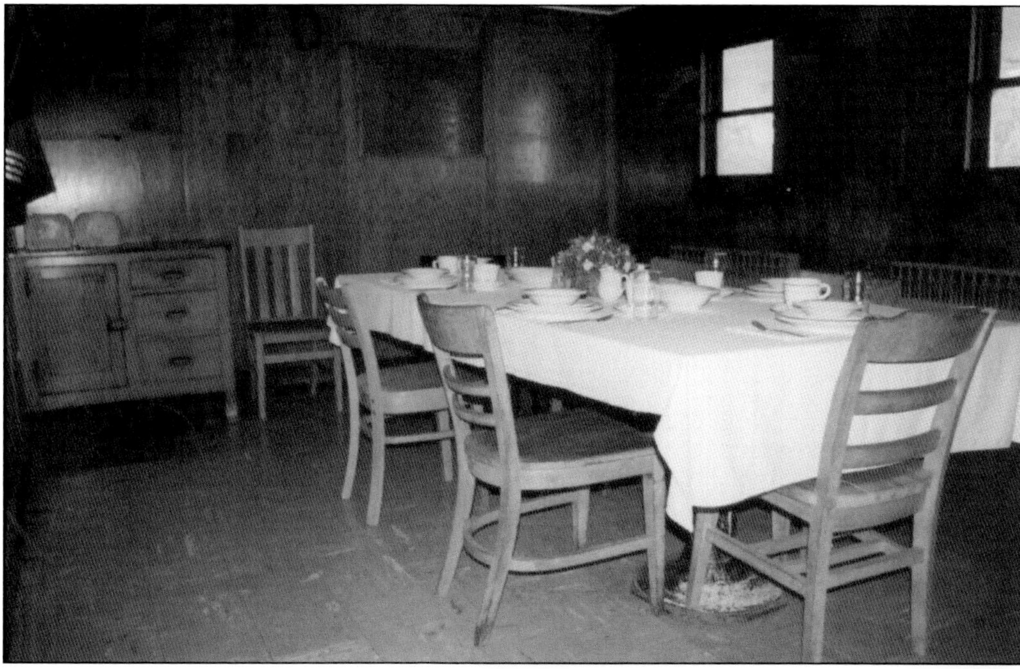

The officers had their own dining room located just aft of the *City of Milwaukee's* galley. As was the custom on Great Lakes boats, the licensed officers—captain, mates, chief, and assistant engineers—had separate facilities from the unlicensed deck and engine crew. (CofM.)

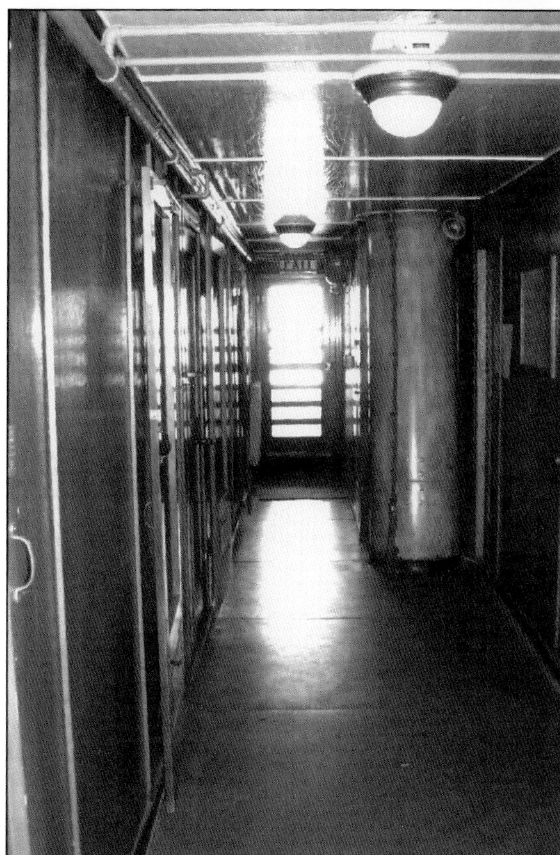

Going aft out of the galley and past the boat's walk-in refrigerator, one enters the Engineers Hallway. On the left are separate rooms for each of the three assistant engineers, with the chief engineer's room at the far end. Through the first door on the right, one finds the second and third cooks' rooms, followed by a large dorm-style "4 Boys" room utilized by the entry-level kitchen help. Located next to the dorm room is the common bathroom. While each of the rooms has a basin with hot and cold running water, all of the crew bunked in this section shared a common bathroom and showers. (Photograph by Bob Strauss.)

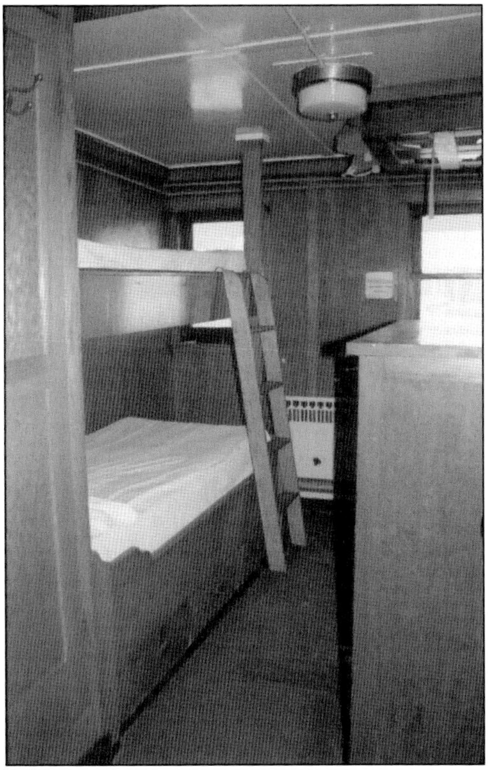

This is a look into the second and third cooks' room. Just beyond the bureau to the right is a small fold-down desk attached to the wall. The closet just visible to the left held the cook's kitchen whites. Cooks often put in long hours, providing three meals a day plus ensuring there was food available for the night watch. The majority of the crew worked a four-and-eight shift—four hours on duty followed by eight hours off. For example, a crewman would work from noon to 4:00 p.m., have eight hours off, then report back to work from midnight until 4:00 a.m. All shifts (or watches) were 12:00–4:00, 4:00–8:00, and 8:00–12:00. (CofM.)

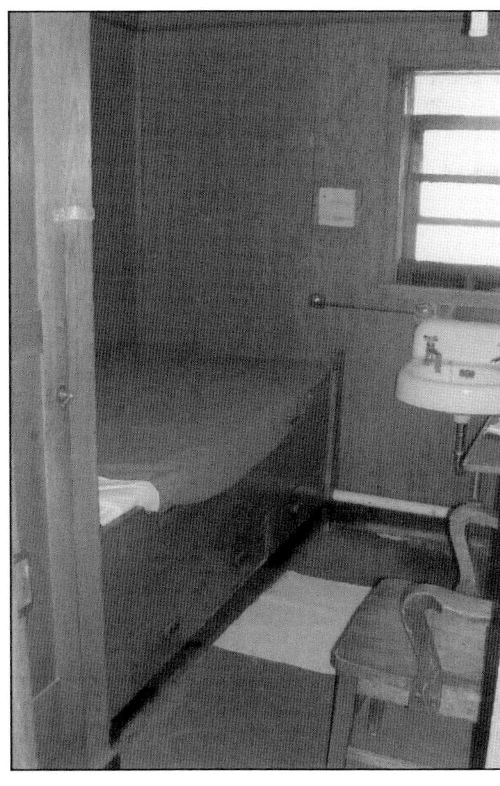

This view looks inside of one of the assistant engineer's cabins. Like the rest of the crew quarters, it is spartan but functional: bed, wash basin, a simple drop-desk, and a chair. In addition to the closet, clothing storage was available underneath the bunk. The chief engineer delegated authority to his assistants, who worked directly with the engine room crew. (Photograph by Bob Strauss.)

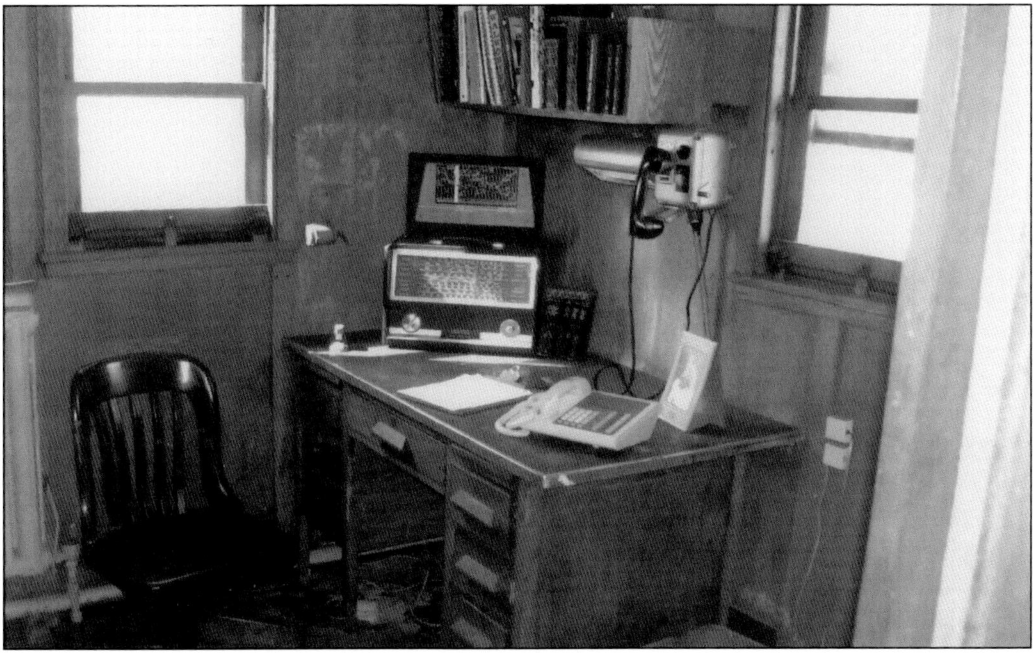

The chief engineer's quarters are twice as large as the assistant's, with the extra space given over for use as an office. With the exception of the newer telephone on the desk—installed when the room was temporarily used as the museum office—this area appears much as it did when the ship was operational. The shelf above the desk was used for technical manuals and parts catalogs needed to keep a 1931 steamship operational. Above the desk is another sound-activated phone. These were scattered throughout the ship. (Photograph by Bob Strauss.)

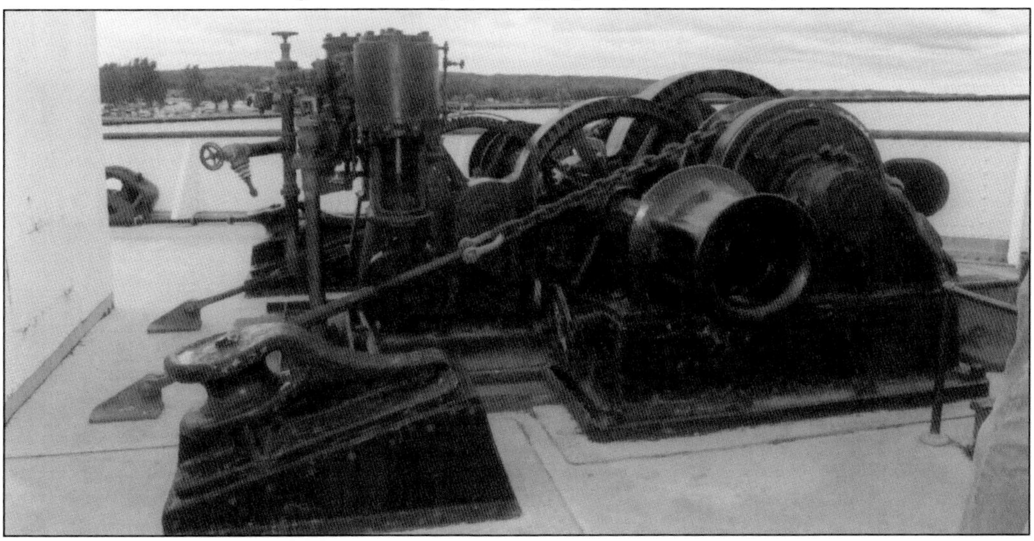

Located on the deck at the very bow of the ship is the steam-powered anchor windlass. The Grand Trunk sisters *Madison*, *Grand Rapids*, and *City of Milwaukee* had their gear such as this located on the open deck. In contrast, the Pere Marquette boats of this design had gear concealed on a lower deck. As the Pere Marquette boats carried a considerably larger passenger load than did the Grand Trunk's, this minor tweak in design was likely done to avoid any mishaps with unwary travelers. (Photograph by Bob Strauss.)

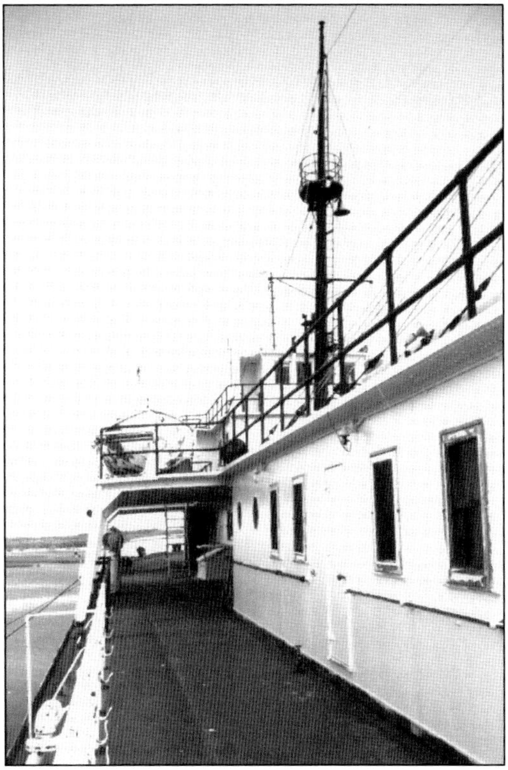

This is the view of the *City of Milwaukee*'s port promenade deck looking forward. The door on the right is an entrance into the passenger dining room. Visible on the deck above is one of the ship's lifeboats. For their own safety, passengers were restricted to this deck, also known as the spar or weather deck. (CofM.)

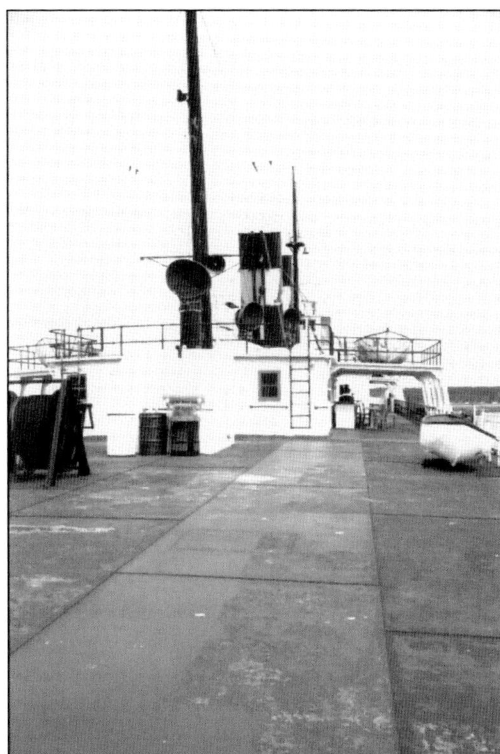

This view of the weather deck was taken from just forward of the aft pilothouse. The small structure in front of the black barrels in the center of the picture covers the stairway to the car deck and also contains the dynamo room. One must walk carefully across the deck, as the deck plates are lapped at their seams, providing a small protrusion for someone to possibly trip on. (CofM.)

A dramatic view shows the forward stack, still in Ann Arbor markings. The whistle mounted on the upper part of the funnel is not the original ship's whistle, but was removed from the Great Lakes steamer *Manitou*. Although the details of the switch have been clouded by time, the crux of the tale is that a past captain and/or some crew members preferred the sound of the *Manitou*'s whistle over their own. The *Manitou* was being scrapped at the time, so an arrangement was made with the shipyard to acquire the steamer's whistle and have it placed on the *City of Milwaukee*. (CofM.)

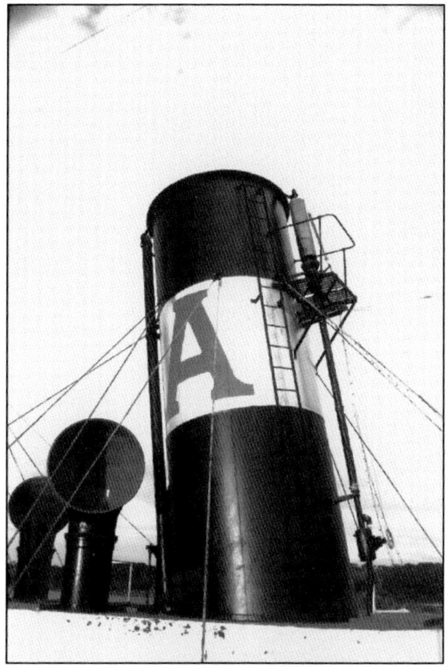

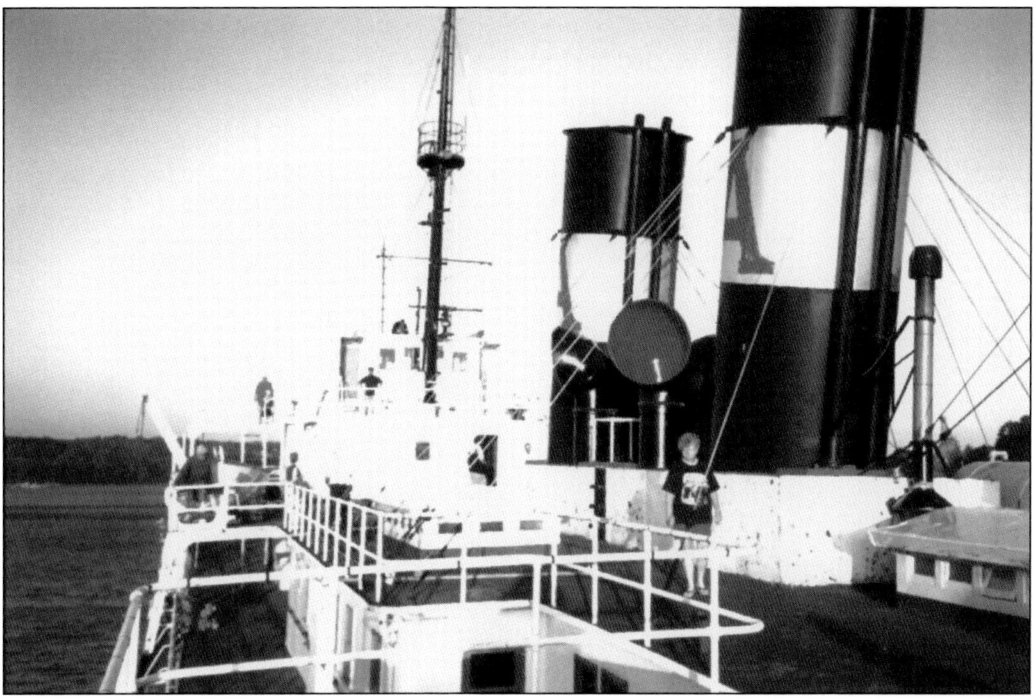

An unidentified teenager standing next to the aft stack gives a sense of the size and dimensions of the stacks. Visible between the stacks are some of the ship's ventilators, which provided much needed fresh and cool air down to the engine and boiler rooms, where temperatures often read a steady 110 degrees. The ventilators could be rotated to face the wind, forcing air down below. Also in sight are the clerestories over the passenger dining room and the galley. The thin stack visible on the right is for the galley stove. (CofM.)

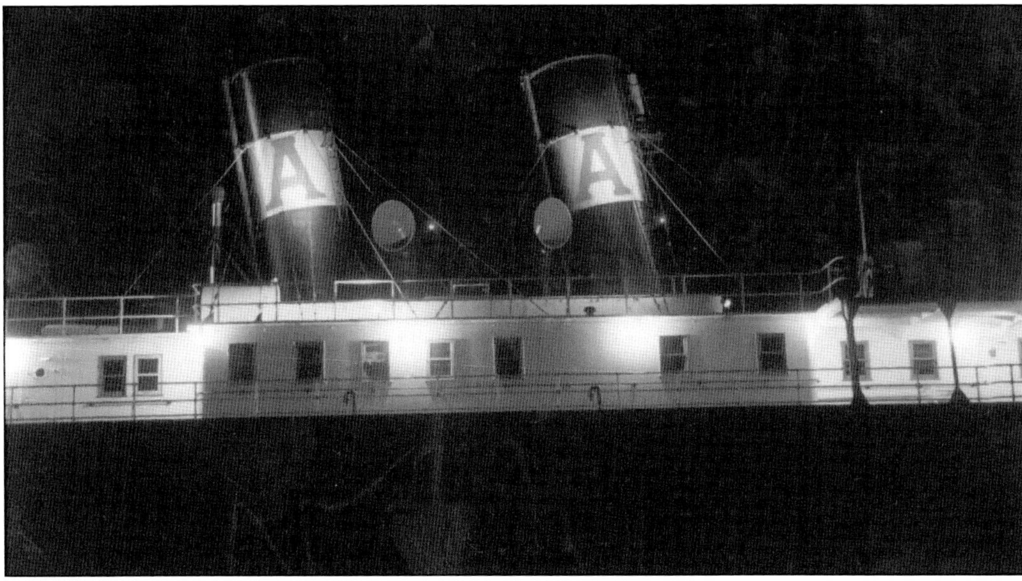

Having a ship "lit up" means turning on every available light at night and can create a rather dramatic sight. This photograph shows the stacks of the *City of Milwaukee* lighted on a dark night. Ships are often lit up for special events and holidays; a daytime version of this, when lights would not be visible, would be to fly flags and pennants from the masts and ship's upper works. (CofM.)

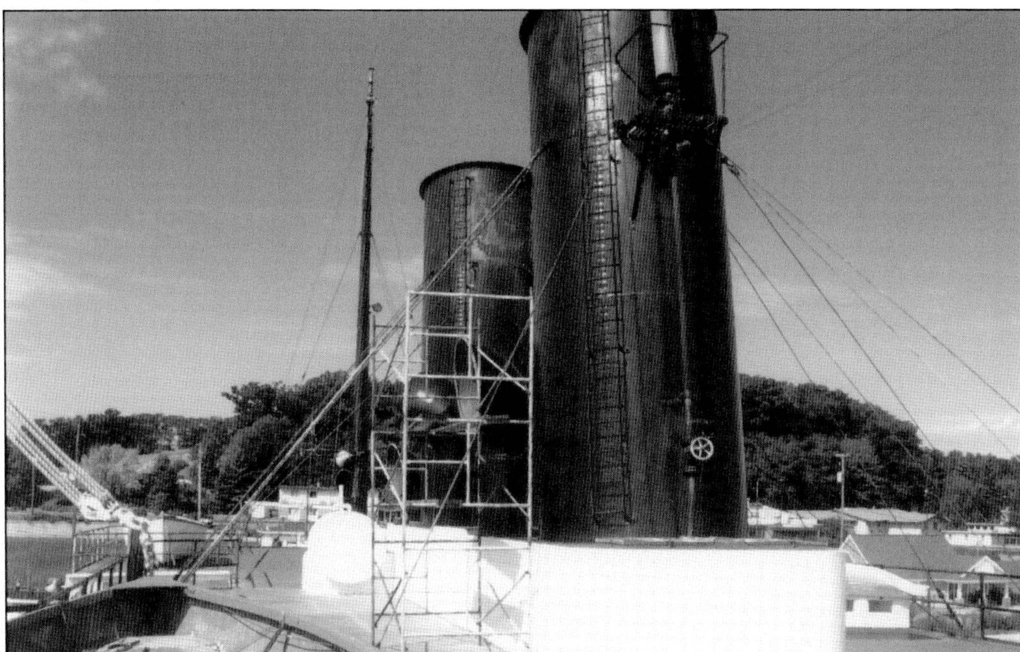

In returning the *City of Milwaukee* to its 1931 appearance, the stacks were repainted all black, discarding the silver-and-black Ann Arbor color scheme. The scaffolding alongside the stacks is mute testimony to the continuous need for upkeep and preservation. Volunteers are always welcome to come and wield a scraper and paintbrush, as well as tackle any other available job, to continue the preservation. (CofM.)

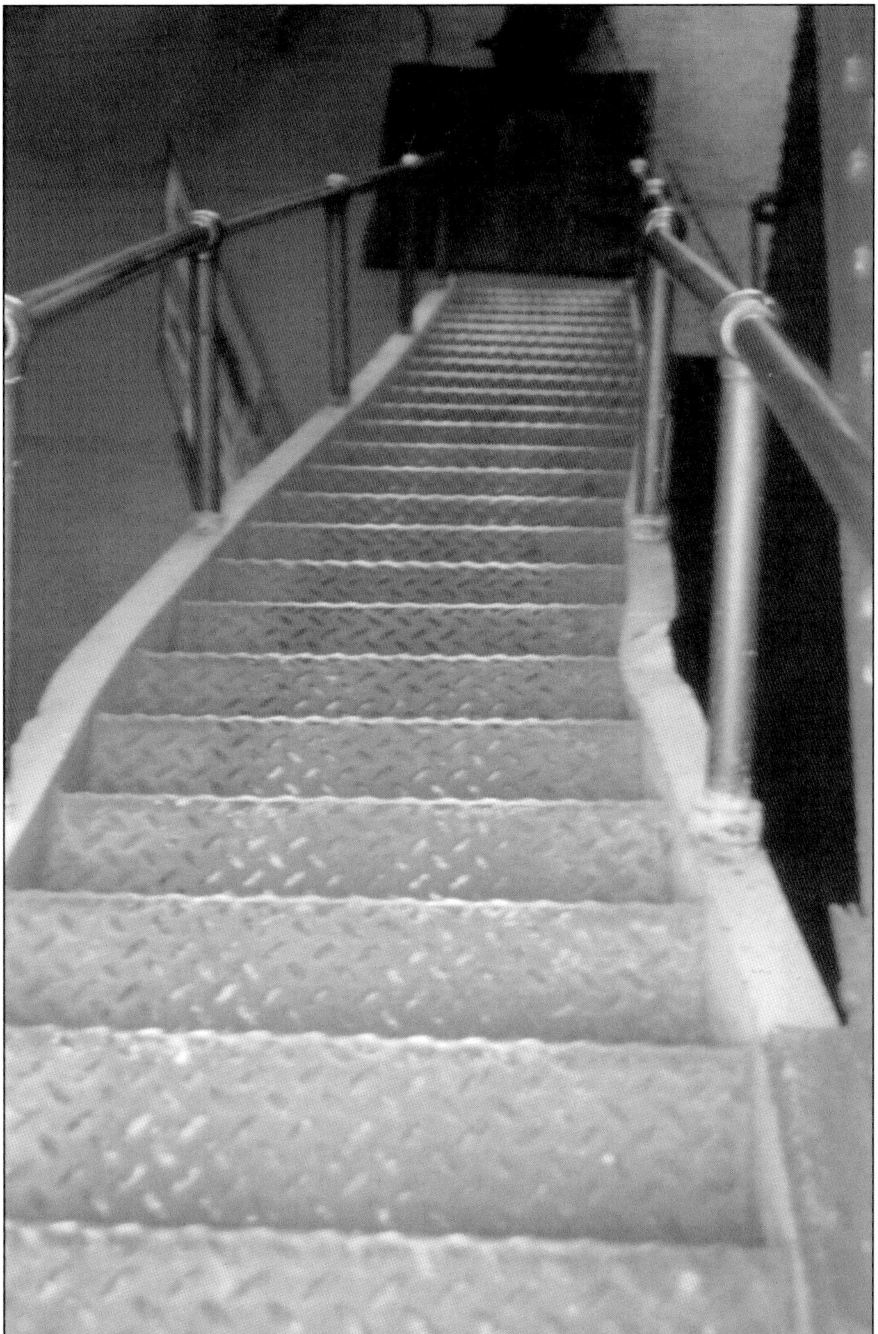

Mishaps on a working boat are not uncommon, and the *City of Milwaukee* has seen her share. Here is a permanent reminder of one such incident. On one stormy winter crossing, a railcar worked free of its restraints and toppled against the stairway leading from the car dock to topside. The stairway held its own, and the railcar was soon righted, but the resulting kink remains as a visible reminder of that perilous night. The structural integrity is a tribute to the craftsmanship of the workers at the Manitowoc Shipbuilding Company. (CofM.)

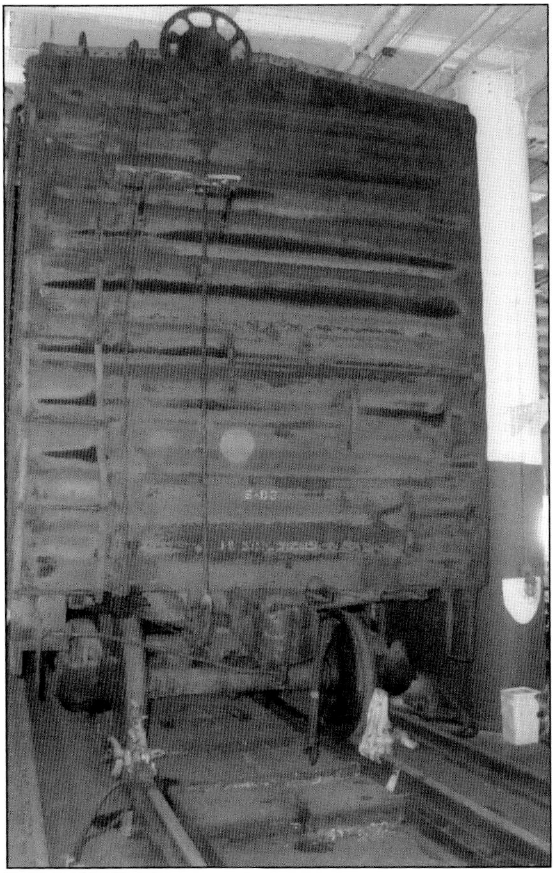

Heavily loaded boxcars took up all available room, leaving little side-to-side and overhead clearance. When the car deck was full, crew members often would have to crawl on hands and knees to secure jacks and chains to restrain the railcars. Using the brakes alone was not considered a safe practice during severe weather (CofM.)

The standard method of securing railcars to prevent tipping and rolling was to first fasten the last car on a string with a set of wheel clamps to prevent the string from rolling. Second, a set of four screw jacks, one on each corner of a car, would be set to take the weight of the railcar off its trucks (wheels). Finally, and especially if weather were expected to be severe, a chain and turnbuckle would pull down against the upward pressure of the jacks, rendering the cars immobile. (CofM.)

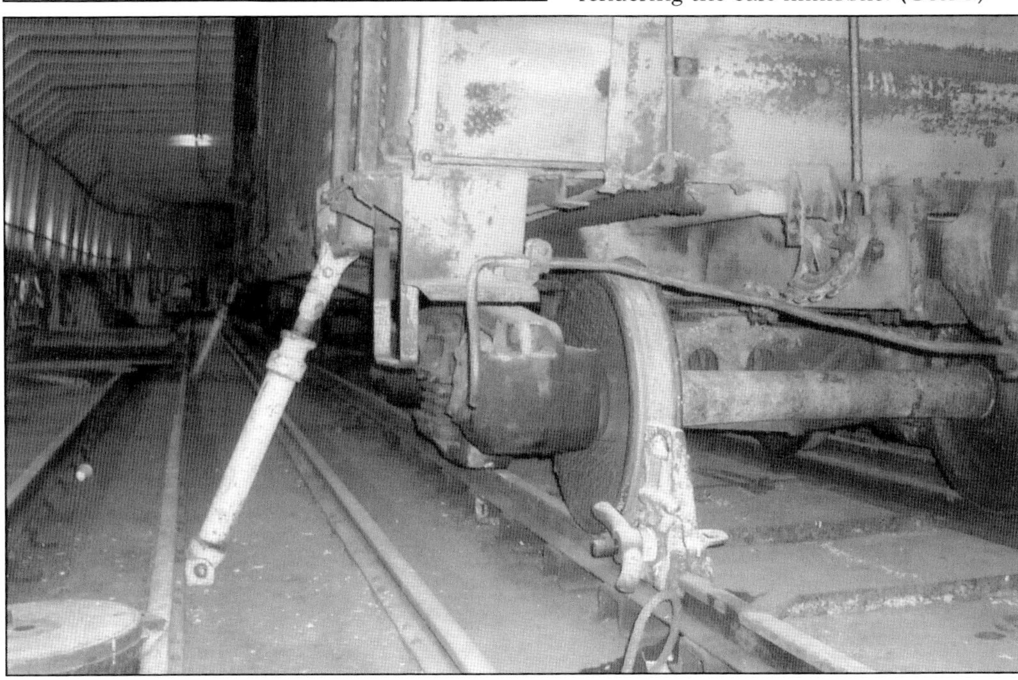

The engine and boiler rooms are located below the car deck along with the crew quarters, known as the flicker, shown here pre-restoration. It is thought that the word *flicker* was derived from the fact that the lights, particularly on the early ferries, flickered. This was the realm of the "black gang"—coal passers, firemen, and oilers who tended the triple-expansion engines and four Scotch boilers in the 110-degree bowels of the ship. (CofM.)

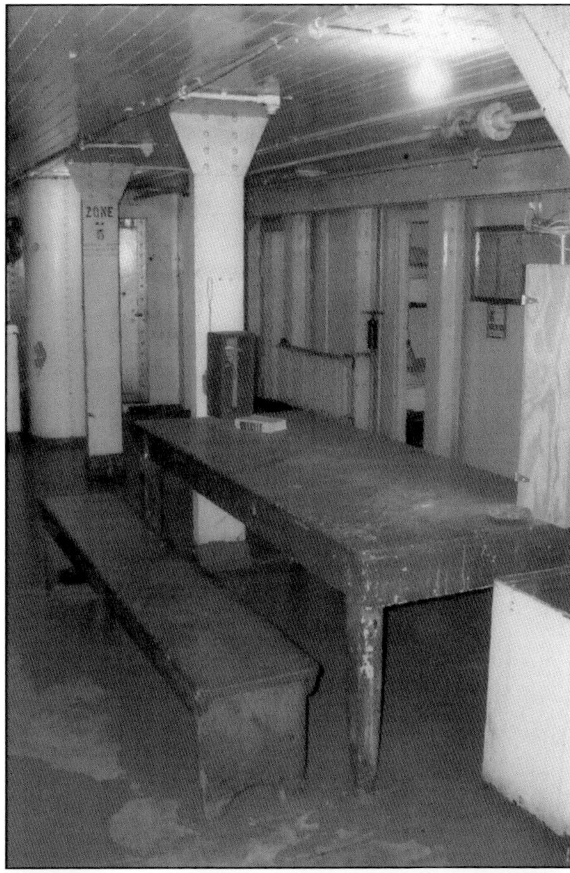

Looking aft, crew cabins line either side of the flicker, with two bunks per cabin. Walls are stark white, and floors and a table are red. Washbasins are visible along the aft bulkhead. Unlike their counterparts above deck, the flicker cabins did not have basins. A bathroom and shower are located to the left of the basins. At the end of the table, stairs lead up to the car deck, and two decks up is the crew's mess. The flicker doubled as a rec room for the black gang, with card games and storytelling favored during downtime. (Photograph by Bob Strauss.)

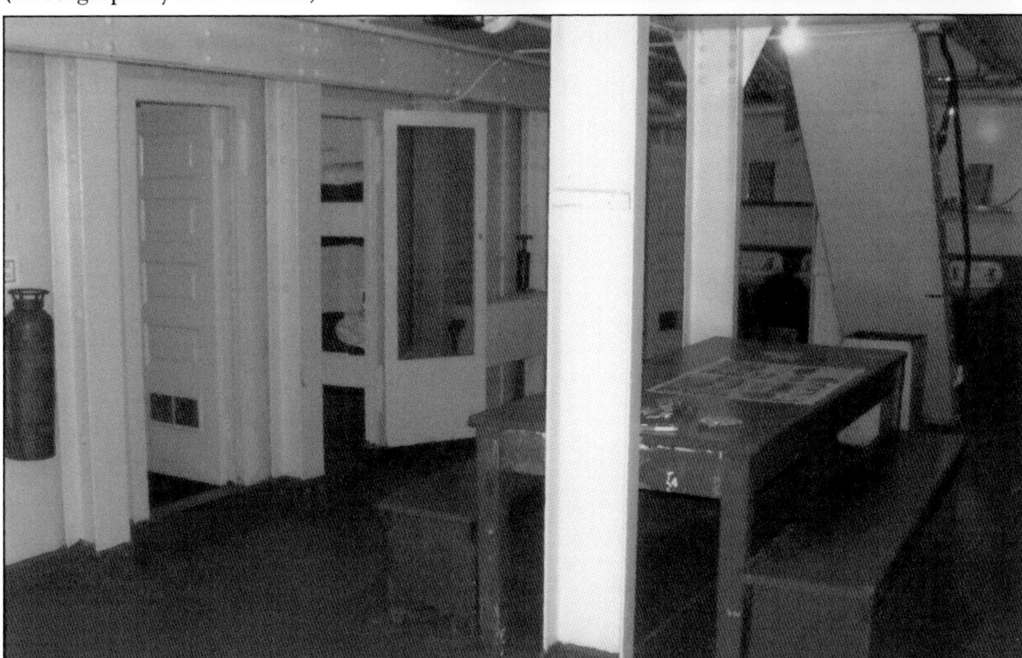

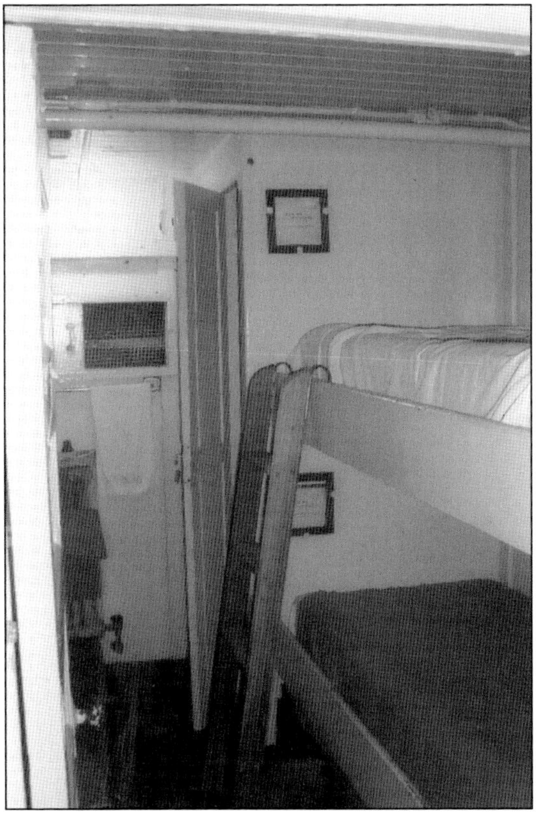

To say that the engine room crew quarters were spartan would be an understatement. They were painted white and had no windows, and the sounds of the lake's waves or ice chunks were often heard as they rushed by alongside the ship's hull, accompanied by the oily smell often wafting in from the engine room. Privacy was at a minimum. (CofM.)

This desk located in the engine room was used by the engineer as a below-decks office, which enabled him to take care of administrative duties without having to run up two decks to his own workstation. On the other side of the bulkhead behind the desk is a combination storage/workroom, which is full of parts, nuts, bolts, small machine lathes, and other tools that allowed the engine room to properly function. (Photograph by Ken Ottmann.)

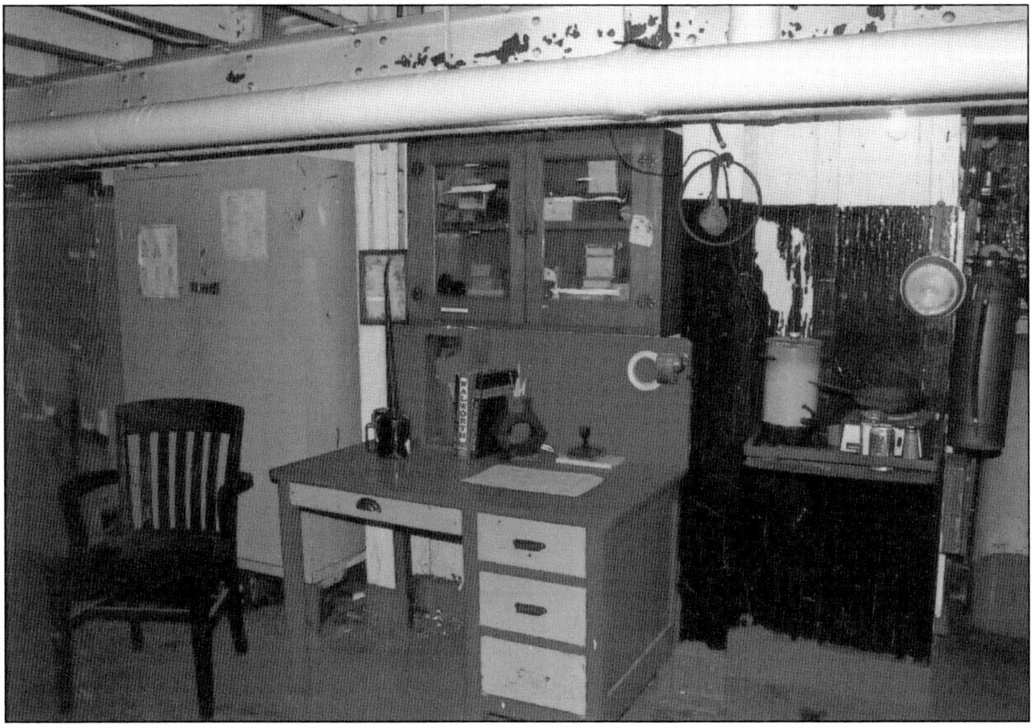

On this engine-room chadburn (telegraph), engineers received their maneuvering orders from the captain in the pilothouse. The captain would "ring down" the orders, which would be acknowledged by the engineer, who would then set the engine controls for the desired performance. (Photograph by John Brandt.)

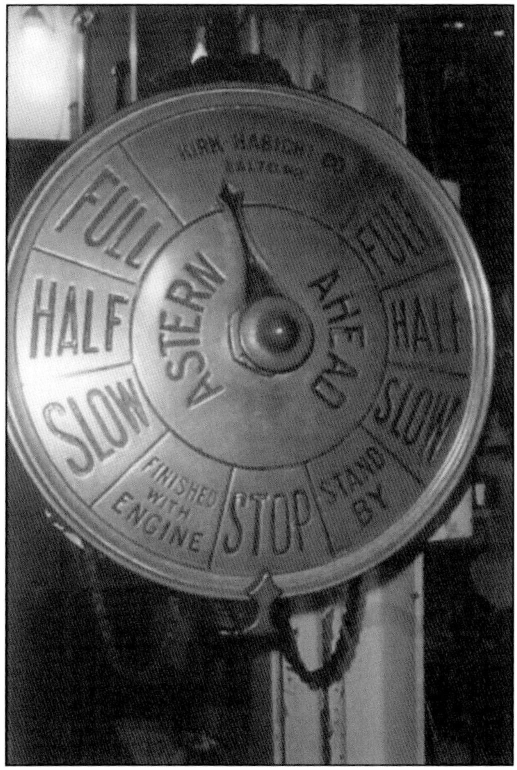


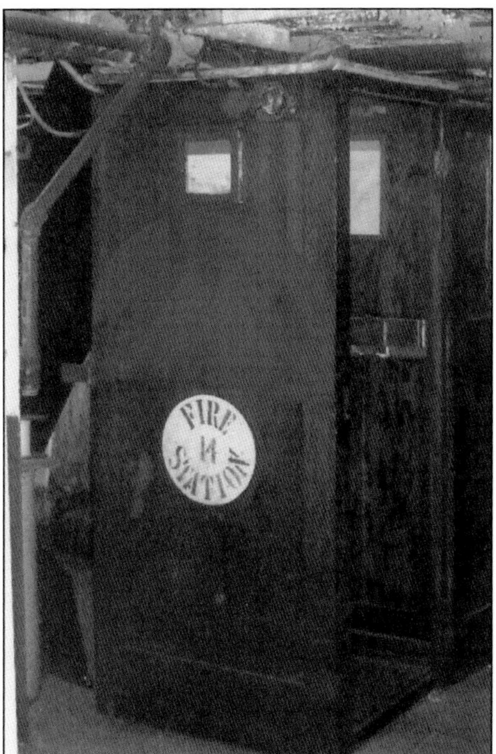


This wooden phone booth is located in the engine room. Should the engineer have need to telephone the captain or anyone else, he would use the phone in here to escape the sometimes deafening noise of the engine room that would make a normal phone conversation impossible. (CofM.)

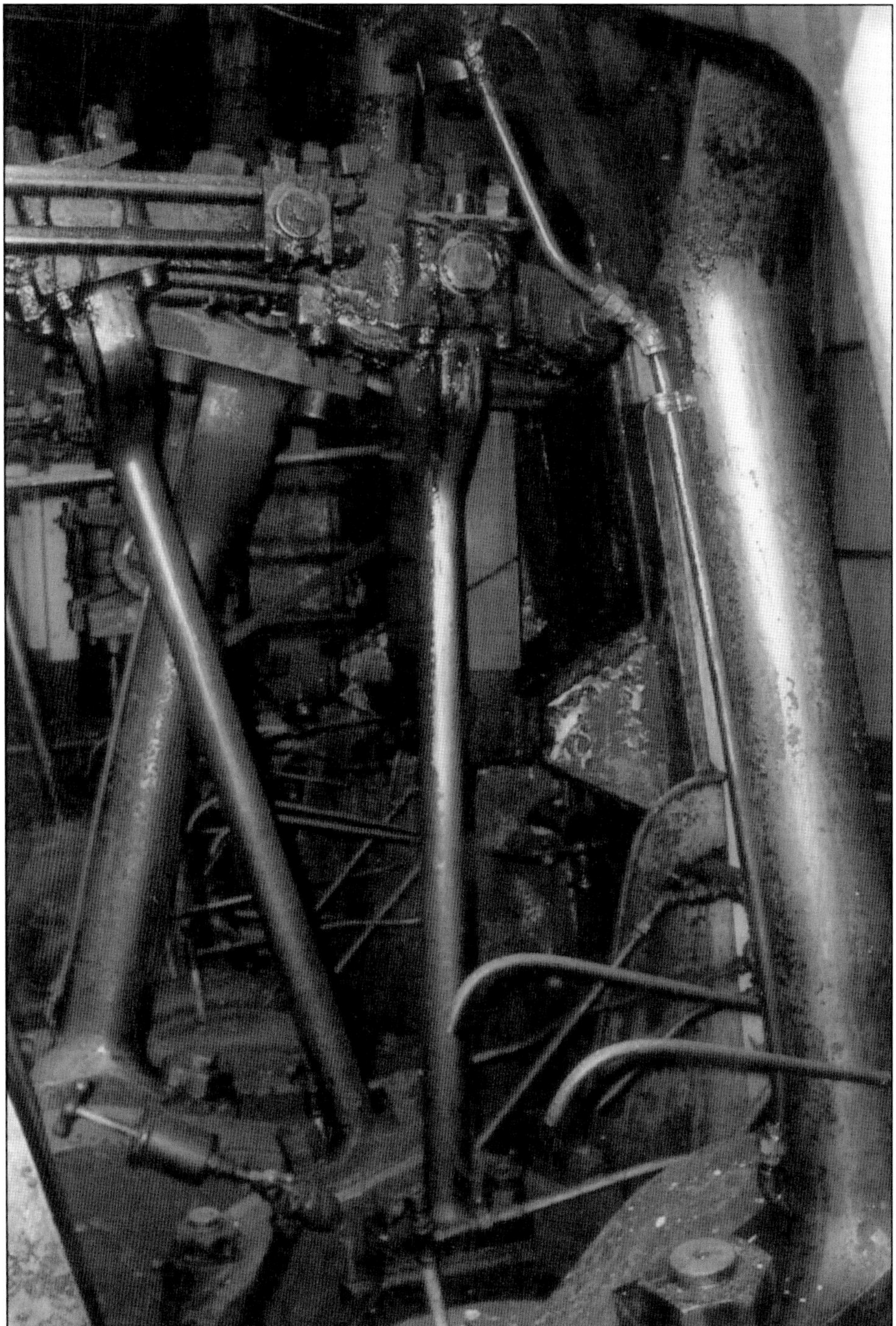

This photograph offers a close-up of the inner workings of one of the two triple-expansion steam engines. A single engine was rated at 1,350 horsepower, each pair providing each ship a total of 2,700 horsepower, propelling the vessel at a speed of 14 miles per hour. Oilers would make their rounds of the engines at 20-minute intervals, making sure the bearings were properly lubricated. (CofM.)

# *Eight*

# Fundraising Efforts

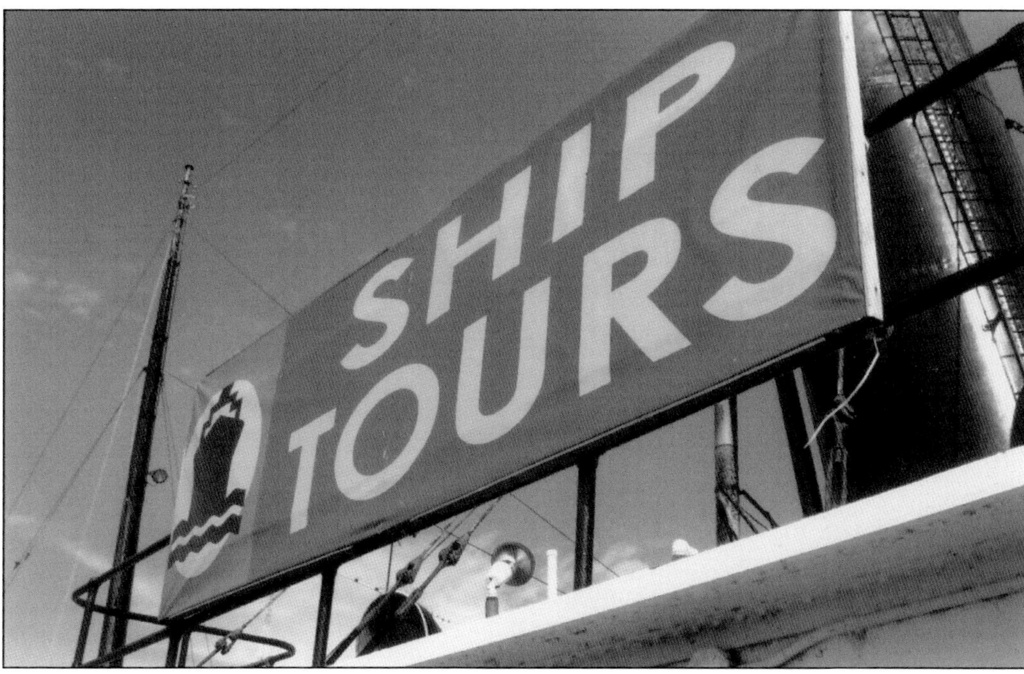


An important—and necessary—aspect of any museum venture is fundraising to continue the essential work of restoration and preservation. In addition to paid memberships, means used to obtain funds for the museum include special events, overnight stays, and various other activities. (CofM.)

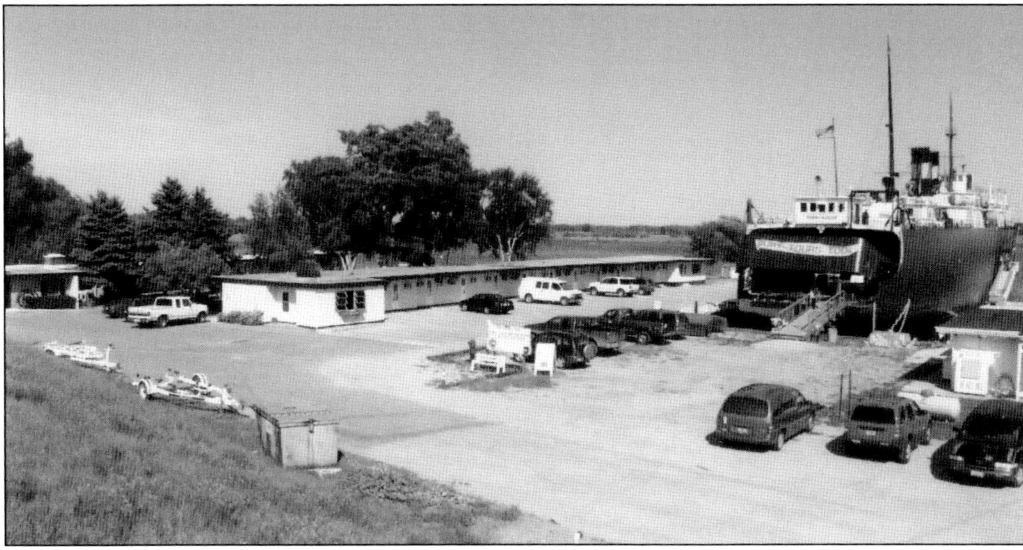

The Moonlite Motel and Marina was acquired by the society in 2003. The site, which included a motel, marina, and campground, was obtained in an attempt by the society to gain a more visible location on a major highway. It was hoped business from the acquisition could be used to subsidize museum operations, but unexpected expenses involving the motel resulted in that portion of the property being sold to developers. The society retained the marina and campground portions of the property. (Photograph by Tom Cubberly.)

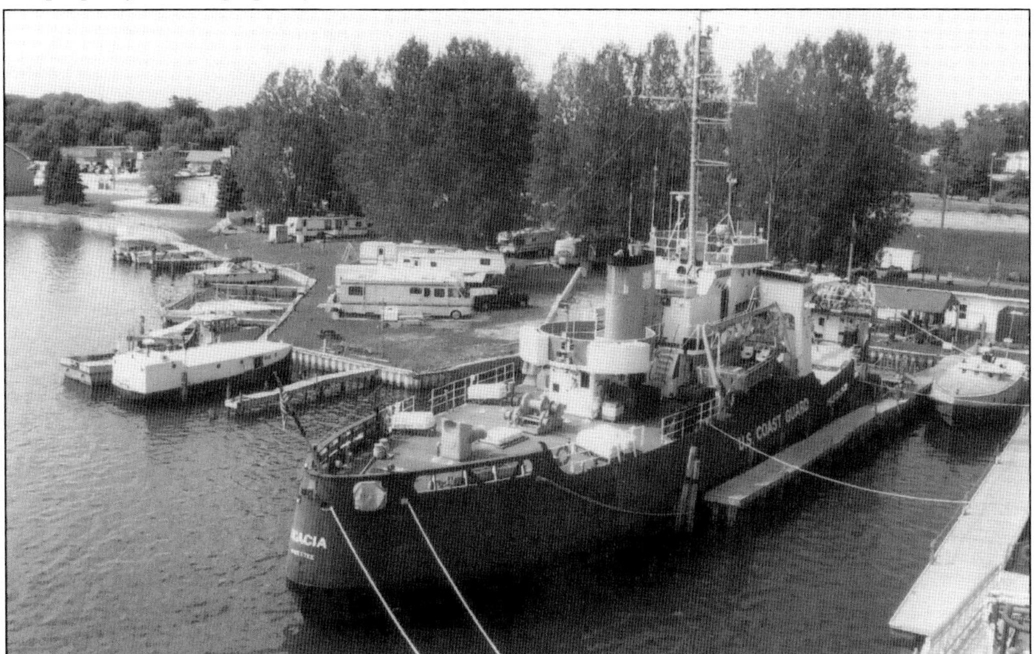

A portion of the marina was removed to create a berth for the USCGC *Acacia*, but plenty of berths are still to be had. Beyond the *Acacia* is the campground portion of the grounds. Many of the campers have had their sites for years, but transient spots are still available. The *Acacia* will be available for group overnight stays, while the *City of Milwaukee* will be open for group and individual stays. (Photograph by Bob Strauss.)

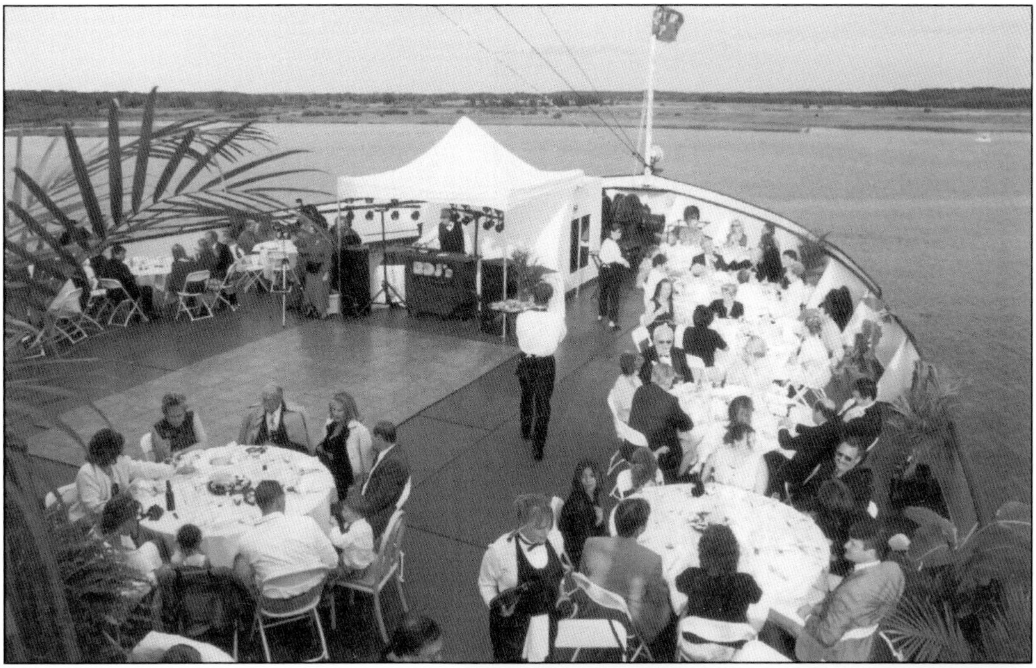

In recent years, the *City of Milwaukee* has been host to wedding receptions, anniversary celebrations, birthday parties, and other get-togethers. Here, a wedding reception is using the open area on the bow to its advantage. A uniformed waitstaff tends to the needs of the guests as a DJ prepares his playlist for the evening's festivities. (CofM.)

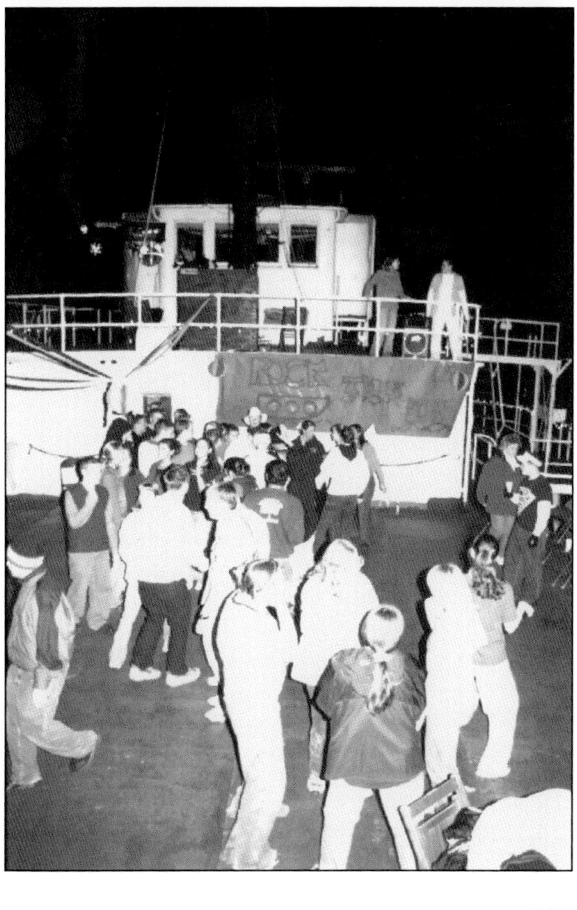

Local youth are entertained at an evening Rock the Boat event. A good time is had by all as a DJ, from his perch behind the pilothouse overlooking the Texas deck, selects tunes to be played. (CofM.)

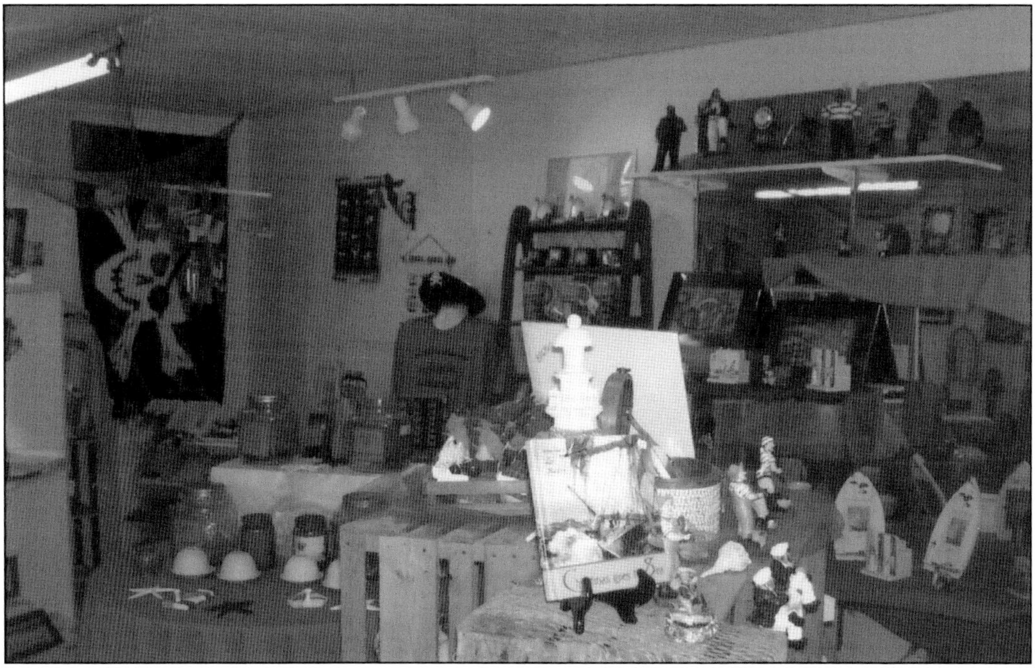

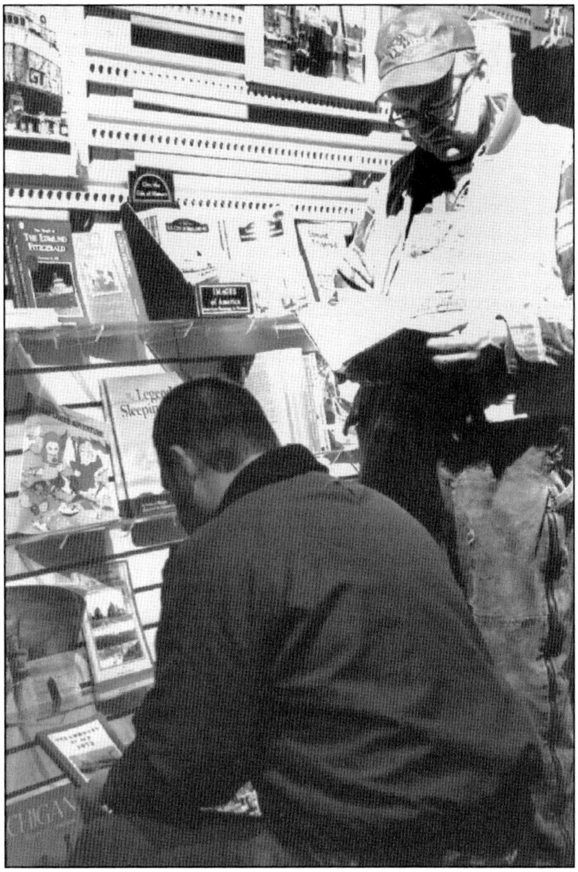

A well-supplied gift shop is a normal part of any museum, and the *City of Milwaukee* is no exception. Postcards, pictures, coffee mugs, shirts, and a wide assortment of various nautical knickknacks are for sale. Some items are also available through the online gift store, accessible on the museum website at www.carferry.com. (CofM.)

Here, two patrons peruse the books available in the gift shop. Items to interest the young, the old, and everyone in between are sure to be found there. With every new year, many fresh and different items find their way onto the shop's shelves. Water, soft drinks, and assorted snack chips are also available for a nominal price. (CofM.)

A uniformed docent conducts a tour outside of the purser's office. In addition to providing tourists and maritime and railroad enthusiasts the opportunity to experience and explore a unique historical landmark, tours are the mainstay of fundraising efforts. (CofM.)

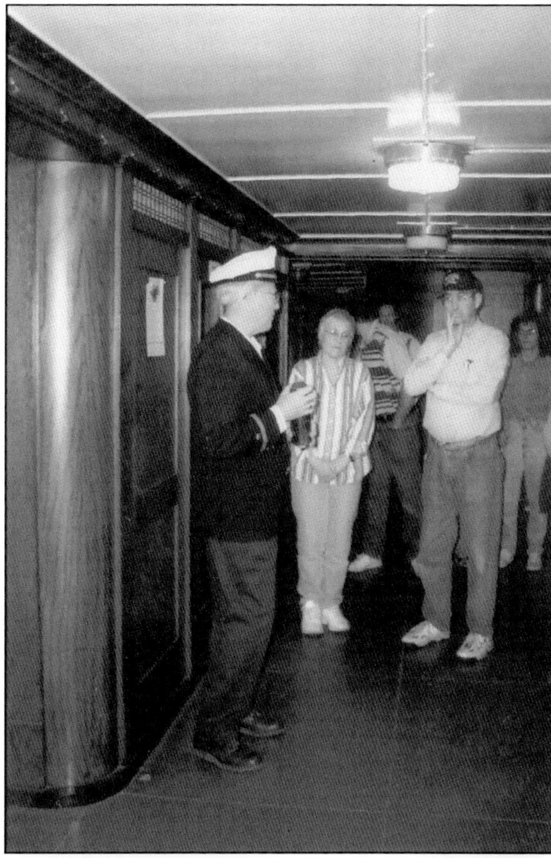

Board president George Micka mans the table at Trainfest in Milwaukee, Wisconsin. Held annually in November at Wisconsin State Fair Park, this model railroad event, the largest of its type in the Midwest, provides an outlet for the *City of Milwaukee* and other like-minded historical groups to raise awareness and funding. Through the sale of gift shop items and historical memorabilia donated by society members, events such as these provide much needed funds for ongoing preservation and restoration efforts. (Photograph by Bob Strauss.)

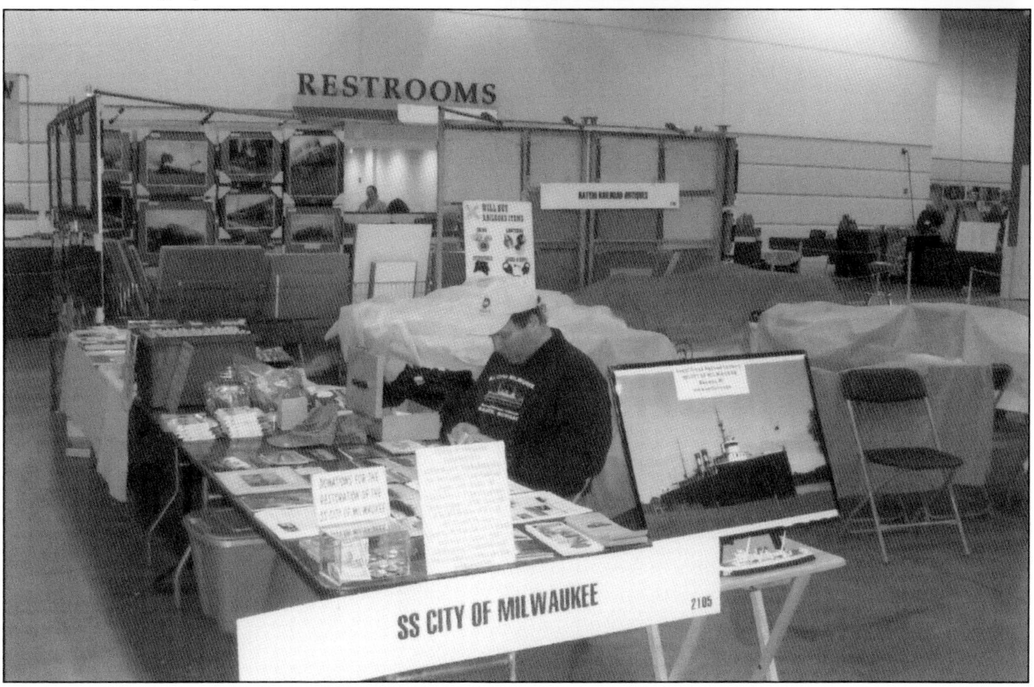

Each October, the *City of Milwaukee* receives a makeover into Manistee's "Ghost Ship." Friendly tour guides give way to spooks and goblins and other nefarious rapscallions. During the course of the month, scores of people file on board, daring the crew to scare them silly. (CofM.)

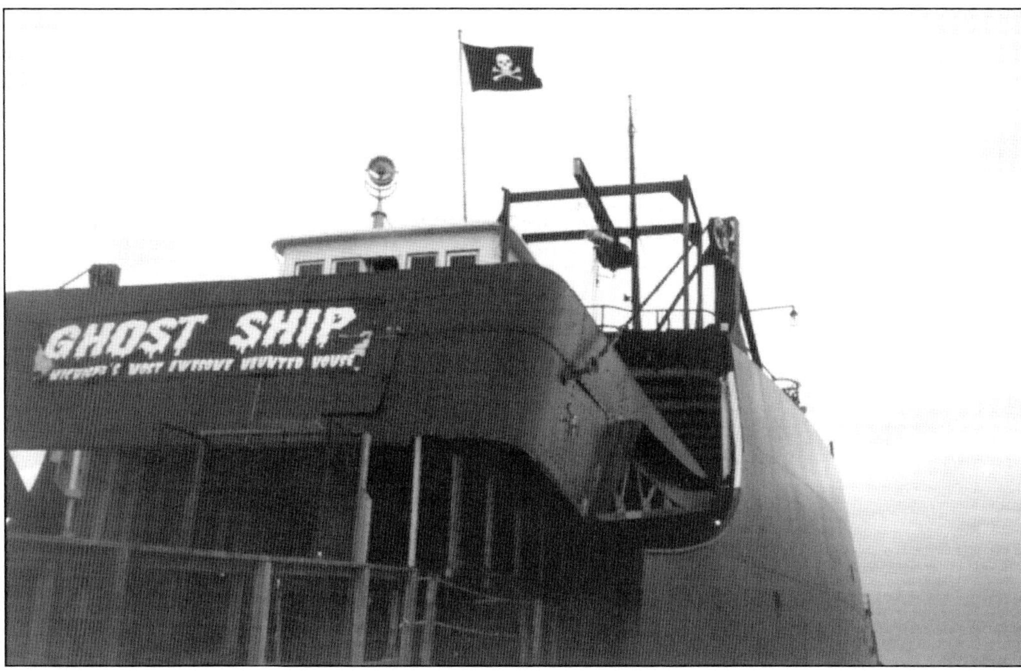


A Jolly Roger flies high on the stern of the boat as a sign of welcome for new victims, er, "guests." A not-so-jolly reception awaits the unwary members of the public who dare to venture aboard. The sign on the stern gate advertises Manistee's Ghost Ship as "Michigan's Most Awesome Haunted House." (CofM.)

Young and old alike enjoy serving on board the Ghost Ship. Here, "Mrs. Tumbs" and her loving daughter eagerly await their expected guests. Many of the volunteers have multiple years of service for this event under their belts, all for the price of a post-event pizza party. (CofM.)

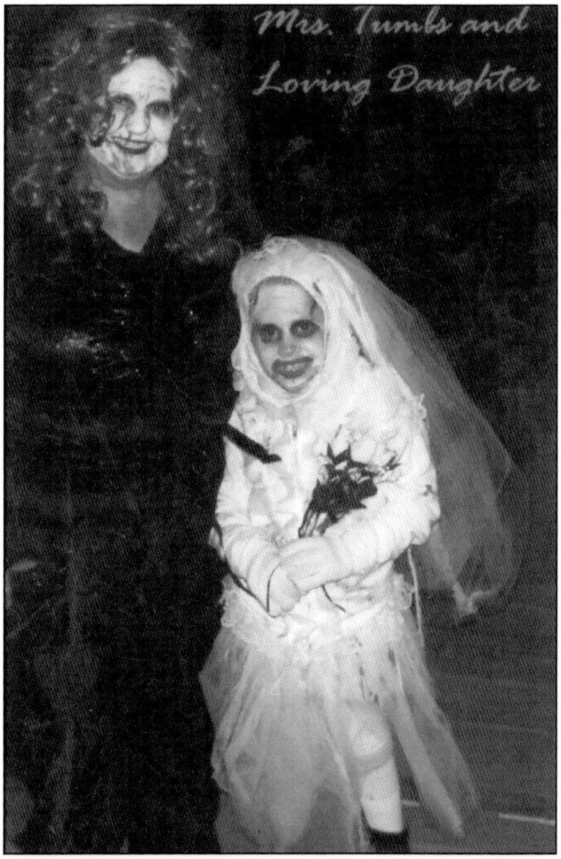


A line of people winds its way on board an early Ghost Ship. The annual event has become a popular attraction in the Manistee area during October, known well enough that it now has its own Facebook page. (CofM.)

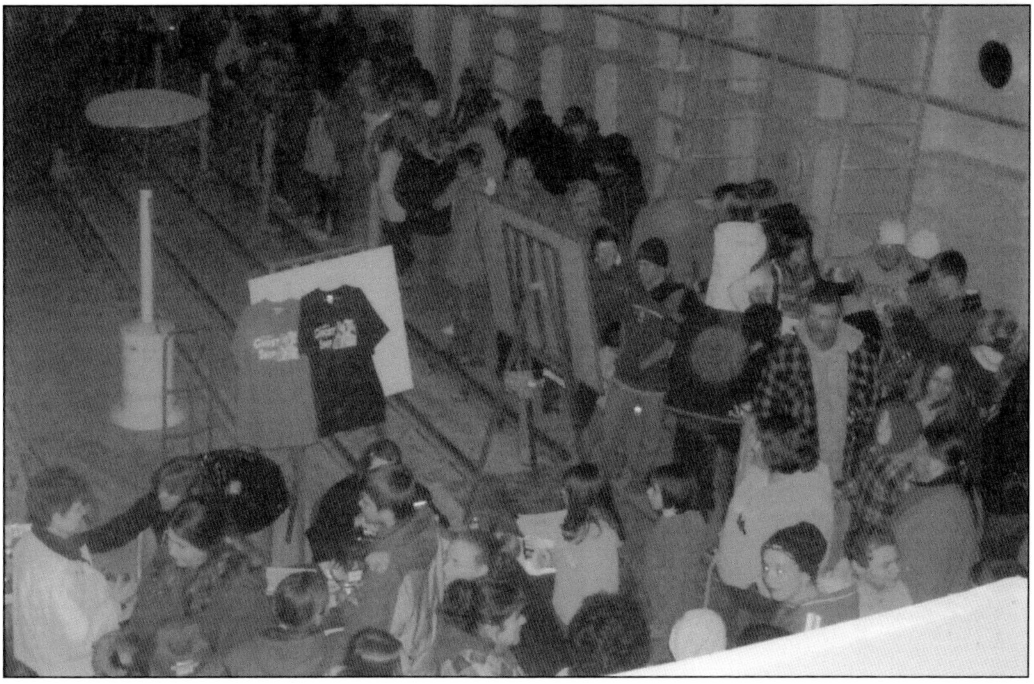

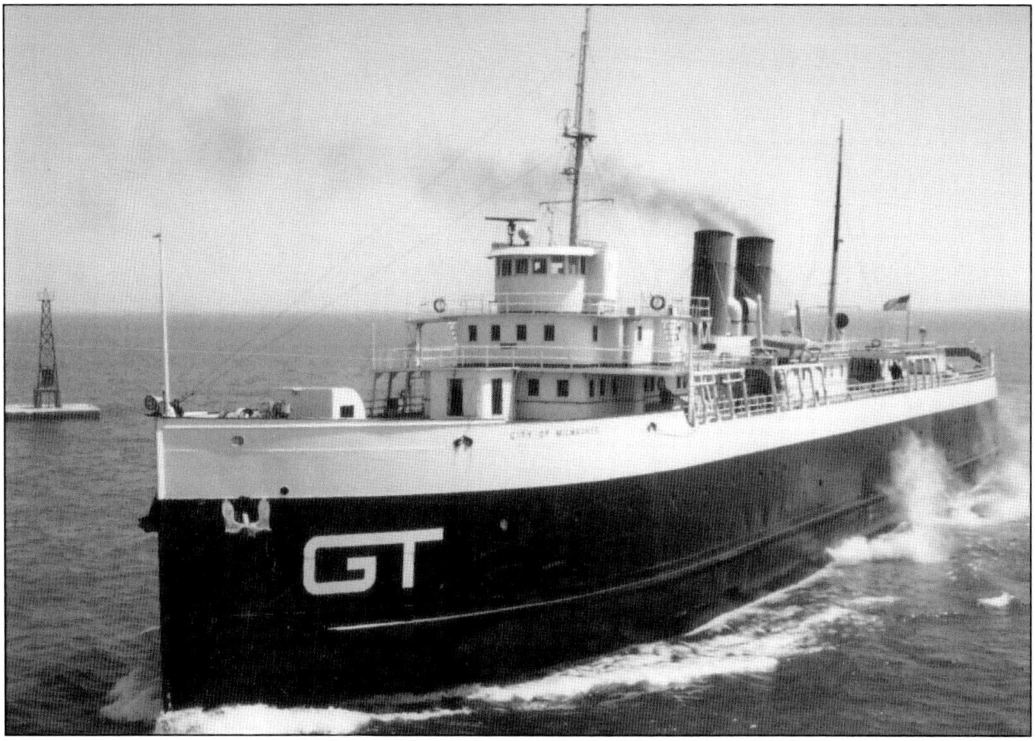


The *City of Milwaukee* is shown wearing her Grand Trunk colors entering Kewaunee, Wisconsin, during the late 1970s while on lease to the Ann Arbor fleet. (Photograph by Andrew LaBorde.)

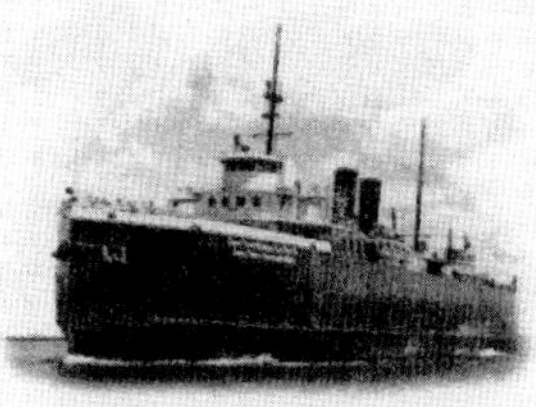

**S.S. CITY OF MILWAUKEE**
**NATIONAL HISTORIC LANDMARK**

**Address**
111 Arthur Street (US-31 N)
Manistee, Michigan 49660

**Telephone**
231-723-3587 voice
231-723-3589 fax

**Internet**
www.carferry.com
info@carferry.com

**Please help us complete the handicapped walkway to the theater boxcar.**
For a donation of $100 we will dedicate one gangway plank. 50 characters are allowed.

_ _ _ _ _ _ _ _ _ _ _ _ _ _ _ _ _ _ _ _ _ _ _ _ _ _ _ _ _ _

_ _ _ _ _ _ _ _ _ _ _ _ _ _ _ _ _ _ _ _ _ _ _ _ _ _ _ _ _ _

Number of Planks as above: ____
Mail this form with your donation to: **S.S. City of Milwaukee**
**99 Arthur St.**
**Manistee, MI 49660**
The S.S. City of Milwaukee is a 501(c)(3) nonprofit organization. Donations are tax deductible as permitted by law.

A fundraising effort that has been implemented is the Plank Program. For a $100 donation, one can commission a plank, which will be laid along a walkway on the car deck and can be used to commemorate anniversaries, birthdays, or other special events; as a memorial for a loved one; or even advertising for a business. (CofM.)

# *Nine*

# MISCELLANEOUS DRAWINGS

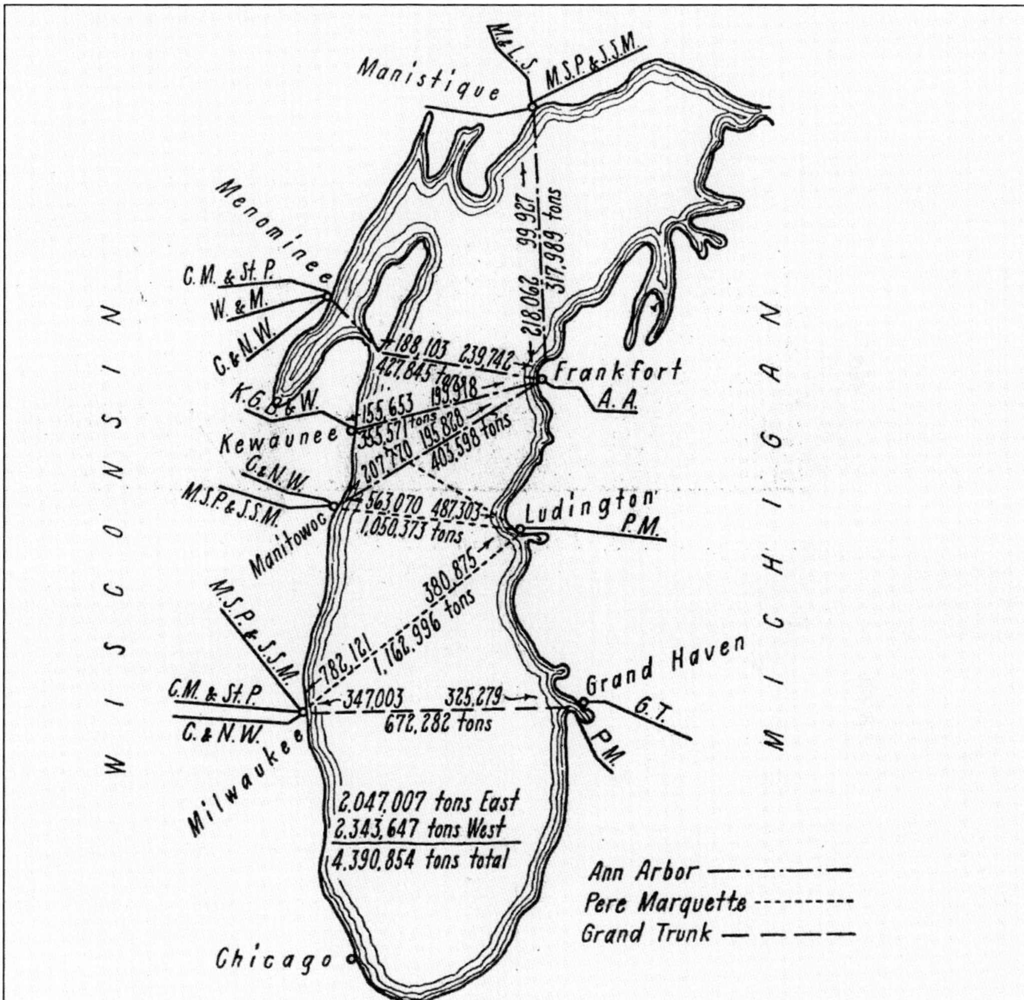


**Eight Car Ferry Routes Cross Lake Michigan**

Overall eastbound and westbound freight tonnage on the Lake Michigan car ferries was increasing during the 1920s, prompting all three of the Lake Michigan car ferry operators to expand their fleets by ordering additional ferries from the Manitowoc Shipbuilding Company during the middle of the decade. Note that on this 1924 tonnage map, the Grand Trunk fleet had the smallest tonnage numbers, but it only ran a single route out of Grand Haven. Pere Marquette had three routes running out of Ludington, and the Ann Arbor ran four routes out of Frankfort. (*Railway Age*/Simmons-Boardman Publishing.)

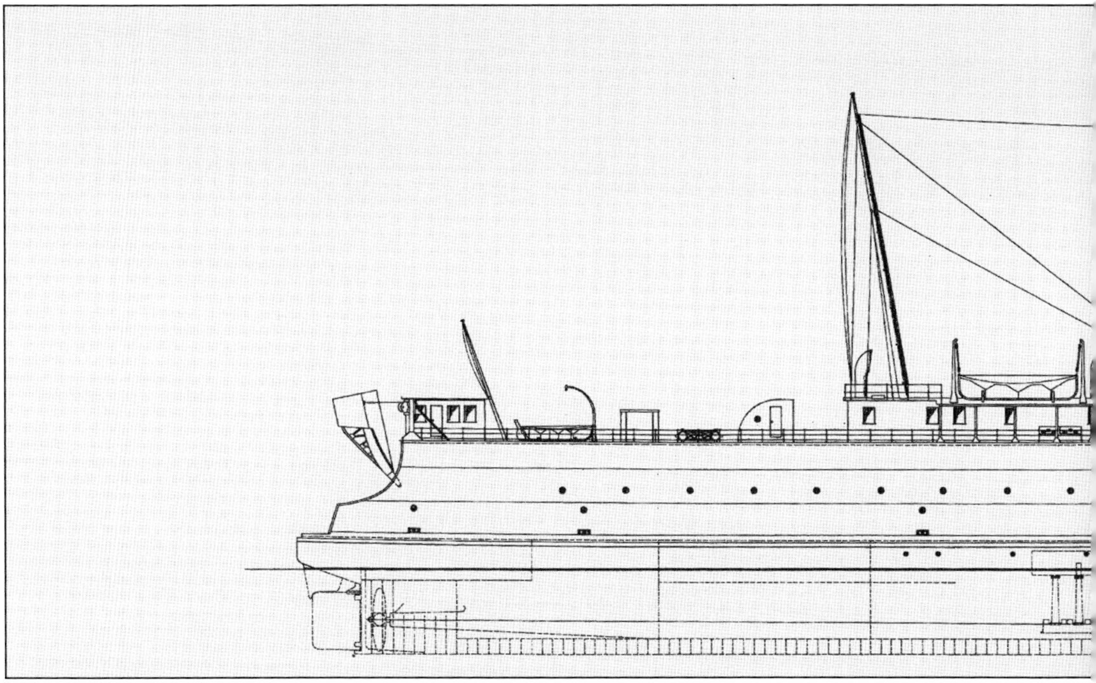

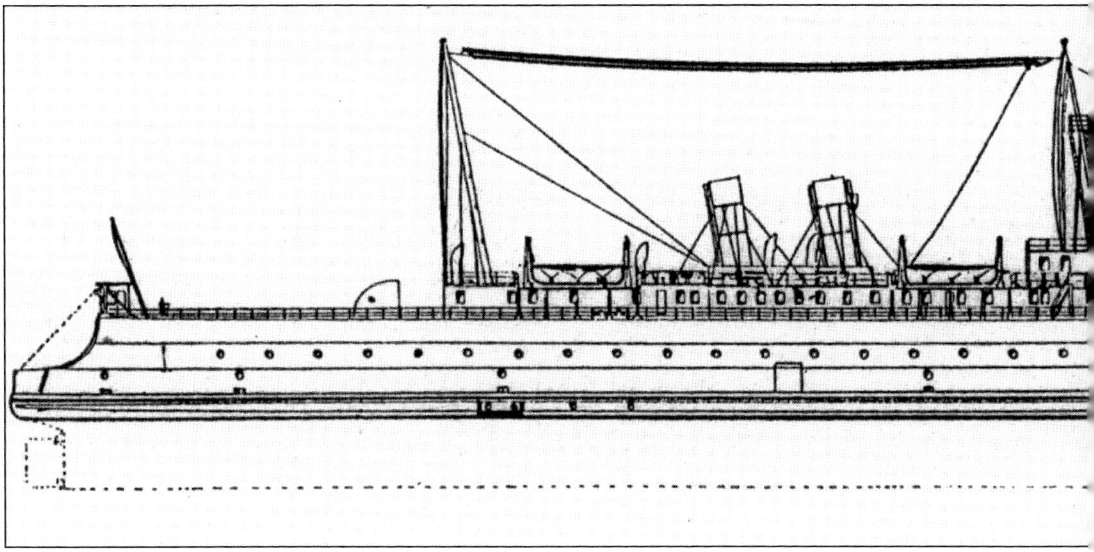

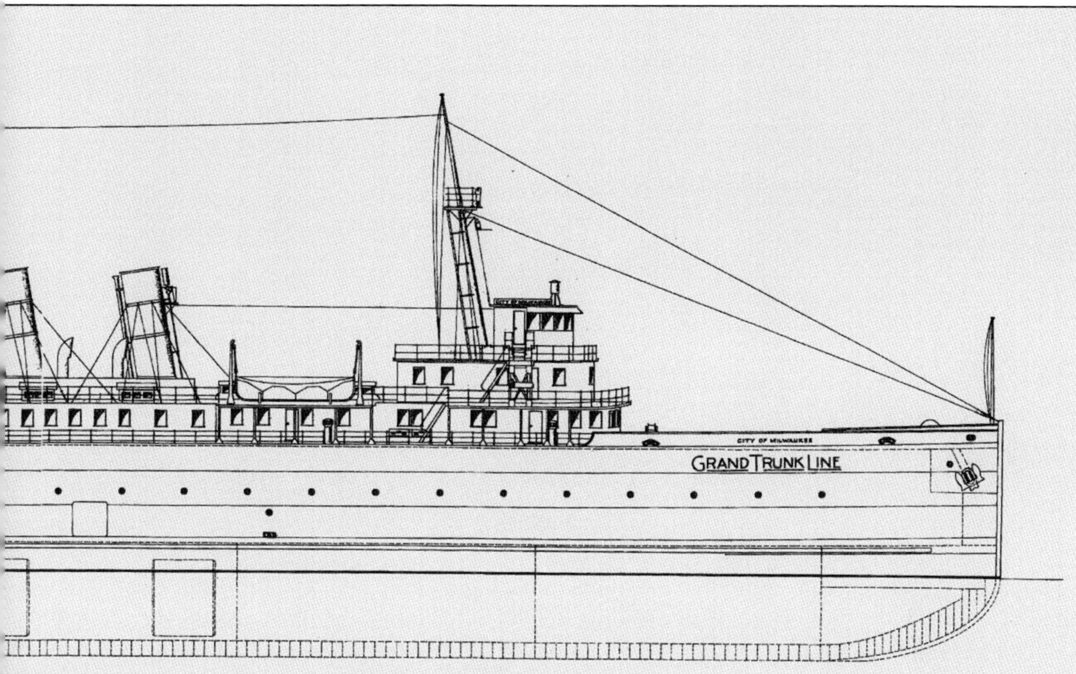


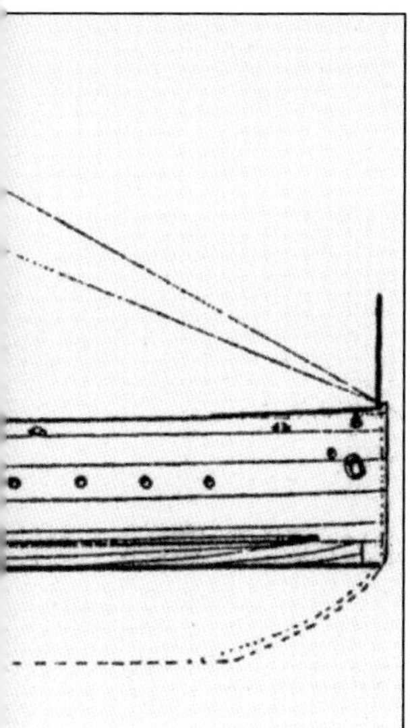

The *City of Milwaukee* was the last of a six-ship class of railroad-car ferries designed and built by Manitowoc Shipbuilding Company. The ship's clean, uncluttered lines, twin stacks, and balanced cabin layout support a low and lean profile that is widely considered to be the pinnacle of Great Lakes car ferry design. Grand Trunk's three sister ships—*Grand Rapids* (1926), *Madison* (1927), and *City of Milwaukee* (1931)—were nearly identical and likewise were nearly so with Pere Marquette Railway's first-of-class *Pere Marquette 21* and *Pere Marquette 22*, built in 1924. The most distinctive departure from the standard design of the six sisters was *Ann Arbor No. 7* (1925) Characteristic of the Ann Arbor Railroad's custom-ordered ships, the *No. 7* (at left) had a cutaway, spoon-shaped prow to aid in navigation on Ann Arbor's ice-choked routes on northern Lake Michigan. Another notable difference was *Ann Arbor No. 7*'s distinctive and unusually tall paned pilothouse windows, presumably installed to provide additional visibility while traversing the narrow, icy waters of the Sturgeon Bay ship canal. (Above, SS *City of Milwaukee* archives; left, courtesy *Marine Review*/Simmons-Boardman Publishing.)

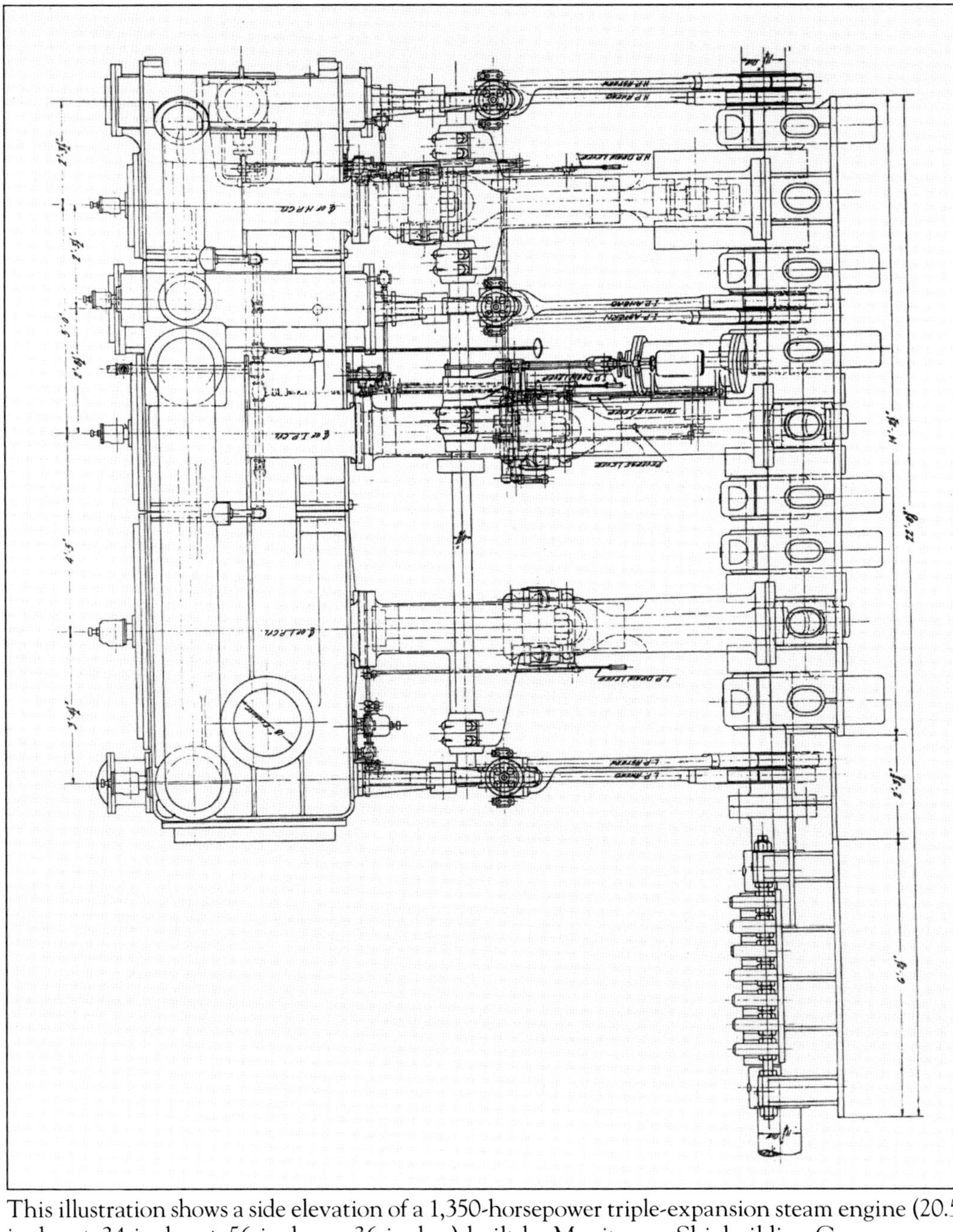

This illustration shows a side elevation of a 1,350-horsepower triple-expansion steam engine (20.5 inches + 34 inches + 56 inches x 36 inches) built by Manitowoc Shipbuilding Company and installed on the six *Pere Marquette 21*-class railroad-car ferries. At the time this vessel class was built, Manitowoc Shipbuilding was a full-service, highly capable yard developing a reputation for building, servicing, modifying, and retrofitting Great Lakes car ferries. The shipbuilder designed and constructed all of the major components on the ferries, including engines, boilers, anchor windlass, mooring winches, steering engine, sea-gate winch, and propellers. A proud and resourceful company with an immense pool of talent, Manitowoc Shipbuilding did as much of its work as possible in-house. (Art Chavez.)

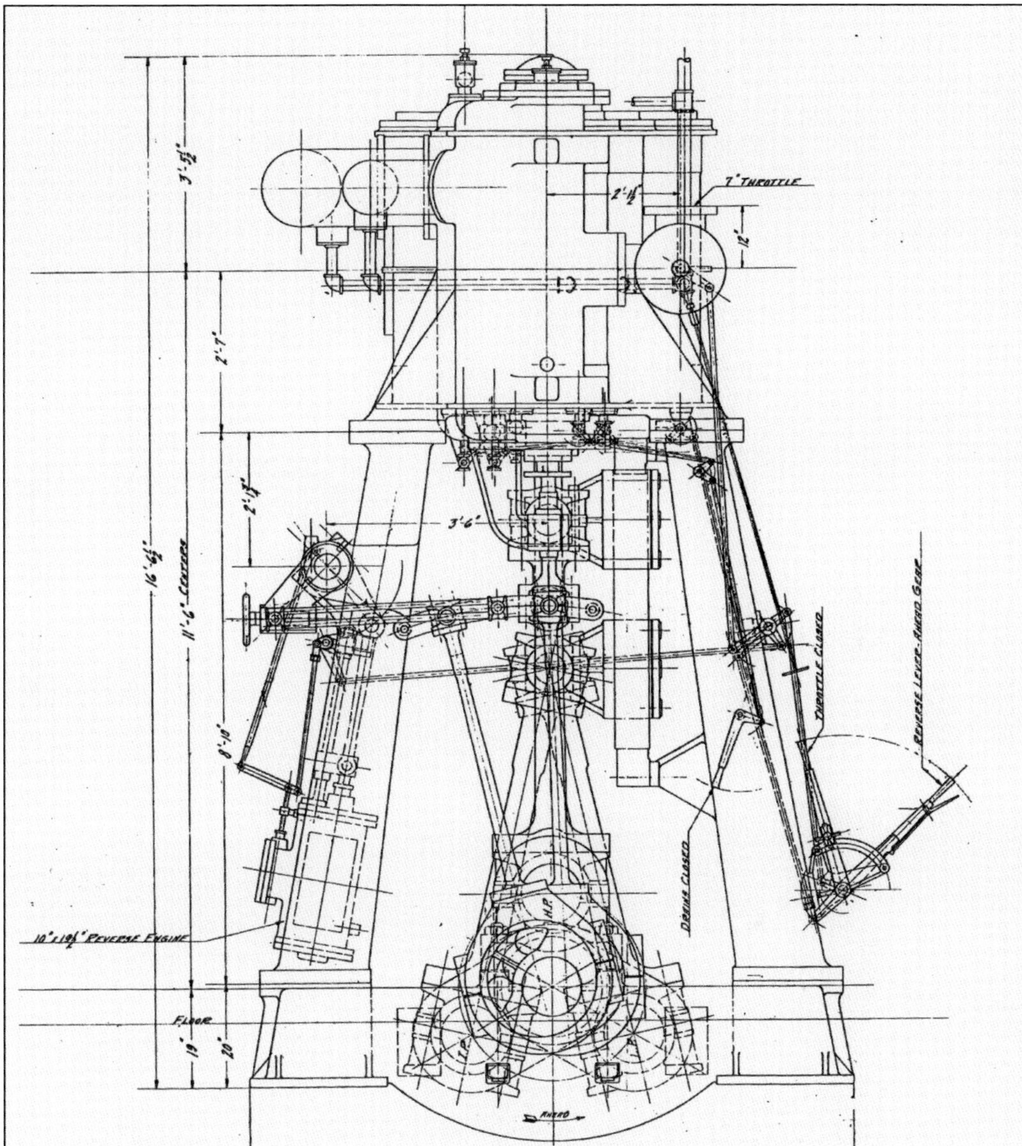


This shows a front elevation of the triple-expansion steam engine. Built by Manitowoc Shipbuilding Company, two each were installed on the six *Pere Marquette 21*–class railroad car ferries, providing each vessel with 2,700 indicated horsepower. All six ships in the class were equipped with four Scotch boilers with a working pressure of 190 pounds per square inch. Originally coal-fired by hand, the boilers of the *City of Milwaukee*, *Grand Rapids*, and *Madison* were converted to burn oil in 1947. The work was carried out one ship at a time in the old car ferry slip at Grand Haven, Michigan. According to logbook notations, the ferries typically loaded 12,000 gallons of No. 5 or "Bunker C" fuel oil every 24 to 48 hours when in service. (Art Chavez.)

## CITY OF MILWAUKEE—Carferry—Great Lakes—Twin Screw—Steam

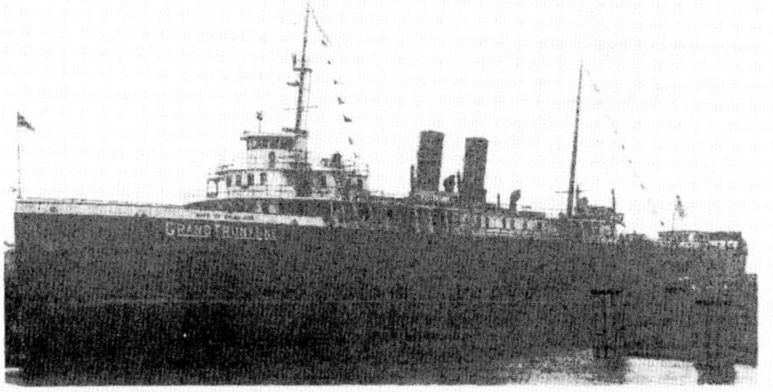


**DESCRIPTION**

For service on Lake Michigan between Milwaukee and Muskegon. Can carry 30 loaded 42-foot freight cars and 100 passengers. Propelled by two triple expansion marine engines of 1400 horsepower each at a service speed of 15 miles. Similar to the CITY OF MADISON and CITY OF GRAND RAPIDS. Total cost of this carferry is about $1,000,000.

**Name**—CITY OF MILWAUKEE
**Owner**—Grand Trunk Railway Co.
**Builder**—Manitowoc Shipbuilding Corp.
**Naval Arch.**—Manitowoc Shipbuilding Corp.
**Launched**—Nov. 25, '30; comp. Jan. 15, '31
**Classification**—American Bureau of Shipping

**HULL PARTICULARS**

Length over all, 360 feet; length between perpendiculars, 348 feet; breadth molded, 56 feet; depth molded, 21 feet 6 inches; draft, mean, designed, 16 feet; displacement loaded, (designed), 6300 short tons; gross tonnage, 2942; net tonnage, 1488; passenger capacity, 100; cargo capacity, 26 to 30 loaded freight cars; bunker fuel capacity, in tons of coal, 375 (short tons); speed, 14 statute miles per hour.

**MACHINERY PARTICULARS**

**Main Engines**—Two, 3-cylinder triple expansion steam engines, built by Manitowoc Shipbuilding Corp. Size, 20½ x 34 x 56 inches and 36 inches stroke; indicated horsepower each engine, 1400 at 96 revolutions per minute.

**Boilers**—Four, scotch marine type, built by Manitowoc Shipbuilding Corp. Size, 14 feet 6 inches in diameter by 12 feet in length; working pressure, 190 pounds per square inch; fuel, coal hand fired.

**Auxiliary Generators**—Two, Engberg, reciprocating engine driven, 20 kilowatts each. Built by Troy Engine and Machine Co.

**AUXILIARY EQUIPMENT**

**Pumps**—Union; Dean; Kingsford
**Windlass**—Manitowoc Shipbuilding Corp.
**Steering Engine**—Manitowoc Shipbuild. Corp.
**Propellers**—Manitowoc Shipbuilding Corp.
**Refrigeration**—Copeland
**Radio Compass**—MacKay (Kolster)
**Telegraphs**—Chas. Cory Corp.
**Marine Hardware**—The Dayton Mfg. Co.
**Oil Purifiers**—De Laval
**Deck Covering**—Selby, Battersby & Co.
**Shaft Sleeves**—Shenango-Penn Mold Co.
**Generator** (Emergency)—One 5 k.w. Kohler

The CITY OF MILWAUKEE is the latest of a long series of carferries built by the Manitowoc Shipbuilding Corp. for service on the Great Lakes. She is now in use by the Grand Trunk system for ferrying cars across Lake Michigan. Of orthodox design throughout, the new vessel is practically a duplicate of two recently constructed carferries for the same company and is heavily constructed for severe winter operating conditions. Construction began early in 1930 and was carried out under the supervision of Capt. C. E. McLaren, marine superintendent in charge of carferry operation.

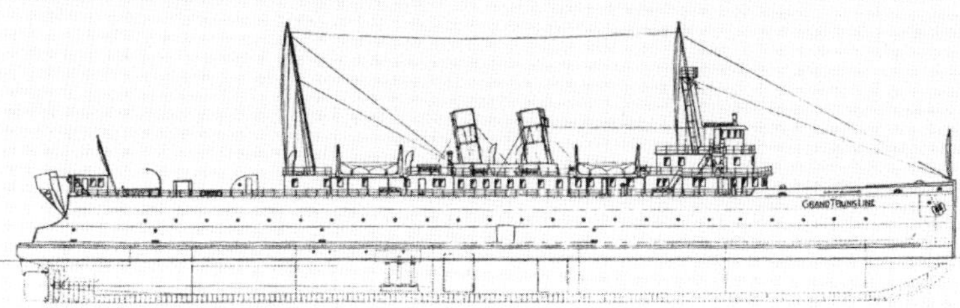

The *City of Milwaukee* was a noteworthy vessel at the time of her launching at Manitowoc Shipbuilding Company in 1931. While larger, faster ferries of a more modern design were built two years before the *City of Milwaukee* by the same shipyard for the rival Pere Marquette Railway, the Grand Trunk Line opted for the more simple, economical, yet classic design that was proven reliable in the five previous ships in the vessel class. (*Marine Review*/Simmons-Boardman Publishing.)

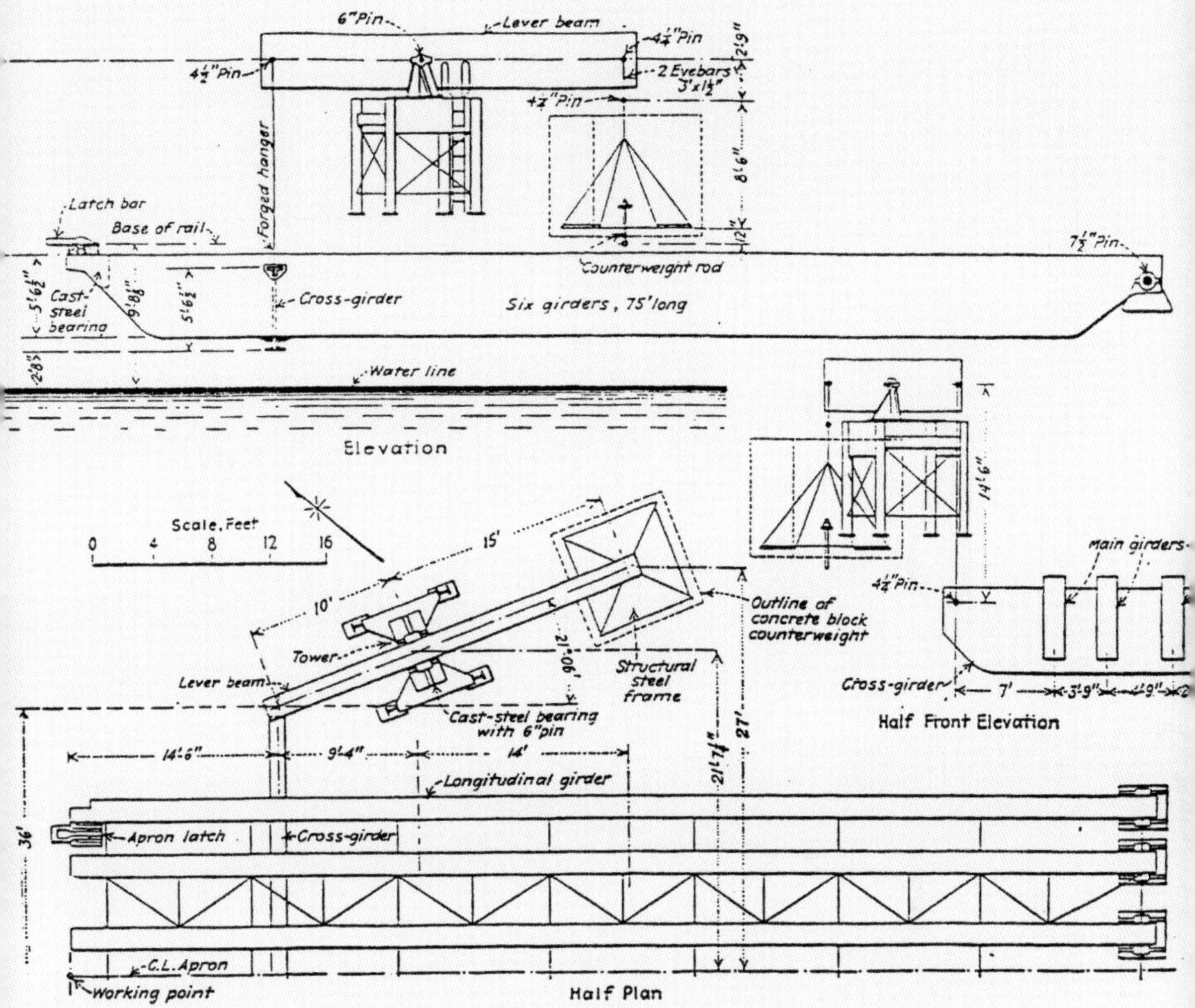

FIG. 2—GENERAL DESIGN OF CAR-FERRY LANDING FOR GRAND TRUNK RY.

This is a profile and layout of Grand Trunk Railroad's Kinnickinnic River loading apron at Milwaukee in 1927. With Grand Trunk expanding its fleet with the recent addition of the car ferries *Grand Rapids* and *Madison*, it was decided to add an additional car ferry slip and loading apron on the Kinnickinnic River at Milwaukee in 1927. The four-ship fleet was headquartered at Milwaukee, with one slip at Grand Haven. When the Grand Trunk ferry fleet's base of operations was switched to Muskegon, it again got along with only one slip on the Michigan side of the lake. (*Railway Age*/Simmons-Boardman Publishing.)

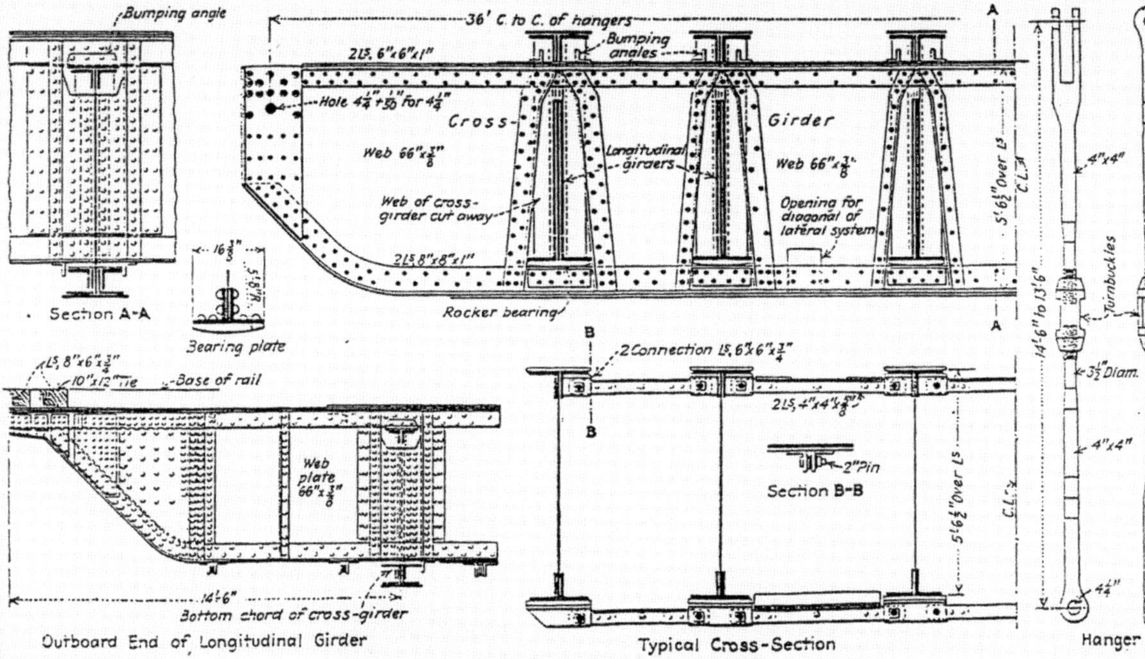


FIG. 3—FLEXIBLE FRAMING OF LANDING APRON

This image shows framing details of Grand Trunk Railroad's Kinnickinnic River loading apron. Grand Trunk's new loading apron was far stronger and more durable than the older, typically 50-foot-long ferry slips that were then common on the Great Lakes. The new slip was 75 feet in length and able to take more flexing action as the ship listed to port or starboard with the weight of the cars as they were switched from one side of the ferry to another. The end of the apron affixed to the shore remained on a straight plane, while the apron's mid-structure bore the side-twisting movement as it aligned on the far end with the stern of the listing car ferry. This view shows the heavy steel construction of the apron's main structure, with the only wood being the planking laid on the deck of the apron between the railroad tracks and fender pilings. (*Railway Age*/Simmons-Boardman Publishing.)

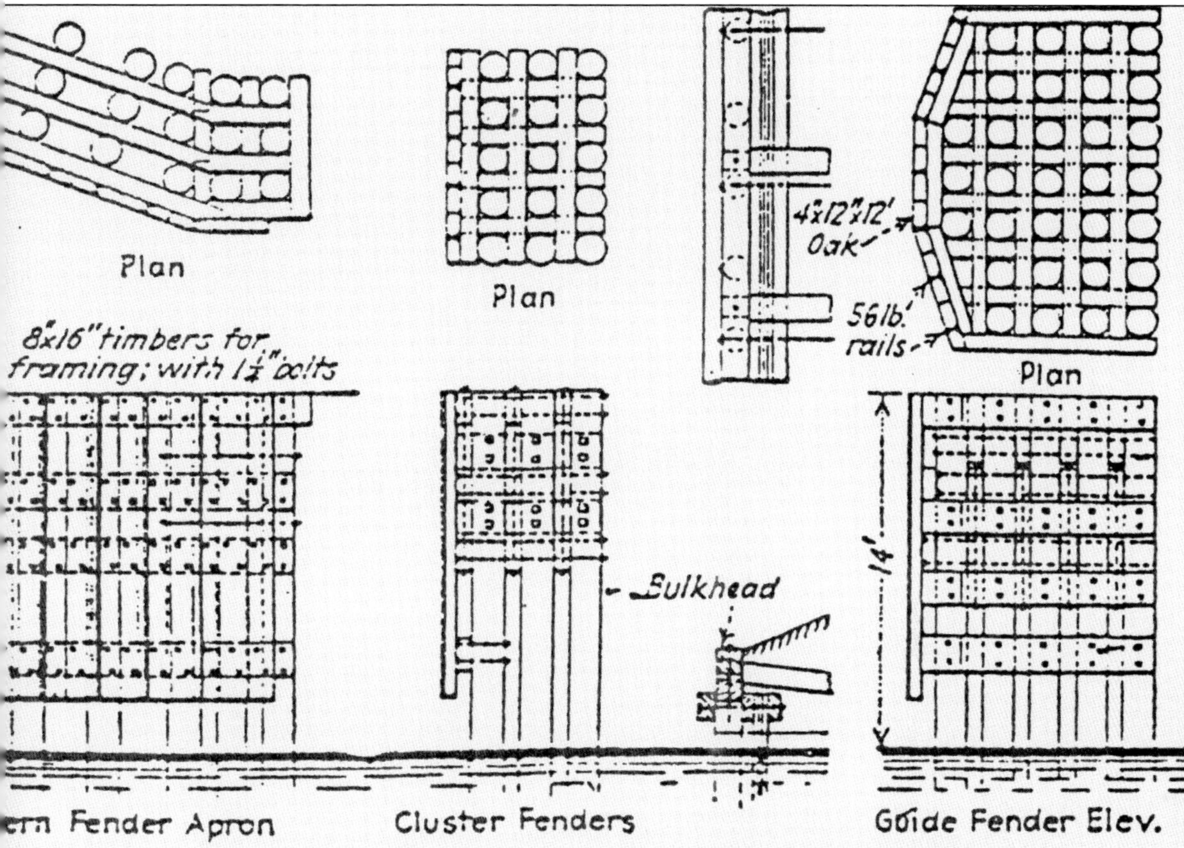


FIG. 4—PILE AND FRAME FENDERS

These are timber and piling details of Grand Trunk Railroad's Kinnickinnic River car ferry slip. Fender pilings were built to correspond with the shape of a car ferry's aft hull form as a guide in aiding the captain's approach when the vessel was maneuvered toward the loading apron. At this stage in the docking procedure, the ferry was steered with the twin propellers and not the rudder, which was set amidships. Working the twin engines made the ferries highly maneuverable and eliminated the need for a tug as required for other large freight vessels approaching a tight docking location. Once the ferry was aligned against the apron, two large locks were lowered onto the ship's stern, mooring cables were attached, and the ferry's engines running slow astern, thus securing the connection. (*Railway Age*/Simmons-Boardman Publishing.)